9.25

W9-BRN-477

NEW DIRECTIONS IN MUSIC

Dedicated to my wife, without whom this book would not have been written; and to my parents, whose faith started it all.

NEW DIRECTIONS IN MUSIC

David H. Cope

Miami University, Oxford, Ohio

Second Edition

WM. C. BROWN COMPANY PUBLISHERS

Dubuque, Iowa

wcb

Copyright © 1971, 1976, by
Wm. C. Brown Company Publishers

Library of Congress Catalog Card Number: 79-149410

ISBN 0–697–03556–5

All rights reserved. No part of this publication may
be reproduced, stored in a retrieval system, or trans-
mitted, in any form or by any means, electronic, me-
chanical, photocopying, recording, or otherwise, without the prior written permission of the publisher.

Third Printing, 1978

Printed in the United States of America

Consulting Editor
Frederick W. Westphal
Sacramento State College

Contents

Foreword

Most music history or literature courses beginning with 1750 proceed to Prokofieff (or perhaps to Penderecki, if the course is given by an enlightened professor). Twenty-five years ago this course would have culminated with Debussy. Due in part to the considerable volume of recent writing about the new music (by way of periodicals such as *Source, The Composer,* and *Perspectives of New Music*), and to its vastly expanded availability through various media and recordings, it has become a matter of urgent necessity to present relevant updated information about the subject, in textbook form. No longer can the new music of our time be disregarded particularly since so many of the techniques of the avant-garde of the 1940s and 1950s are now part of the mainstream! My study of the manuscript of this book makes it clear that David Cope presents the music of the recent decades in a most articulate and balanced manner. In fact, much of this material existed for some time "underground," and we owe to this book a debt of gratitude for moving that material out into the open and presenting it in a vital way to students, educators, and professional muscians.

Is it presumptuous to write a book about 1950 to 1975 when the later year is only partially spent? Where is the perspective that is a by-product of time and research? Frankly, it isn't always in evidence, *nor should it be,* as the author (a composer and not a musicologist or critic) does not seek to present definitive judgments, and therefore does not need such time-honored perspective. One of the great joys of this book is that it does not "sit in judgment," but reports what happened: how and why. The author's avoidance of partisanship and pomposity help make this text eminently readable. It contains, moreover, so much information for its size that it can and will, I am sure, function as a valuable source book. This is a rare combination, readability and reference value, and *New Directions in Music* combines both attributes with style, empathy, and lucidity.

As an American musician, I cherish these years during which we stepped into the international music scene, not as the "noble savage" but as a leader. The influence of Ives, Cowell, Cage, and Varèse (who considered himself a composer of the "New World") have been felt and heard so markedly and repeatedly that I feel the so-called "international" style is in large part a Europeanization of the American style. This notion is easily documented by the influence of John Cage alone, for one. Add Ives, Cowell, and the others and the picture becomes quite clear. The missing part of the picture is post-Webern serialism, which has been a dead issue for some time and a small part of the total scene. In considering any recent movement or tendency, the origin is almost always American. This is quite the reverse of the musical scene at the beginning of the century!

Some of the concepts and music discussed may take many readers to personal limitations of what music means. All these controversial ideas are presented with clarity, balance, and understanding. The restraint of the author is most commendable, and I am often amazed at the way he adroitly sidesteps main "traps" and too-often fought battles.

If this foreword seems more in the style of a positive review, please consider these words as a recommendation for a most important book that will, I hope, inform students, educators, and professional musicians alike about some of the more adventuresome movements in the music of our time.

Bertram Turetzky
Del Mar, California

Preface

This, the second edition of *New Directions in Music*, contains three major additions. A new chapter, The Post *Avant-Garde*, is dedicated to the clearly evidenced demise of the *avant-garde* as a movement, and the resultant combinations of mainstream and experimental traditions—focused less on their differences and more on their shared "musical" ecology. Two new appendices supplement the final pages. The first of these (Appendix 3) acts both as a springboard to further study of notation, and as an aid in the understanding of many of the musical examples in the text. The second (Appendix 4) leads the reader directly to many of the sources discussed in the book (names and addresses of record companies, music publishers, and periodicals, as of January 1975).

As part of the expanded and revised text are additions and changes in both title and content of two chapters: from "Sound-Mass," to "Sound-Mass, Rhythm, and Microtones"; and from "Electronic Music" to "Electronic and Computer Music." Moreover, there has been a photo complement to each chapter which, the author hopes, will lend a more personal touch and add a new dimension of character to the book. And too, quite a few examples have been added to further supplement the reader's understanding of the text. The book has been reorganized within chapter subheadings which are intended to clarify both the outline and the direction of each chapter.

The annotated chapter bibliographies have been reorganized and considerably expanded. Each includes not only materials discussed in the chapter itself, but supplemental materials which would be of use to the reader seeking out specifics in greater detail. Each chapter bibliography is divided into two categories:

1. Readings: books and articles relevant to the subject matter of the chapter (listed alphabetically by author, or subject). Also included are reference materials for in-depth biographical study of the composers mentioned in the chapter.
2. Recordings and Publishers: these include record numbers and publishers (when available) of works referred to in the chapter as well as such other works as the author feels might demonstrate chapter content (listed by composer alphabetically).

Though by no means all-inclusive, these bibliographies are sufficiently comprehensive to serve the reader quite adequately. They are intended to be used as lists of information selected for its importance and relevance to chapter material, and as *sources* in themselves for bibliographical information to support more intensive research. The bibliographies have been extensively updated and their scope broadened since the first edition. This, combined with the updating of the composer biographies (Appendix 2), the expansions of terms and their definitions (Appendix 1), and the source addresses of Appendix 4, should make the materials discussed more easily understood by and accessible to the reader. Composition or publication dates are included if available. They are mentioned with the first appearance of the name of the work and not thereafter (i.e., if the work is discussed and date listed in the body of the chapter the date will not be included in the chapter bibliography under *Recordings and Publishers*).

When on tour, a situation in which authors and composers are frequently to be found, one is ofttimes confronted by readers holding a variety of misconceptions, two of which this composer-author would like to dispel with brevity and singular decisiveness. First of all, just as writing about Greek mythology does not make one either a Greek or a believer in myths, so writing about various types of *avant-garde* musics does not *necessarily* make one a composer of those selfsame musics. Secondly, due to the volatile nature of much of the subject matter under discussion, one must weigh carefully a most important statement in the *Preface* to the first edition:

The lack of material related herein to more traditional (mainstream) techniques is not intended to reflect or suggest their unimportance (they are *most* important), but is rather due to both the fact that there is a wealth of material already available on these subjects, and to the necessarily limited scope of this text to reasonable length and coverage of the material discussed.

Whether one agrees or disagrees with the concepts, philosophies, and resultant sound activities and/or silences discussed herein is simply beside the point. These musics *do* exist and to avoid either their manifestations or significance is simply playing ostrich.

It is quite possible that more compositions have been brought into the world during the past 25 years than had been brought in during the entire previous 120-year period. A large part of these works are experimental, some destined to become, like P.D.Q. Bach, "hopelessly lost," others perhaps to help found a broader and more creative base for artistic endeavor. In any event, they can no longer be considered external to the history of this era, or to its future existence.

Directions seem as numerous or as diverse as composers or works. And yet there exists behind these directions historical motives and constant aesthetic values, traceable and uniquely observable due to their singularly radical nature. Electronic instruments and techniques, aleatoric methods, adoption of scientific procedures and theatrical participation, once held as highly controversial and innovative, have entered a large number of current mainstream compositions, due in part to the recent sophistication of international communications media. It was not always so. Berlioz's innovations in orchestration waited half a century for recognition and acceptance. Charles Ives's experiments took many years to be discovered—many more to be considered even rational.

The purpose of this book, then, is to explore the history, philosophies, materials, composers, and works pertaining to those directions of music since the late 1940s which express a radical departure from tradition in concept and/or production, with special emphasis on the relationship of these to significant and realistic directions of style and thought.

New Directions in Music is intended as an introduction and general survey of *avant-garde* and post *avant-garde* music in the twentieth century to 1975, in the hope that it will serve to stimulate the reader to further listening and research. Designed for music students at the college and graduate level, it may be suitably integrated into any course incorporating the study of various aspects of twentieth-century composition: forms, techniques, philosophy; and it can be a valuable supplement to the well-rounded education of any serious musician. By the very fact that most of the years discussed have not yet become "history" in the academic sense, the author has intentionally avoided the standard historical approach and rhetoric in order to develop *concepts* and *interest* in the *New Directions in Music.*

The lack of deep analysis of works included reflects the author's belief that to do so would inherently imply an artificial judgment of their importance, something which only time can determine. The works are discussed only as they relate to, demonstrate, or evolve a concept.

D. C.

1 Some Thoughts on Beginnings

Overview

Each of the chapters that follow this one presents an historical outline of the development of one or more aspects of contemporary music, and culminates in discussions of a series of relatively recent works the author feels best exemplify one or more of that chapter's subject matter. "Some Thoughts on Beginnings" is intended to serve as a correlative overview of the interactions of origins and notable early examples of *New Directions* paralleling the chapter order of the book.

By 1950, the majority of performers and audiences were just beginning to react to twelve-tone procedures as something other than *avant-garde*, although these had already been accepted as commonplace by most composers. Webern's pointillism had already affected the European younger generation (Boulez, Stockhausen, Pousseur, Dallapiccola, and others), creating the so-called post-Webern School. Serial techniques had invaded all aspects of composition: color, dynamics, rhythm, meter, tempo; and the breakdown of the row into groups of three (trichords), four (tetrachords), six (hexachords), and so on, pointed towards consummate intellectual control by the composer of all the related aspects of his music. Even older than Machaut's isorhythm, this concept did represent a new and clear-cut breach between two opposing ideals: more control vs. less control. The roots of this disagreement seem to lie, both nationalistically (Europe vs. America) and compositionally, in the concept that extremely highly organized music sounds very often like extremely unorganized music, the row and total serialization representing the parting of the ways (see fig. 1.1).

Total Control: The Parting of Ways

Pantonality (this, not *atonality*, was the term used by Schoenberg), or "inclusive of all tonalities," is not important because of the row, for twelve-tone series have existed for centuries in all types of music (see fig. 1.2). Nor does its importance lie in chromaticism (again, note fig. 1.2), but in its efforts to create extreme control over compositional elements, a control which is predominantly inaudible and recognizable in general stylistic terms only.

1

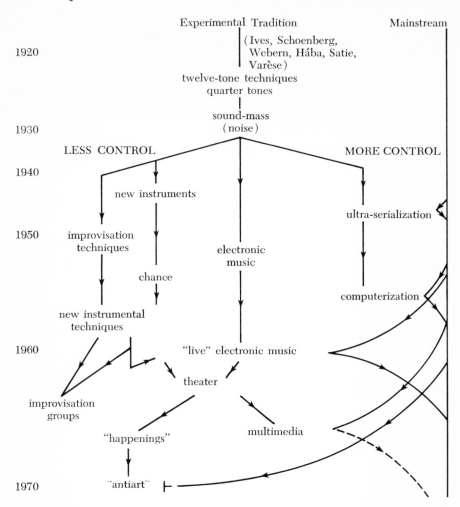

Figure 1.1.   An *Avant-Garde* mobile

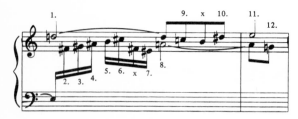

Figure 1.2.   J. S. Bach: *Well-Tem-
pered Clavier*, Book 1, Fugue 24.

Color pointillism (*Klangfarbenmelodien*) introduced a unique approach for timbre serialization which added greatly to the corporealization of total serialization of all sonic elements (see fig. 1.3).

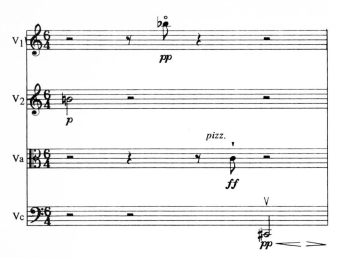

Figure 1.3. *Klangfarbenmelodien*

Figure 1.4. Anton Webern (noted pointillistic composer and one of the originators of *Klangfarbenmelodien*).

Range pointillism, in and of itself, represented no real new concept; like note serialization, it had existed with no adverse effects for centuries (see fig. 1.5).

Figure 1.5. Collaggiani's aria from
Pergolesi: *Il Maestro di Musica*.

Very few directions during this period have been able to avoid some
derivation (intentional or otherwise) from the concept of total control
and/or color pointillism. Again, however, it is necessary to point out that
very few of the works and ideas expressed beyond this chapter involve
actual dodecaphonic techniques.

The following piano composition by Milton Babbitt demonstrates serialized control of dynamics, rhythm, and pitch:

Figure 1.6. Milton Babbitt: *Three
Compositions for Piano*, 1947 (measures 1-8, Piece No. 1). Published
by Boelke-Bonart, Inc., Hillsdale, N.Y.

key: O = original; R = retrograde
(backwards); I = inversion;
IR = inverted retrograde

A. *Row* (original): see fig. 1.7.

The twelve-tone row upon which the work is based is constructed such that the first six notes (hexachord) are the same as the second six notes (hexachord) transposed an augmented fourth (six half steps). Inversions, retrogrades, and inverted retrogrades work in like manner, creating an extremely organized chromaticism.

B. *Rhythm:* The hexachords are divided into "duration sets" (groups of notes) with the various combinations of 4 + 2 and 5 + 1 creating the total row. In this case, Babbitt has chosen 5 1 4 2 as the original (that is, notes grouped together rhythmically with first a set of five, then one, then four and finally two: twelve). The retrograde then becomes 2 4 1 5, the inversion 1 5 2 4 (the inner subsets reversed: 5 1 becomes

Hexachord No. 1   Hexachord No. 2
(bottom voice mea. No. 1)   (top voice mea. No. 1)

Figure 1.7. Row of Milton Babbitt's
Three Compositions for Piano.

1 5; 4 2 becomes 2 4) and the inverted retrograde 4 2 5 1. Figure 1.6 shows the rhythmic analysis of the first eight measures in detail (note that the number 5 above a bracket does not mean quintuplet here but rather a grouping of five notes as a part of the rhythmic row). Two versions of the rhythmic row occur simultaneously here: one voice stems up, the other stems down.

C. *Dynamics:* Dynamics are related to the rhythmic row occurring in each voice: original form at *mp;* retrograde with *mf;* inversion with *f;* inverted retrograde with *p.*

Oliver Messiaen (b. 1909 in France) was one of the first to use rigid rhythmic control (augmentation, diminution by one half, one third, one fourth, etc., of the original) over his materials. His *Quatre études de rythme* (especially number 2, *Mode de valeur et d'intensités*), published in 1949, was one of the first works to include integral organization of the "whole." Though based more on modal than twelve-tone principles, it did in fact serialize the basic musical components (36 sounds; 24 durations; 7 dynamics; 12 articulations).

Messiaen's influence over the younger composers of France, combined with twelve-tone theory, enabled Pierre Boulez to arrange twelve different durations, twelve articulations, and twelve dynamics in row forms, thus creating serialization possibilities over more compositional elements. This is particularly effective and noticeable in Boulez's *Structures* (1952) and *Second Piano Sonata* (1948). Bernad Alois Zimmer-

Figure 1.8.   Pierre Boulez

mann's *Perspectives* for two pianos (1956) is row controlled from an aggregate of procedures pertaining to pitch, density, rhythm, dynamics, attacks and pedaling representing somewhat of a landmark in its degree of systematic composer control (see the article on the work in *die Reihe* #4 for complete analysis). Ruth Crawford's (1901-53) innovative String Quartet (1931) employs procedures of total organization. The third movement of this work, especially, includes an obvious systematic procedure of control in which the compositional elements (pitch, duration, dynamics, and rhythm) are related and serialized. In conjunction with the organizational principles, there exists as the foundation of the movement a double canon in dynamics only (first canon in the viola and 'cello and the second in the two violins). The resulting dovetailing of dynamics (one voice in crescendo and the other in simultaneous diminuendo) foreshadows yet another technique of the *avant-garde:* timbre modulation (the instruments for most of the opening are at intervals of major and minor seconds from one another with the undulating dynamics creating timbre movements one instrument to another).

In his now-famous article "Who Cares if You Listen," Milton Babbitt speaks of this "high degree of determinacy":

In the simplest terms, each such "atomic" event is located in a five-dimensional musical space determined by pitch-class, register, dynamic, duration, and timbre. These five components not only together define the single event, but, in the course of a work, the successive values of each component create an individually coherent structure, frequently in parallel with the corresponding structures created by each of the other components. Inability to perceive and remember precisely the values of any of these components results in a dislocation of the event in the work's musical space, an alternation of its relation to all other events in the work, and—thus—a falsification of the composition's total structure. For example, an incorrectly performed or perceived dynamic value results in destruction of the work's dynamic pattern, but also in false identification of other components of the event (of which this dynamic value is a part) with corresponding components of other events, so creating incorrect pitch, registral, timbral and durational associations.[1]

This necessarily scientific or mathematical approach is new only in its applications, for since Pythagoras and his followers, music theory has evolved through a process of scientific formula applied during, though more often after, the compositional process. The increased requirements on both the performer and audience must certainly have been in part responsible for the replacement of one by tape, and the diminishing size of the other to fellow professionals and interested, but often confused bystanders. Even without the row, performance conflicts appeared to Charles Ives who, in the Postface to his *114 Songs* (1922) explained: "Some of the songs in this book, particularly among the later ones, cannot be sung, and if they could, perhaps might prefer, if they had a say, to remain as they are; that is, 'in the leaf'—and that they will remain in this peaceful state is more than presumable."[2]

In America the colleges and universities have replaced the courts, the church, and patrons of earlier times, offering the composer his only realistic terms for physical survival. The need in this academic environment to present composition as an ordered and intellectual pursuit, and the close physical proximity of so-called "disciplines" of scientific teachings, have contributed no small part to the large volume of systems and aesthetics in the past forty years. Pierre Boulez, in an interview with the author, referred thus to this environment:

1. Milton Babbitt, "Who Cares if You Listen," *High Fidelity* 8, no. 2 (February 1958):38-40, 126-27.
2. Charles Ives, "Postface to 114 Songs," in *Essays before a Sonata, and Other Writings*, ed. Howard Boatwright (New York: W.W. Norton & Co., 1961), p. 131.

Yes, academic, and in the strong sense of the word. It does not matter whether the academic is after Schumann, after Bach, after Wagner, or after a new serial type; the academic is something which I cannot accept at any time. The main problem, to my mind, is to find a purely musical way of thinking and not something which is parascientific.[3]

Dane Rudhyar's 1926 prediction in *The Foreword* contradicts this point: "It is in America that this new music will take root. There is no room for it in the old Europe which has become a soul-less form."[4] Regardless of the continuing battle for artistic supremacy and chauvinism, it was events in *both* Europe and America that led to the impact of *Sound-Mass* on the musical world.

Sound-Mass

Sound-mass, in contrast to "total control," minimizes the importance of individual notes (and their order) while maximizing the texture, rhythm, dynamics, and/or timbre of a given passage. This refocusing of importance is of great significance in the development of the *avant-garde* movement, for certainly it is with sound-mass that one confronts directly that fine thread between traditional concepts of "noise" and "music" (often fluctuating aesthetic identities).

Early songs of Charles Ives predate most deliberate "clusters" of sound if such *discovery* be important in itself. Sound-mass is also evident in fragments of works by such composers as Gustav Mahler in his unfinished *Tenth Symphony* (1910: panchromatic chords), and Béla Bartók in his 1926 *Piano Sonata*.

It is possibly most challengingly utilized, however, in Igor Stravinsky's *Le Sacre Du Printemps* (1912), where a driving and repetitive string mass of sound is "charged" with unpredictable harsh accents. The rhythm of the accents becomes the thrust of the work at this point ("Danses des Adolescentes") and pitch becomes meaningless except in its being there. Figure 1.9 shows the "Danses" and the resultant increase in importance of rhythm (accents) and decrease in importance of pitch as an integral linear (melodic) or vertical (harmonic) contributor to the work at this point.

Research and experimentation in the breakdown of tonality progressed as well along lines separate and distinct from twelve-tone procedures and sound-mass.

Many composers felt that the creation of temperament, especially equal temperament, and the arbitrary resolution of the octave into twelve

3. Galen Wilson and David Cope, "An Interview with Pierre Boulez," *The Composer* 1, no. 2 (September 1969): 79-80.
4. Dane Rudhyar, "A New Philosophy of Music," *The Foreword*, March 1926.

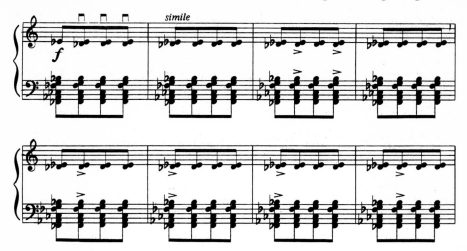

Figure 1.9. Igor Stravinsky: *Le Sacre Du Printemps:* "Danses des Adolescentes." Piano reduction of the string parts.

parts, had created equally arbitrary musical systems. Alois Hába (1893-1972) constructed a quarter-tone piano in the early twenties[5] and experimented with a sixth-tone system in the late thirties. Charles Ives (1874-1954) with *Three Quarter Tone Pieces* (1918?) for two pianos tuned a quarter tone apart, and Harry Partch (1901-74)[6] who, in the process of working with microtones (a practical and acoustical division of the octave into 43 tones), developed new instruments necessary for the realization of his experiments, worked more in isolation than Hába, but have received much attention in the past few years.[7] Composers such as Teo Macero, Calvin Hamilton, Donald Lybbert, and Ben Johnston have recently continued similar experimentation.

Though quarter tones had been used sparsely by Bartók (especially in his *Violin Concerto,* 1938) and Milhaud in the late thirties and forties, their true import had not fully been discovered; the use of twenty-four or more divisions of the octave requires abandonment or total revision of techniques of traditional instruments; creation of new or revised systems of notation; and implications of increasingly complex harmonic and melodic vocabularies. New instruments (e.g., the tape recorder), nota-

5. See Alois Hába, *The Theory of Quarter-tones* (out of print).

6. See Harry Partch, *Genesis of a Music* (Madison: University of Wisconsin Press, 1949).

7. See also Elliott Friedman, "Tonality in the Music of Harry Partch," *The Composer* 2, no. 1 (June 1970):16-24.

tions (graphs, punch cards), and scientific vocabularies developed in the early fifties, not so much as a direct result of experiments with intonation, but retrospectively in direct confrontation with the same problems.

Microtonal music (the term "microtone" is used here because the term "quarter tone" is as binding as twelve-tone: 24 tones to the octave being not that much less restrictive) is being used by a large number of composers today. Notation and performance are the primary roadblocks to consistent usage (see Appendix C). Ben Johnston (who has used micro-tones extensively in his *String Quartet #2*, 1964, and later works) has explained the situation quite accurately in his "How to Cook an Albatross": "In our laziness, when we changed over to the twelve-tone system, we just took the pitches of the previous music as though we were moving into a furnished apartment and had no time to even take the pictures off the wall. What excuse?"[8]

Instrument Exploration

Surprisingly, it seems, the desire for new and different sounds is probably the least significant of the driving forces behind the experimental or *avant-garde* composers in the past twenty years. Yet it is within this area that the contemporary composer has had the most serious division with his audience. John Cage referred to this in his 1937 lecture "The Future of Music: Credo": "Whereas, in the past, the point of disagreement has been between dissonance and consonance, it will be, in the immediate future, between noise and so-called musical sounds."[9] Philosophically, it is not "new" sounds (since no significant new sounds have been developed that had not coexisted with music since the beginning), but the concept that these sounds were potentially valuable as a musical resource, that has disturbed the music world.

A group of Italian composers, called Futurists, wrote music for machine guns, steam whistles, sirens, and other "noisemakers" as early as 1912. Deriving their name from Marinetti's 1909 term *futurismo* (referring to extreme radicalism in all the arts), the Futurists were among the first composers to include noise as an inherent part of the music, not merely as a side effect. Francesco Pratella's theoretical "Musica Futurista" (reprinted in Nicolas Slonimsky's *Music Since 1900*) describes the "music" of steamboats, automobiles, battleships, railways, shipyards, and airplanes. Luigi Russolo (1885-1947), the most noted Futurist composer, constructed many of his own "noise instruments." Though his and the majority of the music of this movement was completely without popular success and

8. Ben Johnston, "How to Cook an Albatross," *Source* no. 7:65.
9. John Cage, *Silence* (Cambridge, Mass.: The M.I.T. Press, paperback edition, 1961), p. 4.

approval, its significance lies in the fact that it proposed a concept and laid a foundation for other composers (though no *direct* relationship is implied) such as Varèse, who employed sirens and anvils, and Mossolov who, in his more imitative *Symphony of Machines—Steel Foundry* (1928), added to the traditional orchestra the constant rattling of a metal sheet throughout the work. Equally unsuccessful was the Futurist movement in France (*bruitisme*); again, however, it enlarged the concept of noise as a viable source for music to draw upon. George Antheil's *Ballet mécanique* (1924) is probably the most "infamous" of noise pieces, and is largely influenced by the French movement. Its first Carnegie Hall performance (April 10, 1927) brought about a violent audience reaction reminiscent of that which occurred at the first performance of Stravinsky's *Le Sacre du Printemps*. Antheil established the paradigm for the *avant-garde* to come, the "predictable" unpredictability of which is expressed in "An Introduction to George Antheil" by Charles Amirkhanian:

Here is a man who once drew a pistol during a piano recital to silence a restive audience; a man who, in 1923, composed a piece of music calling for the sound of an airplane motor; a man who was mistakenly reported by the news media to have been eaten alive by lions in the Sahara Desert; and a man who collaborated with Hedy Lamarr in the invention and patenting of a World War II torpedo.[10]

Figure 1.10. George Antheil arriving in New York for the U.S. premiere performance of his *Ballet mécanique* (1927).

10. Charles Amirkhanian, "An Introduction to George Antheil," *Soundings* 7-8:176. Originally printed in a KPFA Folio of November 1970.

Ezra Pound remarks that Antheil was possibly the first American-born musician to be taken seriously in Europe. This might explain John Cage's later successes there. The *Treatise on Harmony* by Antheil is a twenty-five-page book repetitively dwelling on the need for a reappraisement of rhythmic ideas equal to those of melody and harmony: "A sound of any pitch, or combination of such sounds, may be followed by a sound of any other pitch or any combination of such sounds, providing the time interval between them is properly gauged; and this is true for any series of sounds, chords or arpeggios."[11]

Electronic Music

In light of the vast technological progress of the past fifty years, it was inevitable that electronic sound sources would become viable materials from which the *avant-garde* composer could draw his new musics. The "Tapesichordists" (as Otto Luening and Vladimir Ussachevsky were termed in a November 10, 1952 review in *Time* of their renowned Museum of Modern Art concert of October 28, 1952), while not taken seriously until the early sixties, have steadfastly and consistently improved their working conditions, equipment, and technical knowledge to the point at which very few observers now claim the creation of music by "electrical means" to be a *passing fancy*.

In the first experiments with electronic music it was the potential "parameter expanding" advantages of the instruments themselves which attracted the composers, rather than the "noise" and program music, which seemed to be not of paramount interest. In France it was Pierre Schaeffer who developed the potentials of the first "electronic instrument": the tape recorder. By rerecording "natural" sounds at various speeds and splicing in composer-controlled rhythms this *musique concrète* became the first truly serious music of this genre. Likewise in France, Pierre Henry continued work with the tape recorder while in America it was the works of John Cage, Vladimir Ussachevsky, and Otto Luening that brought attention to this new sound source (all during the five-year period 1948-52—the years of real discovery and experimentation). "Electronic" sound sources soon added an entirely fresh potential of new materials to the sonic vocabulary.

Too soon, however, the new sounds became old and the new control (the composer becoming the performer, and indeed with the advent of computer realization capable of literally any microcosm of controllable elements in time) became available equally to those preferring lack of control. This latter point is strikingly evidenced by such contrasting works as Milton Babbitt's *Vision and Prayer* (1961) and Karlheinz Stockhausen's

11. Ezra Pound, *Antheil* (New York: Da Capo Press, 1968), p. 10.

Mikrophonie I (1965). The former, in pure electronic sounds (with "live" voice), is detailed by the composer in every available way, while the latter is a work derived from two performers acting on one six-foot gong with the score composed primarily of verbal descriptions of how the sounds should affect the listener ('grating,' 'scraping,' etc.) and two other performers controlling directional microphones, filters, and potentiometers (electronic timbre and volume control respectively).

Certainly the aforementioned need for new, nonequal-tempered scales combined with nearly limitless rhythmic possibilities (no longer restricted to the ten fingers of the pianist or the thousand of an orchestra), present opportunities that many composers cannot resist. Few, however, would agree with "New Music for an Old World Dr. Thaddeus Cahill's Dynamophone An Extraordinary Electrical Invention for Producing Scientifically Perfect Music" titling a *McClures' Magazine* article of July 1906.[12]

Nourished by the 1948 invention of the long-playing record, electronic music has become accessible to every listener's living room despite the singular neglect shown it by "serious music" radio stations. Moreover, electronic music's lack of visual interest in the concert hall has helped spawn a whole genre of interesting combinations of "live electronics"—tape with "live" performers—and has contributed greatly to the refinement and growth of *Media-Forms.*

Media Forms

Alexander Scriabin's *Prometheus—The Poem of Fire* (1910) is one of the first examples of mixed-media compositions with origins not directly related to opera or ballet. The scoring calls for large orchestra, chorus, piano, organ, and *clavier à lumières,* a nonexistent instrument with a keyboard-controlled lighting console. The part for the *clavier à lumières* employs traditional musical notation, and each key is associated with a color. Scriabin directly ascribed keys and tonal regions with colors (e.g., f was blue, *the color of reason;* F, *the blood red of hell;* D, *the sunny key;* etc.) and with *Prometheus* he envisioned far more than a superfluous "light-show." His concepts embodied a deeply philosophical and religious symbolism with beams and "clouds" of light moving throughout the hall. The chorus is to be draped in white robes and vocalize on ritualistic closed lips or vowel sounds. Unfortunately, *Prometheus* (which was completed in early 1910) was premiered in 1911 without the *clavier à lumières*—without any lighting, in fact. It waited until March 20, 1915 (just five weeks before the composer's death) to receive any mixed-

12. Elliott Schwartz, *Electronic Music: A Listener's Guide* (New York: Praeger Publishers, 1973), p. 241 (from Otto Luening's remarks).

media complement at all, and then received only weak color projections moving on a small screen, falling considerably short of the composer's intentions.

Schoenberg's *Die glückliche Hand* (opus 18, 1910-13) was to be presented with lighting effects, which proved to be technologically unfeasible, and the resulting presentation proved to be a poor realization of the composer's intent. *Prometheus*, at least, has had a media "revival" in the past few years, with numerous attempts made at fulfilling the composer's wishes. Unfortunately, most of the results seem diluted by the architecture of the concert hall's interior, or by the lack of real musical translation of sound into light.

Theatrical elements in new music seem to have closer historical ties with the ballet than with opera or oratorio. Though many mainstream composers (notably William Schuman and Aaron Copland) have created ballets for dance groups (especially for Martha Graham), it was really when John Cage and the Merce Cunningham dance group became associated that theater was again injected into the combination of art forms, with each surviving by its dependence upon the other.

These directions, combined with the television-cinema age, and the need in electronic music for auxiliary visual material, have contributed largely to the contemporary revival of the *Gesamtkunstwerke* concept in the form of "happenings." Richard Maxfield writes: "I view as irrelevant the repetitious sawing on strings and baton-wielding spectacle we focus our eyes upon during a conventional concert. Much more sensible either no visual counterpart or one more imaginatively selected such as lighting, cinema, choreography, fireworks, trees. . . ."[13] The sophistication of equipment and techniques of lighting, still and moving projections, and so on, have made available many new multimedia possibilities to the twentieth century artist-composer. Like all other facets of mid-twentieth century life, the new forms of art must inevitably share responsibility with the electromechanical environment in which they develop.

Improvisation

Improvisation has contributed to the "creative" act of the performer and consequently has become an added element in the growing conflict between "total control" and "lack of control." As such it forms a fertile middle ground between the two. Improvisation reflects a controlled interaction between or among performers, as it is used in jazz, though without the necessarily limited and constricting harmonic and melodic vocabu-

13. As quoted in *An Anthology of Chance Operations*, ed. La Monte Young and Jackson Mac Low (New York: 1963). No page numbers.

lary. Dating from the figured bass of the Baroque age and before, improvisation remains a calculated and constructive method of variation. Likewise, it meets the need and desire of composer and performer alike to share more equally in the joy of creating and communicating with sound. Once it is admitted that any notation, regardless of exactness or precision, must necessarily involve a certain amount of performer choice and decision, there remains only the question, "How much?" The answer is determined by what will obtain the best result, that is, the most *alive* result.

Indeterminate Music

Indeterminate music is the concept that finds least historical precedence. The concept is more philosophical than real. Obviously two performances of Paul Ignace's *It Is* (1946) could vary to extreme degrees in instrumentation, rhythm, harmonic simultaneity; but without prior knowledge of the composer's procedure or visual access to the score, the audience could make no real decision concerning determinability or indeterminability. Figure 1.11 is the full score to *It Is;* that is, there are no performance instructions as to how it is to be interpreted as a musical composition in any way. Earle Brown's later *December 1952* is similar in nature but more visually musical in that its short vertical and horizontal bursts of line of varying thicknesses ignite more easily some form of rhythmic, dynamic, and pitch realization.

Many have suggested that indeterminate concepts of sound return to the most fundamental of primeval thought: "Play sounds and listen to them." Certainly, sophistication of instrumentation and equipment has altered; however, it may be that this "new" concept of sound is indeed the oldest.

Barney Childs has noted that ". . . The means of indeterminacy may be applied in composition, in performance, or in both."[14] The composer may, for example, use chance operations to complete a work in fully traditional notation. On the other hand he may achieve unpredictability by graphic scores with little hint at realization. The degree of "unpredictability," of course, varies with each composer and work. At one end of the spectrum *improvisation* exists as a form of indeterminacy in that a certain degree of indeterminacy exists prior to performance. At the other end of the spectrum one finds works like *It Is* and *December 1952* where little, if anything, is predictable. It is at this latter degree, pushed just a bit further, that one encounters *Antimusic.*

14. Barney Childs, "Indeterminacy and Theory: Some Notes," *The Composer* 1, no. 1 (June 1969):20.

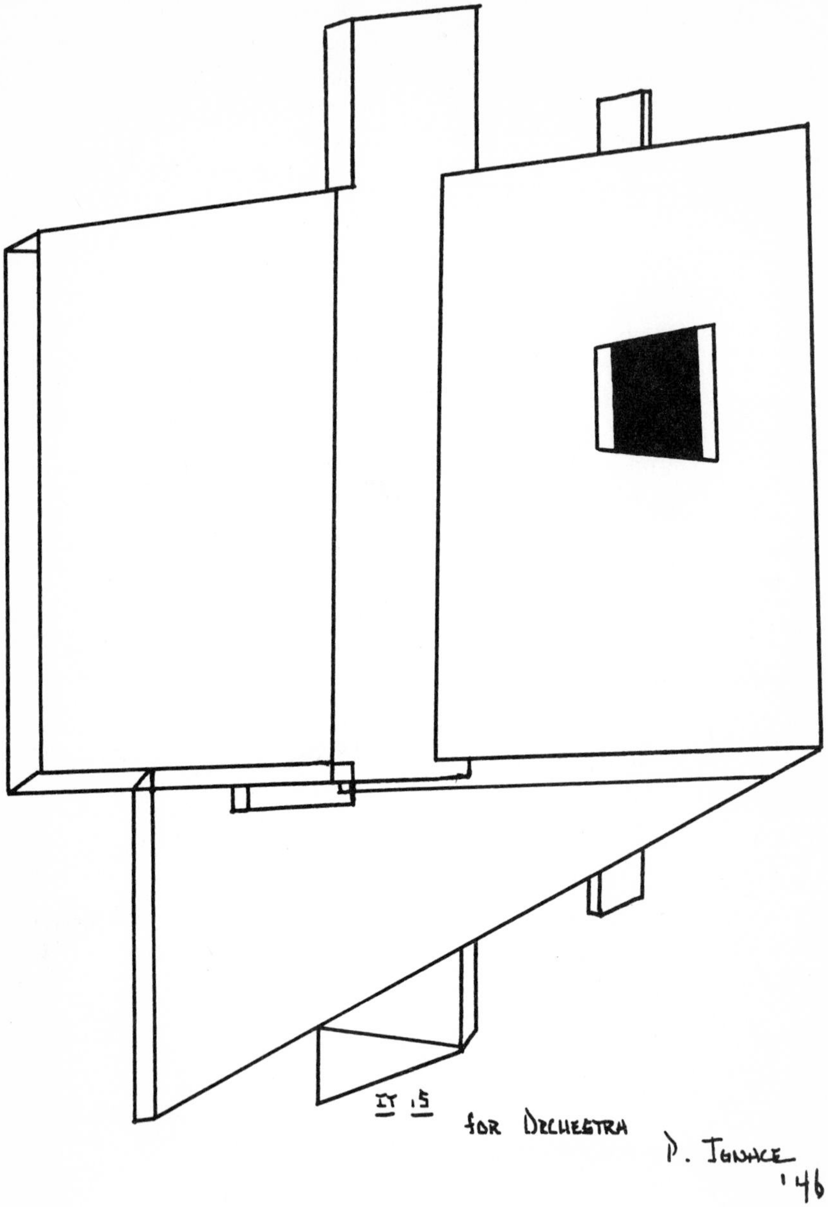

Figure 1.11.   Paul Ignace: *It 1s*
(full score).

Antimusic

Though the scope of this book does not permit fully detailed coverage of the cross-disciplinary aspects of the arts in general, and the added stimulus which the visual arts in particular have given to new music, the impetus generated by artists such as Marcel Duchamp, Man Ray, Robert Rauschenberg, Kandinsky, and many others has been profound. In the mainstream of music one finds it generated by composers like Schoenberg (who was himself an expressionist painter of repute) and Stravinsky. In the *avant-garde* one encounters cross-relationships particularly between such artists and composers as Erik Satie (Man Ray), John Cage (Rauschenberg), and Earle Brown (Alexander Calder) among others.

If one were to draw roots to the antimusic movement, the *Musical Sculpture* by Marcel Duchamp is noteworthy (undated, but shows a direct relationship with current concept musics), as is his early work *The Bride Stripped Bare by Her Bachelors, Even*. Duchamp's *Erratum Musical* (1913) is a work done in numbers whose realization by the composer consists in substituting a note for each number (Petr Kotik has made two current realizations, one for two pianos, the other for five instruments). The dada artists and later the antiart, concept art, and minimal art movements have all preceded the parallel activities in music.

Paul Nougé (active in the surrealistic movement), in his *Music is Dangerous* (written in 1929), points out that the most known "uses" of music (relaxation, forgetting, and pleasure) are but subtle facades for its emotional dangers, drawing proofs from the ancient modal theories wherein each mode provoked distinct emotions (phrygian: excitement; lydian: calming; etc.).[15] His "iatric" music (medicinal music: noting that a great many medical terms end in "iatric" such as pediatric, etc.) further established music's profound remedial capabilities (possibly, in the sense that a witch doctor has therapeutic powers, predating our current fascination with music therapy). Most importantly, however, was Nougé's concept that the audience was indeed not separate from or even "safe" from musical performance: "Our answer is that the concept of *spectator*, which seems to play so important a role in certain minds, is one of the grossest imaginable."[16] It is doubtful that Nougé's writings have had a direct influence over the antimusics of our present era but it is most noteworthy that such expressions as ". . . how we may defend ourselves against music. . . . Evidently, the easiest way is to refuse once and for all to have anything to do with it . . ." are not at all a new thought or light divertissement as might be supposed.[17]

15. Paul Nougé, *Music is Dangerous*, trans. Felix Giovanelli from *View* magazine. Reprinted in book form by *Soundings* (1973).
16. Ibid., p. 17.
17. Ibid., p. 24.

From these concepts, more *about* than *with* sound, questions regarding the most fundamental of ideas about music must inevitably arise. The continual expansion of the definition of music to include *all* sound, regardless of origin or "beauty," and all concepts of sound, may eventually annul the "antimusic" designation used here; but the primary motive behind the antimusic philosophy remains: to destroy the concept of an "immaculate" art separate from life, with all its dangers and temporality. Indeed, the antimusic philosophy returns full circle to the primeval approach to sound.

The Post *Avant-garde*[18]

The struggle, however taut it may have once seemed, grows less and less tangible with each passing year. The post *avant-garde* works of chapter 9, as different in sound and structure as they may seem, hold a fragile but distinctly recognizable common seed among them. Possibly Ben Johnston says it best in his article *On Context:* "Awareness makes free choice possible. Freedom requires responsiveness: responsibility."[19] Later in the same article his optimism is clearly focused:

It is as though we have to cross a chasm. If we are to build a bridge over it we will have to anchor its ends far in the past and far in the future. Tradition thoroughly assimilated will help us anchor in the past; only a sharp eye for where we are going can help us anchor in the future. Technology will help us build the bridge, which will not impose upon nature but will be possible because we understand how things happen and cooperate rather than interfering.[20]

The twentieth century is the age of revolution in music, but for beginnings, it must again be stated that the nearest local relatives, as desirable or undesirable as they may be, rest in serialization, the restriction that founded two ideas of nearly irreconcilable differences: music as thought (control), music as sound (freedom).

18. Note here that what the author means by post *Avant-Garde* is not its literal translation from the French (after the "ahead of its time") but rather the developments after the period known as the *avant-garde* (1940-70: see chap. 9 of this book).
19. Ben Johnston, "On Context," *ASUC Proceedings #3* (1968), p. 35.
20. Ibid.

Bibliography

*Further Readings**

*Addresses for record companies, periodicals, and music publishers mentioned in this Bibliography can be found in Appendix 4.

American Society of University Composers. *Proceedings* I-VIII. A clear cross section of contemporary thought concerning the issues encountered in chapter 1.

Anderson, E. Ruth. *Contemporary American Composers: A Biographical Dictionary*. Marshfield Hills, Mass.: An incredibly complete source for contemporary American composers. (Address: P.O. Box 194, 02051)

Asterisk. A new periodical as of December, 1974, dedicated to presenting the many aspects of new music.

Babbitt, Milton. "Set Structure as a Compositional Determinant." *Journal of Music Theory* 5 (April 1961):72-94. A good study in the thoughts and directions of the materials derived from this "determinate" composer.

Basart, Ann Phillips. *Serial Music: A Classified Bibliography of Writings on Twelve Tone and Electronic Music* (Berkeley: University of California Press, 1961). An excellent reference tool.

Beckwith, John, and Kasemets, Udo. *The Modern Composer and His World*. Toronto: University of Toronto Press, 1961. A series of reports and discussions from the International Conference of Composers (1960) on the various aspects covered in chapter.

Berg, Alban. "Why is Schoenberg's Music So Hard to Understand?" *The Music Review*, (May 1952), pp. 187-96. The first printed translation—a fascinating early source for such information.

Boretz, Benjamin, and Cone, Edward T., eds. *Perspectives on American Composers*. New York: W.W. Norton and Co., 1971.

———. *Perspectives on Contemporary Music Theory*. New York: W. W. Norton and Co., 1972. Both of the above are useful books dealing with issues facing the contemporary composer in articles by contemporary composers.

Cage, John. M. *Writings '67-'72*. Middletown, Conn.: Wesleyan University Press, 1973. The latest book by this innovator of our times.

———. *Silence*. Cambridge, Mass.: The M.I.T. Press, paperback edition, 1961. An excellent primer on *all* facets of the *avant-garde*.

Chase, Gilbert. *The American Composer Speaks*. Baton Rouge: Louisiana State University Press, 1966. Very valuable, especially pp. 184-305. Consists of articles and statements by the composers themselves.

Contemporary Music in Europe. Reprinted from *Musical Quarterly*, January 1965. Valuable but somewhat outdated view of the *avant-garde* on the continent.

Cowell, Henry, ed. *American Composers on American Music*. New York: Frederick Ungar Publishing Co., 1933. An excellent source of material on early composers of *avant-garde* music, such as Henry Brant, John Becker, Ruth Crawford, Carlos Salzedo, and Wallingford Riegger, among others.

Cowell, Henry, and Cowell, Sidney. *Charles Ives and His Music*. New York: Oxford University Press, 1955. An excellent biographical and analytical study of this great innovator of the twentieth century.

Cowell, Henry. *New Musical Resources*. New York: Alfred A. Knopf, 1920. A superb look into the mind of this *avant-garde* genius and his forward-looking ideas, many of which are still considered revolutionary.

Composer Magazine, 1-6. A good source for a wide cross section of articles and interviews concerning subject matter in chapter 1.

Dallin, Leon. *Techniques of Twentieth Century Composition*. 3rd ed. Dubuque, Iowa: Wm. C. Brown Company Publishers, 1974. Includes a wide variety of new musics for discussion in addition to excellent discussion of mainstream musics, presenting a very sensible balance of musical styles.

Hansen, Peter. *An Introduction to Twentieth Century Music*. Boston: Allyn & Bacon, 1967. Includes material to the point of this chapter, especially pp. 359-96.

Hitchcock, H. Wiley. *Music in the United States: A Historical Introduction*. Englewood Cliffs, N. J.: Prentice-Hall, 1969. Quite good as an introduction to new music in America, especially pp. 221-61.

"Hommage to Messiaen." *Melos*, 25: December 1958, entire issue. A good study of this man and his musical contributions.

Journal of Music Theory. Often contains articles pertaining to this subject matter.

Kolneder, Walter. *Anton Webern: An Introduction to His Works*. Berkeley: University of California Press, 1968.

Lang, Paul Henry, ed. *Problems of Modern Music*. New York: W. W. Norton and Co., 1960. A collection of chapters by various individuals involved deeply in the *avant-garde*, inclusive of Babbitt, Carter, Ussachevsky, and Krenek, among others.

Messiaen, Oliver. *The Technique of My Musical Language*. Paris: Alphonse Leduc & Cie., 1950. A complex theoretical and philosophical treatise of his highly specialized rhythmic and control procedures.

Numus West, 1-5. An excellent periodical devoted to the various aspects of *avant-garde* music.

The New Oxford History of Music (The Modern Age 1890-1960). London: Oxford University Press, 1974. Good introductory material on new music by country.

Partch, Harry. *The Genesis of a Music*. New York: Da Capo Press, 1973. An excellent study of this innovative man's work and ideas.

Perle, George. *Serial Composition and Atonality*. Berkeley: University of California Press, 1962. Contains numerous analyses, especially of completely serialized compositions, and lists a large number of them as well for further study.

Perspectives of New Music. Excellent periodical dedicated to new music idioms.

Prieberg, F. K. "Der musikalische Futurismus." *Melos* 25:124-27. Good introduction to the works of Luigi Russolo and the Futurists.

Die Reihe 1-6. Edited by Herbert Eimert and Karlheinz Stockhausen. Released at various dates by Theodore Presser Co. Provides a wide variety of viewpoints and concepts relating to the materials of chapter 1; good readings for the person interested in the European concepts of the *avant-garde* through the mid-sixties.

Rossi, Nick. *Music of Our Time.* Boston: Crescendo Publishing Co., 1969. Excellent source of examples, composers, and photos of new music (unfortunately segregated by country as in so many other books of this type).

Salzman, Eric. *Twentieth-Century Music: An Introduction.* Englewood Cliffs, N. J.: Prentice-Hall, 1967. Extremely good on new music, its only drawback being brevity. Pp. 155-86 especially good in treatment of "ultra-rationality" vs. "antirationality."

Schwartz, Elliott, and Childs, Barney, eds. *Contemporary Composers on Contemporary Music* (New York: Holt, Rinehart and Winston, 1967). Superb book and a continuation in spirit of Cowell's *American Composers on American Music* in that it is a collection of articles by the composers themselves inclusive of a full range of topics relating to *avant-garde* musics (see especially Stefan Wolpe's "Thinking Twice," pp. 274-307, on complex serial and philosophical ideas; and "The Liberation of Sound" by Edgard Varèse, pp. 195-208, as well as a host of other very important articles which will be cited many times later in this book).

Sonorum Speculum. A valuable reference source for information on new music in the Netherlands.

Soundings 1-10 (now, unfortunately, out of publication; see address, Appendix 4 for back issues). A very important periodical on new music. *Soundings* has likewise printed two extremely important books: *Soundings: Ives, Ruggles and Varèse* and *Music is Dangerous.*

Spinner, Leopold. *A Short Introduction to the Technique of Twelve-Tone Composition.* (London: Boosey and Hawkes, 1960). Useful to the uninitiated.

Templier, Pierre-Daniel. *Erik Satie.* Cambridge, Mass.: The M.I.T. Press, 1969.

Tremblay, George. *The Definitive Cycle of the Twelve Tone Row.* New York: Criterion Music Corp., 1974. An extremely complex text dealing in part with the 288 rows of any "cycle" from the 479,001,600 discrete twelve-tone rows possible: an eyeful of complex note control.

Vinton, John, ed. *Dictionary of Contemporary Music.* New York: E. P. Dutton & Co., 1974. An excellent source for subject headings listed in this chapter as well as biographical material on all the composers listed.

Yates, Peter. *Twentieth Century Music.* New York: Pantheon Books, 1967. A superb book dealing with the philosophies and backgrounds of the current *avant-garde*.

Note: At this writing two books on twentieth-century techniques are soon to be released: one by Gardner Read (MacMillan), and the other by Raymond Wilding-White (Holt, Rinehart, and Winston). Nancy Zin's *But There's Nothing in it I can Hum: A Guide to Contemporary Music* should be available by or before publication of *New Directions in Music.*

*Recordings and Publishers**

*Note: Only the recordings and publishers of composers not discussed in later chapters are included here. In addition are "collections" of *avant-garde* music (following the listings of individual composers).

Antheil, George. *Ballet mécanique* (1924). Templeton.

———. *Sonatas* (3). Weintraub. Recorded on Orion 73119.

———. *Symphony No. 4* (1942). Recorded on Everest 3013.

———. *Transatlantic* (1929). Universal Edition. A most interesting and unusual Antheil opera.

Babbitt, Milton. *Quartet No. 2* (1954). Recorded on Nonesuch 71280.

———. *Quartet No. 3* (1969-70). Recorded on Turnabout 34515.

———. *Three Compositions for Piano* (1947). Boelke-Bonart.

———. *Vision and Prayer* (1961). AMP Publishers. Recorded on CRI-268.

Bartók, Belá. (Recordings too numerous to mention here may be found by consulting the Schwann Record Catalog.)

Berg, Alban. *Concerto for Violin and Orchestra*. Universal Edition. Recorded on Columbia MS-6373.

Boulez, Pierre. *Le Marteau Sans Maître* (1955). Universal Edition. Recorded on Columbia MQ-32160.

———. *Second Piano Sonata* (1948). Heugel Publishers. Recorded on FIN 9004.

———. *Structures* (1952). Universal Edition. Recorded on Vox 678.028.

Crawford, Ruth. *Quartet* (New Music Edition). Recorded on Nonesuch 71280 (along with quartets by Perle and Babbitt).

Dallapiccola, Luigi. *Sei cori di Michelangelo Buonarroti il Giovane* (for chorus and orchestra, 1933-36). Carisch Publishers. Recorded on Telefunken S-43095.

Ives, Charles. (Recordings abound; consult Schwann Record Catalog.)

Johnston, Ben. *Quartet No. 2* (1964). Recorded on Nonesuch 71224 (along with Cage's 'live' electronic HPSCHD).

Messiaen, Oliver. *Chronochromie* (1960). Leduc Publishers. Recorded on Angel S-36295.

Rudhyar, Dane. *Granites* (for piano, 1929). Published by Lengnick. Recorded on CRI S-247.

Satie, Erik. *La Belle excentrique* (1920). Sirene. Recorded (with a large group of Satie works) on Vanguard C-10037/8.

Schoenberg, Arnold. *Die glückliche Hand* (1913). Universal Edition. Recorded on Columbia M2S-679. (For further Schoenberg recordings see Schwann Catalog.)

Scriabin, Alexander. *Prometheus* (1910). Belaive Publishers. Recorded on Candide 31039. Like the Schoenberg, lacks its "color" counterpart.

Stravinsky, Igor. (Numerous recordings are listed in the Schwann Catalog.)

Stockhausen, Karlheinz. *Mikrophonie I.* (1964). An electronic work recorded on Columbia MS-7355.

Varèse, Edgard. Scores are available from G. Schirmer. His music is recorded on Columbia MS-6146.

Webern, Anton. Complete works (published primarily by Universal Edition), including his pointillistic orchestration of Bach's "Fuga" from *The Musical Offering*, are recorded on Columbia's four-record set, K4L-232.

        ❂   ❂   ❂   ❂   ❂

Collections of new musics offering the listener different perspectives on the *avant-garde* include: Odyssey 32160162, five works in quarter tones; The Cornell University Wind Ensemble Recordings, offering a wide variety of different types of new musics (fifteen records to date); *The New Music,* consisting of three Victrola albums by RCA (VICS-1312, VICS-1239, and VICS-1313) which cover a wide gamut of *avant-garde* literature.

Spectrum is a series of new music records (three to date: H-71219, H-71220, and H-71221) on Nonesuch which, like the RCA *New Music* series, offers a wide range of new styles. Nonesuch as well presents *The New Trumpet* (H-71275) and *The Contemporary Contrabass* (H-71237). *The Sounds of New Music* (Folkways FX 6160) contains, among other works, *Dance* by Cage (published by C. F. Peters), *Ionisation* by Varèse (published by Ricordi), and Henry Cowell's *Aeolian Harp* and *Banshee* (both published by AMP).

For further works one should consult the separate chapter bibliographies along with the following important sources: *Internationales Musikinstitut Darmstadt Informationszentrum für zeitgenössische Music: Katalog der Abteilung Noten* (Druckerei und Verlag Jacob Helene KG., Pfungstadt, Ostendstrasse 10), a very fine listing of works of new music by *avant-garde* composers, published yearly; *New Music* (quarterly of modern compositions which Henry Cowell edited for many years; now out of print, it is still a fascinating source of music of twentieth-century American *avant-garde* composers); *Source Magazine* which, like *New Music,* publishes music, not articles, is an excellent source for new music.

2 Sound-Mass, Rhythm, and Microtones

Sound-Mass Evolution

One of the most profound aesthetic technicalities of the musical world is that fine differentiation between sound and noise (noise being generally a derogatory term applied to sounds incapable of making music). One of the prime movers in fracturing this elitist concept is the cluster chord or what has become known as sound-mass.

With Henry Cowell's *The Tides of Manaunaun* (1911) and Charles Ives's *Majority* (piano and voice, 1921), the cluster chord (on piano in both of these works) came into focus. Both present some of the first uses of traditional "noise" as an acceptable musical element and, as such, assign greater philosophical importance to contemporary music than many have suggested.

In *The Hero Sun* (1922) Henry Cowell uses the right forearm on the black keys (see fig. 2.1: note that the $\sharp$ above indicates black keys while a $\natural$ would indicate white keys) strikingly using sound-mass as both a melodic and percussive device against the open consonances of the left-hand harmonies. Cowell's notations for clusters deviated occasionally from piece to piece, but the basics are shown and explained in figure 2.2, taken from *What's This* (also 1922). These works, along with a large number of other innovative pieces (such as *The Banshee* discussed under *Instrument Exploration*) did indeed impress a large number of composers (Béla Bartók in particular) and culminated in his writing of *New Musical Resources* (1930). Figure 2.3 from this book reveals the depth to which Cowell studied both the musical properties and notation of sound-mass. About this example he has written: "Clusters that do in a certain sense move are, however, quite possible, and it is interesting to consider the various ways in which such movement can be introduced."[1] He notes both additive and subtractive clusters (subtractive in fig. 2.3), and thus predates a great deal of music (especially that of Penderecki) and articles (especially Kagel's "Tone-clusters, Attacks, Transitions" in *die Reihe* #5).

John Becker (1886-1961), regrettably a relatively unnoticed innovator of the twenties and thirties, includes large clusters in most of his works.

---

1. Henry Cowell, *New Musical Resources* (New York: Alfred A. Knopf, 1930), p. 126.

Allegro con brio

Figure 2.1. Henry Cowell: *The Hero Sun* (1922). Page 3. © Copyright Breitkopf and Härtel, Inc. Permission granted by the publisher. Associated Music Publishers, Agents in U.S.

His Third Symphony (1929) derives large sound-mass structures from long sustained chords built of seconds with instruments of similar color. In other sections the clusters are used to turn an entire section of the orchestra into a single percussion instrument sound by means of articulation (short, very loud, heavy accents).

Wallingford Riegger's *Music for Brass Choir* (1949) is one of the first large ensemble works to use large "closed" clusters. The work opens with ten trombones, each with a different chromatic note, encompassing the range of a diminished seventh.

The Symbol (◊, ◊, ◊, etc.) represents a silent pressing down and holding of the key in order that the open string may be subjected to sympathetic vibration.

It will be noticed that half and whole notes are written open, or white; while notes of other time values are written closed, or black.

When such tone clusters are small, the fist or open hand is to be used (The symbol **x** indicates the use of the fist).

In the larger tone clusters the forearm is to be employed. Care should be taken to play all the tones exactly together, and in legato passages to press the keys rather than strike them, thus obtaining a smoother tone quality.

Tone clusters to be played in the manner indicated by the symbol (◊) will be written as:

An arrowhead is used in connection with arpeggiation marks to indicate **whether** the arpeggiation is to be from the lowest tone upwards, as is customary, (↑) or from the highest tone downwards (↓)

R. F. Stands for right fist; L.F. for left fist.
R. A. Stands for right arm; L. A. for left arm.

Figure 2.2.   Explanation of symbols from *What's This* (1922), by Henry Cowell © Copyright Breitkopf and Härtel, Inc. Permission granted by the publisher. Associated Music Publishers, Agents in U.S.

Most noteworthy in this work is the subtlety with which even the panchromatic final chord of the full ensemble (ten trumpets, eight horns, ten trombones, two tubas, and percussion) is expressed in terms of dy-

Figure 2.3. Henry Cowell: *New Musical Resources* (1930), page 128.
© Copyright Alfred A. Knopf, Inc.
All rights reserved. By permission.

Figure 2.4. Henry Cowell.
BMI Archives. Used by permission.

namics. Instead of the more than usual blasts of sound, these (both beginning and end) are soft with the final four bar *lento a pianissimo*.

Twelve-note or panchromatic chords were logically derived from
twelve-tone music; wide spacing avoided "cluster chord" terminology, but
the effect is the same, as in *Sonate Harmonique* by Galen Wilson which
contains a near-panchromatic (nine-note) cluster effect.

Figure 2.5.   Galen Wilson: *Sonate
Harmonique*. (Published by Composers' Autograph Publications, 1968.)

Current Examples

Apart from electronic music, pandiatonicism and the aforementioned Becker work, the cluster (or sound-mass) crept slowly into the orchestra in works like *Metastasis* (1955) by Iannis Xenakis, and *Threnody for the Victims of Hiroshima* (1960) by Krzysztof Penderecki. Probably one of the best-known orchestral works of the past twenty years, *Threnody* employs a wide variety of string techniques (fifty-two string parts), surprisingly few of which are actually new. What is more immediately recognizable are the solid bands of sound which widen and contract by means of glissando. These clusters, involving quarter tones, create a "white sound" effect resolved by movement to a single pitch, and contain such heavy overtone influence that, even though only the area of a fifth may actually have been covered, the aural impression is that of all audible sounds occurring simultaneously.

Figure 2.6 is the final 54 seconds of *Threnody*. Noteworthy is the fact that even though the notation is proportional (see Appendix 3) the visual cluster bands are extremely similar to those that were suggested by Cowell in his *New Musical Resources* thirty years earlier (refer to fig. 2.3).

Penderecki's *Passion According to St. Luke* (1965) is more traditional in form and construction than *Threnody*. The *Passion* constantly involves a compounding of simple structures into dense bands of twelve-tone or panchromatic clusters. A continuous thread of contrapuntal material, even during these cluster effects, represents a unique approach to sound-mass construction. Half-sung, half-spoken backgrounds to crowd scenes create equally massive constructs of sound which owe their intensity to drama as well as to dissonance.

Penderecki's *Capriccio for Violin and Orchestra* (1967) as it appears in fig. 6.13 in the chapter on improvisation shows the cluster band of *Threnody* expanded by its visual potential to the extremes of performer control and theatrics in terms of sound.

Iannis Xenakis utilizes sound-mass as a result of his stochastic procedures (see chapter 7 for more detailed discussion of these). Most of his works employ large "clouds" of sound incredibly dense as a result of large numbers of individual voices usually of like timbre (pizzicato or glissando clusters, for example). Indeed it is difficult to pick out a single one of his works which does not employ sound-mass to a high degree of sophistication (both in terms of rhythm and pitch). Xenakis has had considerable impact in Europe and many have attributed Penderecki's and the Polish School's use of sound-mass to his influence. In a 1955 article "The Crises of Serial Music," Xenakis remarks:

Linear polyphony destroys itself by its very complexity; what one hears is in reality nothing but a mass of notes in various registers. The enormous com-

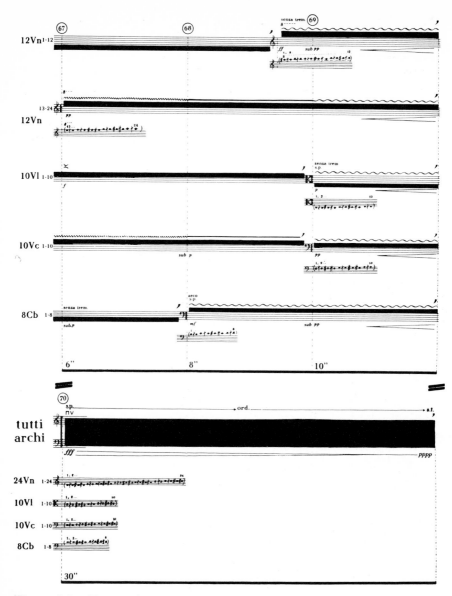

Figure 2.6.   Krzysztof Penderecki:
Threnody for the Victims of Hiroshima
(final page of score). Showing how
the notes for each cluster band are
written out in traditional form beneath
them, in this proportional notation.
Copyright © 1961 Deshon Music, Inc.,
& PWM Editions. Used with permission. All rights reserved.

plexity prevents the audience from following the intertwining of the lines and has as its macrocosmic effect an irrational and fortuitous dispersion of sounds over the whole extent of the sonic spectrum. There is consequently a contradiction between the polyphonic linear system and the heard result, which is surface or mass.[2]

György Ligeti's *Atmosphères* (1961) involves the full complement of winds, strings, and percussion, with more spaced structures of sound orchestrated in such a manner as to create unique "clusters" of sound by overtones and resultant tones filling in the spaces. In *Lux Aeterna* (1966) and *Requiem* (1965) (for soprano, mezzo-soprano, two mixed choirs, and orchestra), Ligeti achieves similar choral clusters approaching an effect in which instruments and individual voices are unrecognizable.

Ligeti's *Lontano* (1967) for orchestra often employs over fifty separate instrumental voices (Ligeti's music, unlike Penderecki's, is notated by traditional means) to create an ever-evolving and developing sonic texture seeming to lack recognizable melodic direction yet maintaining

Figure 2.7.   Edgard Varèse. BMI Archives. Used by permission.

2. Iannis Xenakis, "The Crisis of Serial Music," *Gravesaner Blätter,* no. 1 (1955).

an enormous musical impact in terms of the other available parameters (dynamics and timbre in particular).

Edgard Varèse uses brass, organ, and Ondes Martenot in his *Equatorial* (1934) to achieve sound-mass. In reference to the work of Varèse, Robert Erickson writes: "These highly individual sound-blocks are images, ikons, in their own right. They exist as entities in the same way as a melody can be felt to be an entity."[3] Most of Varèse's output (primarily wind ensemble and percussion music) is developed in terms of "ikons." Many have considered Varèse the extension of Stravinsky's "primitive" period (e.g., *Le Sacre du Printemps;* period extending to the mid-twenties of this century when Stravinsky's so-called *neoclassic* period began) and as such many of the massive dissonances of his *Hyperprism* (1923) and *Octandre* (1924) are strikingly percussive and rhythmic in nature.

Henryk Górecki (b. 1933 in Poland), in his *Scontri* for orchestra (1960), includes massive blocks and bands of tones throughout, at times graphically notated as large black boxes overlapping entire sections of the score.

Luigi Nono's three choral works *Il canto sospeso* (1956), *La terra e la campagna* (1957), and *Cori di Didone* (1958) are based almost entirely on twelve-tone aggregate choral clusters creating masses of white sound within which the voices move as "fish through water."

"The important tones, the ones that are most plainly heard, are those of the outer edges of a given cluster."[4] Thus the composer and performer both realized that order and exact notation of clusters of tones were not sufficiently important to warrant exact notation. They could be described verbally or graphically so that clusters of sound, or sound-masses, were inevitable. Theodore Lucas, in *Aberrations No. VII* for piano (fig. 2.8), evolves a system of cluster notation (white and black keys) which shows duration by horizontal length. Graphic structures show only approximate pitch and relative motion (notice here that the two sets of clusters remain static). Various cluster effects are dramatically notated by Stanley Lunetta in his *Piano Music*. Notice here, especially with the indication "wiggle all fingers," the obvious interpretative possibilities for the performer. See *Piano Music* on page 36.

Figure 2.10, a dramatic portion of Karel Husa's *Apotheosis of This Earth* (1971) for concert band, demonstrates another means of achieving sound-mass: clusters achieved by rhythmic densities so thick as to produce a vibrating column of sound. This approach allows for continuous development of motivic and melodic fragments.

---

3. Robert Erickson, "Varèse: 1924-1937: Sound-Ikon," *The Composer* 1, no. 3 (December 1969):144.

4. Henry Cowell, *New Musical Resources* (New York: Alfred A. Knopf, 1930), p. 122.

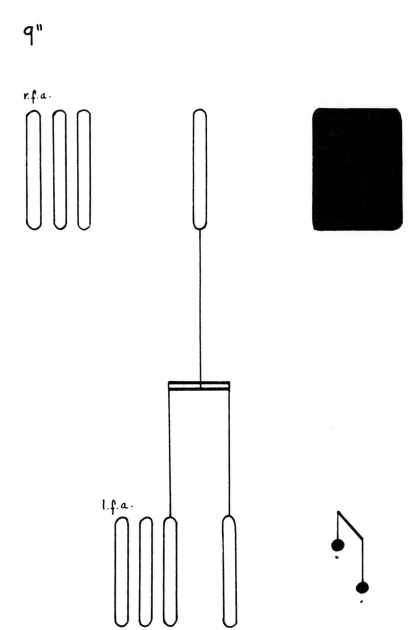

Figure 2.8. Theodore Lucas: *Aberrations No. VII* for piano. Copyright 1969 by the composer. (Published by Composers' Autograph Publications.)

[121 cont'd]

Figure 2.9. Karel Husa: *The Apotheosis of This Earth.* © Copyright 1971 by Associated Music Publishers, Inc. Used by permission.

INSTRUCTIONS:

♪̥ natural

♪ sharp

♪♪ short note

○━━━━ long note
●━━━

♪ white key cluster
▯

♪ black key cluster
▮

♪ black and white key cluster
▯▮

🌀 written-out cluster
♭

cover the area indicated and rapidly wiggle all fingers—
interpret the shape

▱ glissando

♫ spaced evenly

Great care has been taken to space all other notes to indicate
the rhythmical relationships. After each page-turn play each
system completely, following all instructions and playing all
visible notes.

Figure 2.10.   Stanley Lunetta:
Piano Music. Performance instructions.
Permission granted by *Source: Music
of the Avant-Garde* Composer/Per-
former Edition, Davis, California.

Pauline Oliveros's *Sound Pattern* (1965?) creates cluster sound-mass effects with voices, employing whispers, tongue clicks, lip pops, and similar effects, and allowing improvised pitches within areas of high, middle, and low registers. The results here are often similar to choral effects in Penderecki's *Passion* and Ligeti's *Requiem*, yet exist more as timbre clusters than as pitch clusters.

In the last few years, it has become increasingly difficult to ascertain whether the composer's motive for cluster effects has developed improvisational (partially aleatoric) procedures, or whether they came about as a result of such procedures. *Improvisation ajoutée* (1962) by Mauricio Kagel, for four-manual organ and two or three adjunct performers, includes huge block clusters of sound, performed with hands, forearms, and feet, and rapid multichanges in registration with, as the composer states, "the improvisation arising through the statistical nature of timbre transformations."

In *Sonant* (1960), Mauricio Kagel calls for speaking and whispering from the ensemble at various pitch levels *ad libitum,* the result being a huge block or "cluster" sound-mass. The consequence of such experimentations was not only new notations, but a direct result and application of partially indeterminate procedures: though clusters are inevitable, exact duplication of numerous highly variable factors creates widely unpredictable results.

Stockhausen's *Mixtur* (1964) demonstrates huge cluster effects (spatially, as the five groups are placed around the audience) as a result of traditional notation approximated by lack of staves or other exact pitch identification. Obvious motivic structures occur, yet each performer's independent decision regarding pitch height or depth, and rhythmic variety, results in extremely complex sound-mass structures.

The *Trois Poèmes d'Henri Michaux* for mixed chorus and orchestra (1963) by Witold Lutoslawski includes cluster chords derived of approximate pitch notation. An important technique employed in the second part ("Le grand combat") in the choir is the use of rhythmic clusters created by extremely complex composite rhythms.

Rhythmic Developments

It is with these last rhythmically motivated sound-mass structures that the manifold facets of twentieth-century rhythmic development become increasingly more important. While not singularly identifiable as an organic evolution of new rhythms (and one could most certainly devote a book and more to this one aspect of the twentieth-century *avant-garde* alone), the sound-mass has contributed greatly to the breakdown of vertical and horizontal traditions to the point where rhythm has become an ever-increasing area of necessary development.

Rhythm, viewed without a melodic or harmonic drive as in most works prior to this century, becomes a rather simply used parameter of musical structure: static and noninventive, often strangled by the bar line or tied down to basic repetitions related to dance forms. It is with these problems that sound-mass brought rhythm to an ever-increasing complexity both in terms of notation and concept. Note Ligeti's comments about *Lontano* (1967): "The bar lines serve only as a means of synchronization; bar lines and beats never mean an accentuation, the music must flow smoothly. . . "[5] The score is filled with double- and triple-dotted notes, entrances on inner positions of triplets, quintuplets, septuplets, etc., as shown in fig. 2.11, ever diffusing the bar line and beat and giving the

Figure 2.11. György Ligeti: *Lontano*.
Typical rhythmic entrances.

rhythm a development and tangible diversity it had rarely experienced before.

Boulez speaks to this point in his *Boulez on Music Today:*

The rational use of the opposition between multiplication and division of the [beat] unit will, moreover, give rise to striking contrasts due to the broader span of values brought into play . . . interaction of these various methods of organization can be extremely fertile, and will create an inexhaustible variety of objects—in the same way as in the field of pitch.[6]

Some composers, Penderecki among them, have turned to proportional notation to avoid the accent implications of bar lines and simplicity of beat structures. Thus a section is marked 30 seconds and the notations within performed as they reach the eye (as if the visual action of reading would take 30 seconds). No accents, other than those specifically marked, are implied by such notation, and a great deal of rhythmic variety is obtained. By the same token, this inexactitude of notation disturbs some composers due to the fact that results often differ markedly from one performance to another.

5. György Ligeti, *Lontano* (New York: Schott Music Corp., 1969), from the performance notes in the score.

6. Pierre Boulez, *Boulez on Music Today* (Cambridge, Mass.: Harvard University Press, 1971), p. 58.

Rhythmic Control

Attempting the same goal, but from quite a different direction, is Elliott Carter. In *Flawed Words and Stubborn Sounds* Carter speaks of his directions: "The result in my own music was, first of all, the way of evolving rhythms and continuities now called 'metric modulation,' which I worked out in the composition of my *Cello Sonata* of 1948." Later in the same book he speaks of new music in general: ". . . what is needed is never just a string of interesting passages, but works whose central interest is constituted by the way everything that happens in them happens *as* and *when* it does in relation to everything else."[7]

Metric modulation, though not an entirely new concept to Eastern musics or music in the Western World prior to the advent of the so-called "common-practice period," is a highly complex procedure when applied in Carter's works. In his *Double Concerto* (1961) for harpsichord and piano with two chamber orchestras, Carter has many such modulations, two of which are shown in figure 2.12. As is seen here, very often both

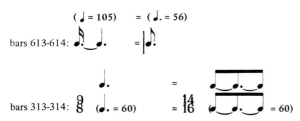

Figure 2.12.   Metric Modulations
from Elliot Carter's *Double Concerto*.

the meter and the tempo change along with the basic equalization across the bar lines. This, combined with a rich variety of complex rhythmic development within the bar, achieves a highly structured yet bar line free momentum of sounds (though many of Carter's critics express grave doubt as to whether such "metric modulations" can actually be performed). The much earlier *Cello Sonata* (1948) has surprisingly few metric modulations and upon comparison with the highly technical complexities of the renowned *Double Concerto* (1961) one can easily see the development of the rhythmic concept.

Most composers take somewhat of a middle road between the proportional and "modulation" principles examined here. Some utilize both

7. Allen Edwards, *Flawed Words and Stubborn Sounds* (New York: W.W. Norton and Co., 1971), pp. 91-92.

Figure 2.13.   Elliott Carter. BMI Archives. Used by permission.

within a single work as does Ligeti in his *Aventures* (see in fig. 3.10 under Instrument Exploration).

Possibly an ever-growing potential source for complex rhythmic structures and rhythm freed from bar lines and their inherent accents and subaccents is electronic and computer music. The author discusses this in his own contribution to *Electronic Music A Listener's Guide* by Elliott Schwartz:

The major advantage to working with electronic equipment and sounds which seem undiminished by overdone "exploration" is rhythmic freedom. No other ensemble of instruments is equally capable of fractioning time into controllable particles as the components of a well-equipped electronic music studio. While some listeners feel that the opportunity to free rhythm from any immediately recognizable meters is removing some inalienable musical basic, it must be pointed out that to a large degree meter was introduced and continued only to keep performers together in ensembles; while necessary, it was certainly not particularly musical in itself. The disposition of time is much more controllable in the electronic studio.[8]

8. Elliott Schwartz, *Electronic Music A Listener's Guide* (New York: Praeger Publishers, 1972); from "Observations by Composers," p. 214.

Microtones

While notation and performance continue to beset the composer bent on freeing his music from the rigidity of the bar line, it is in like manner continuing to block his interests in microtonal possibilities. While twelve-note scales and the search for a single *stable* tuning system have existed for many centuries,[9] it seems to many contemporary composers that this search is a fruitless one, indeed one which results in a hybrid intonation (equal temperament) lacking the multifold potentials of flexible tunings. It is important to note here that while the piano may remain "fixed" in equal-tempered tuning, other instruments do not: indeed orchestral performers create a wide range and variety of tunings, usually a combination of *just* (based on the overtone series) and *equal* (each semitone equidistant from the next) temperaments (applied at the discretion of their "musical ears"). Similarly, tonal key regions with "leading tones," sevenths of dominant seventh chords and the like call for *adjusted* intonations.

Eastern music for centuries has created wide varieties of tunings, and instruments capable of easily adapting to such varieties. Western music, though couched in its secure twelve divisions of the octave, has (but to a much lesser extent) had its proposals, experiments, and protagonists for new intonations. Gerhardus Mercator's (sixteenth century) fifty-three tones per octave scale is a particularly notable example.

In the twentieth century, systems of more than twelve notes to the octave have been produced by Alois Hába, Ivan Wyschnegradsky, and Julian Carrillo among others. Carrillo in "The Thirteenth Sound" divides the octave into ninety-five different pitches and utilizes a fascinating system of numbering each pitch at the end of the stem where one would ordinarily find the note head.[10] Harry Partch (discussed as well under *Instrument Exploration*) utilizes a forty-three-note system but is much freer with it, and through his creation of an entirely new set of instruments has been able to create a virtually "infinite" variety of both timbres and tunings. Most of these approaches, however, seemed doomed to either extremely limited usage or complete neglect. The main problem is that most theorists and composers continue to search for new *systems* not realizing that the devising of any such system is little better than the *system* in present use (a restricted set of pitches). It is indeed the flexi-

9. See Fred Fisher, "The Yellow Bell of China and the Endless Search," *Music Educators Journal*, April 1973, p. 30.

10. Julian Carrillo, "The Thirteenth Sound," trans. Patricia Ann Smith, *Soundings* 5, p. 64. This volume also contains a number of works by Carrillo using his number notations.

bility or "nonsystematic" use of intonations which is most valuable and composers such as Ben Johnston, Lou Harrison, James Tenney, Kenneth Gaburo, and many others are writing sections, movements, or works to

Figure 2.14.   Ben Johnston

multiple sets of intonations. Ben Johnston's Fourth String Quartet is just such a work. It uses a varying number of proportional octave divisions from five to twenty-two, thus creating a flexible set of intonations based on the composer's ear and musical intuitions.

Johnston has written extensively on microtonal music and in writing about his Fourth String Quartet he sums up a great complexity in a few concise words:

Over the whole of the historical period of instrumental music, Western music has based itself upon an acoustical lie. In our time this lie—that the normal musical ear hears twelve equal intervals within the span of an octave—has led to the impoverishment of pitch usage in our music. In our frustration at the complex means it takes to wrest yet a few more permutations from a closed

11. From the April 28, 1974 program notes of a concert at the University of Wisconsin-Milwaukee by the Fine Arts Quartet.

system, we have attempted the abandonment of all systems, forgetting that we need never have closed our system.[11]

The potential of microtones is nearly limitless, bounded only by the ability of the composer to hear his ideas, the notation to express these ideas (see Appendix 3) and the performer to accurately perform the results.

Bibliography

*Further Readings**

Babbitt, Milton. "Twelve-Tone Rhythmic Structure and the Electronic Medium." *Perspectives of New Music* 1, no. 1 (1962):49-79.

Boatwright, Howard, ed. *Essays before a Sonata, The Majority, and Other Writings by Charles Ives.* New York: W. W. Norton & Co., 1962. A superb and fascinating study of the writings and thoughts of this man, many of which relate to sound-mass and rhythm.

Boatwright, Howard. "Ives' Quarter-Tone Impressions." *Perspectives of New Music* 3, no. 2 (1965):22-31. A good study of Ives's thoughts on the subject.

Boulez, Pierre. *Boulez on Music Today.* Cambridge, Mass.: Harvard University Press, 1971. Sheds a good deal of light on his own personal "controlled" approach to rhythmic structures.

Carter, Elliott. "The Rhythmic Basis of American Music." *Score* 12, no. 27, June, 1955.

Christiansen, Louis. "Introduction to the Music of György Ligeti," *Numus West* 2, Feb. 1972. Excellent overview of the works of this man and his contributions both in terms of sound-mass and rhythm.

Cowell, Henry, ed. *American Composers on American Music.* New York: Frederick Ungar Publishing Co., 1933. Gives excellent insight into two composers using sound-mass: John Becker on p. 82, and Wallingford Riegger on p. 70.

Cowell, Henry. *New Musical Resources.* New York: Alfred A. Knopf, 1930. Contains an entire chapter devoted to the structuring and techniques of clusters and sound-mass.

Creston, Paul. *Principles of Rhythm.* New York: Franco Columbo, 1964.

Dallin, Leon. *Techniques of Twentieth Century Composition.* 3rd ed. Dubuque, Iowa: Wm. C. Brown Company Publishers, 1974. Part of a chapter is devoted to "New Rhythmic Concepts" (p. 66).

Erickson, Robert. "Time Relations." *Journal of Music Theory* 7 (Spring, 1963): 174-92.

Edwards, Allen. *Flawed Words and Stubborn Sounds.* New York: W. W. Norton & Co., 1971. Subtitled: *A Conversation With Elliott Carter,* this is an excellent source book for the thoughts on rhythmic complexities and development of this American composer.

Forte, Allen. *Contemporary Tone-Structures.* New York: Columbia University Press, 1955. Has brief discussions of sound-mass.

*Addresses for record companies, periodicals, and music publishers mentioned in this Bibliography can be found in Appendix 4.

44

Johnston, Ben. "Proportionality and Expanded Pitch Relations." *Perspectives of New Music* 5, no. 1:112-20.

Johnston, Ben, and Kobrin, Edward. "Phase 1-a." *Source* 7.
With the article above, and his article in Vinton's *Dictionary of Contemporary Music* on microtones, an excellent exposition of Johnston's learned ideas on microtonality.

Kagel, Mauricio. "Tone Clusters, Attacks, Transitions." *Die Reihe* 5 (1959): 40-55. Interesting as a source of notations for opening and closing keyboard clusters and concepts.

Kirkpatrick, John. "The Evolution of Carl Ruggles: A Chronicle Largely in His Own Words." *Perspectives of New Music* 6, no. 2:146-66. An excellent study of this man of few works embodied in highly chromatic polyphonic sound-mass.

Marquis, G. Welton. *Twentieth Century Music Idioms*. New York: Prentice-Hall, 1964. Contains brief discussions of sound-mass.

Messiaen, Oliver. *The Technique of My Musical Language*. Paris: Alphonse Leduc & Cie., 1950. Excellent source for information on the extremely intricate and involved combination of proportional and metrical rhythmic language. Also a necessity for the understanding of much of Messiaen's rhythmically technical music.

"Microtonal Music in America." *Proceedings* 2, American Society of University Composers. Very good general discussion of the subject.

Nono, Luigi. "Geschichte und Gegenwart in der Musik von Huete." *Darmstädter Beiträge zur Neuen Musik* 3 (1960) pp. 41-47. Most interesting study of all the materials of this chapter as well as the remainder of the book.

Orga, Ates. "Alois Hába and Microtonality." *Musical Opinion*, July 1968. Reflects a distinctly Hába viewpoint but is excellent bibliographical material.

Partch, Harry. *Genesis of a Music*. New York: Da Capo Press, 1973. Includes quite a bit of material on this man's thoughts concerning microtones.

Persichetti, Vincent. *Twentieth Century Harmony*. New York: W. W. Norton Co., 1961. Has brief discussions of sound-mass.

Pound, Ezra. *Antheil*. New York: Da Capo Press, 1968. Contains Antheil's "Treatise on Harmony" which might better be titled "Treatise on Rhythm," as the author-composer spends the majority of the article reflecting on the importance of *when* things happen rather than *what* happens in terms of harmony.

Riegger, Wallingford. "John J. Becker." *Bulletin of the ACA* 9, no. 1 (1959): 2-7. Good study of this iconoclast and his rugged music.

Stockhausen, Karlheinz. ". . . How Time Passes. . . ." *Die Reihe* 3:10-40.

Varèse, Edgard. "New Instruments and New Music." In *Contemporary Composers on Contemporary Music*. Edited by Elliott Schwartz and Barney Childs, pp. 196-98. New York: Holt, Rinehart, and Winston, 1967.

Vinton, John, ed. *Dictionary of Contemporary Music*. New York: E. P. Dutton & Co., 1974. Includes a well-written analysis by Frederic Rzewski of contemporary ideas, pp. 618-25, along with an excellent bibliography.

Weisgall, Hugo. "The Music of Henry Cowell." *Musical Quarterly* 45 (1959). A good source of information on the works of this man and their contrasting of the innovative with the conservative.

"Iannis Xenakis: The Man and his Music." Boosey & Hawkes, 1967. A good if short look into the music of this composer who works almost exclusively with sound-mass.

Yasser, Joseph. *A Theory of Evolving Tonality.* American Library of Musicology, 1932. Quite extensive in its tracing of the history of microtones, but gets bogged down in the author's own equally "bogged" 19-note scale.

Recordings and Publishers

Bartók, Béla. *Sonata* (1921). Universal Edition. Recorded on Capitol P8376.

———. *String Quartet No. 5* (1934). Boosey & Hawkes. Recorded on Columbia ML-4280.

Becker, John. *Symphony No. 3.* Peters. Recorded on Louisville S-721.

Bernstein, Leonard. *The Age of Anxiety.* G. Schirmer. See p. 59. Recorded on Columbia MS-6885.

Blackwood, Easley. *Symphony No. 1* (1958). Recorded on RCA LM-2352.

Blomdahl, Karl-Birger. *Aniara* (1959). Schott. See pp. 1-3.

Boulez, Pierre. *Le Marteau sans Măitre* (1959). Universal Edition. Recorded on Odyssey 32-160154.

Britten, Benjamin. *The Turn of the Screw* (1954). Boosey & Hawkes. See p. 5.

Carter, Elliott. *Double Concerto.* Associated Music Publishers. Recorded on Columbia 7191.

———. *Cello Sonata.* G. Schirmer. Recorded on Nonesuch 71234.

———. *String Quartets* No. 1 (1951) and 2 (1959) AMP. Recorded on Nonesuch 71249.

Constant, Marius. *24 Preludes for Orchestra* (1958). Ricordi. Recorded on Heliodor HS-25058.

Cope, David. *Iceberg Meadow* (1969). Composers' Autograph Publications. Recorded on Capra 1201.

Cowell, Henry. *The Hero Sun.* Breitkopf & Hertel.

———. *The Tides of Manaunaun.* Breitkopf & Hertel.

———. *What's This.* Breitkopf & Hertel.
    (A number of Cowell's piano works are recorded on CRI S-281.)

Crumb, George. *Black Angels* (1970). Peters. Recorded on CRI S-283.

Erickson, Robert. *Chamber Concerto* (1960). Theodore Presser. Recorded on CRI S-218.

Helm, Everett. *Concerto for Five Solo Instruments, Percussion and Strings* (1954). Schott. See p. 15.

Husa, Karel. *Apotheosis of this Earth* (1971). AMP. Recorded on Golden Crest 4134.

———. *Music for Prague* (1968). AMP. Recorded on Louisville S-722. Represents excellent use of sound-mass created both rhythmically in layers and by clusters.

Ives, Charles. *Majority.* AMP.

———. *Sonata #2* (1915). AMP. Columbia MS-7192.

———. *Songs.* New Music Edition. Recorded on Nonesuch 71209.
    (See Schwann Catalog for complete listing of recorded works.)

———. *Chorale for Quarter-tone Piano*. Recorded on Avant 1008.

———. *Three Pieces for Two Pianos Tuned a Quarter-tone Apart* (1924). Peters.

Johnston, Ben. *String Quartet No. 2*. Recorded on Nonesuch 71224.

Kagel, Mauricio. *Improvisation ajoutee* (1962). Peters. Recorded on Odyssey 32-160158.

———. *Sonant*. Peters.

Liebermann, Rolf. *Concerto for Jazz Band and Symphony Orchestra* (1954). Universal Edition. See p. 1.

Ligeti, György. *Atmosphéres* (1961). Universal Edition. Recorded on Columbia MS-6733.

———. *Aventures* (1962). Peters. Recorded on Candide 31009.

———. *Lontano* (1967). Schott. Recorded on Wergo 322.

———. *Lux Aeterna* (1966). Peters. Recorded on DG-137004.

———. *Nouvelles Aventures* (1965). Neues. Recorded on Candide 31009.

———. *Requiem* (1965). Peters. Recorded on Wergo 60045.

Lucas, Theodore. *Aberrations No. VII*. Composers' Autograph Publications.

Lutoslawski, Witold. *Trois Poèmes d'Henri Michaux*. PWM. Recorded on Wergo 60019.

Lybbert, Donald. *Lines for the Fallen* (1968). Peters. Recorded on Odyssey 32-160162. An excellent example of quarter-tone writing.

Macero, Teo. *One-Three Quarters*. Recorded on Odyssey 32-160162.

McPhee, Colin. *Tabuh-Tabuhan* (1936). AMP. Recorded on Mercury MG-50103.

Messiaen, Oliver. *L'Ascension* (1934). Leduc. Recorded on Argo 5339.

———. *La Nativité du Seigneur*. Leduc. Recorded on Everest 3330. An excellent example of his rhythmic procedures.

Milhaud, Darius. *Piano Sonata* (1916). Salabert. See p. 10.

Moryl, Richard. *Chroma for Chamber Ensemble* (1972). Recorded on Desto 7143.

Nono, Luigi. *Il canto sospeso*. Schott.

———. *Cori di Didone*. Schott.

———. *La terra e la campagna*. Schott.

Oliveros, Pauline. *Sound Patterns*. Recorded on Odyssey 32-160156.

Penderecki, Krzysztof. *Capriccio for Violin and Orchestra*. Moeck. Recorded on Nonesuch 71201.

———. *Passion According to St. Luke*. Moeck. Recorded on Phillips 802771/2.

———. *Threnody for the Victims of Hiroshima*. Eulenberg. Recorded on RCA VICS-1239.

Persichetti, Vincent. *Symphony for Band* (1956). Elkan-Vogel. See p. 127. Recorded on Coronet S-1247.

Riegger, Wallingford. *Music for Brass Choir*. Mercury Music. Recorded on CRI S-229.

Ruggles, Carl. *Angels* (1921). Curwen. Recorded on Turnabout 34398. A good example of sound-mass.

———. *Lilacs and Portals* (1926). AME. Recorded on Columbia ML-4986.

Schoenberg, Arnold. *Five Pieces for Orchestra* (1909). Peters. Recorded on Mercury and Columbia MG-50026.

Schuman, William. *Credendum* (1955). Merion Music. Recorded on CRI S-308. Uses sound-mass effectively.

———. *Symphony No. 8* (1962). Merion Music. Recorded on Columbia ML-5912.

Schwartz, Elliott. *Texture* (1966). A. Broude. Recorded on Ars Nova AN-1002.

Stockhausen, Karlheinz. *Mixtur* (1967). Universal Edition. Recorded on DG 137012.

Strandberg, Newton. *Xerxes*. Recorded on Opus One Records 4416. Excellent for use of massive evolutionary sound-mass.

Stravinsky, Igor. *Le Sacre du Printemps* (1913). Boosey & Hawkes. Recorded on Columbia M-31520.

Varèse, Edgard. *Equatorial*. G. Schirmer. Recorded on Nonesuch 71269.

———. *Hyperprism* (1933), and *Octandre*. G. Schirmer. Recorded on Columbia MG-31078.

Wilson, Galen. *Fantasy for Piano* (1968). Composers' Autograph Publications.

Wolpe, Stefan. *Chamber Piece No. 1* (1964). Recorded on Nonesuch H-71220.

Xenakis, Iannis. *Metastasis* (1954). Boosey & Hawkes. Recorded on Vanguard C-10030.

3 Instrument Explorations

Observations

In no other period of music history has the performer played such an important role in the development of new sound resources and instrumental techniques on behalf of the composer. Many instrumentalists have, during the past twenty years, created such a significant impact in determining and exploring the sound capabilities of their respective instruments that they have more than justified the claim that there is an immense potentiality residing within instruments that can be applied as easily and as constructively as by the use of tape.

Bruno Bartolozzi, in his now famous book *New Sounds for Woodwind,* states the concept of the contemporary performer's role in new music as well as the role of his instrument:

Their continued existence in the world of creative composition therefore depends to a very large extent on just what they have to offer the composer, just how much they can rouse his interest and provoke his fantasy. Some composers already show an obvious lack of interest in conventional instruments and have no hesitation in using the most unusual means in an effort to find new sonorities. . . .[1]

No traditional instrument has escaped the imagination of the composer's creative mind. Some performers have steadfastedly maintained that any other than traditional "acts" upon their instrument violate its inherent intention and thus should not be attempted. One must wonder if *plucking* and *muting* do not plunder the instrument's virginity. Certainly, short of physical damage to the instrument itself, even the most critical of traditionalists must admit the impossibility of being "just a little bit pregnant." Donald Erb sums it up well:

Music is made by a performer. It comes from him rather than from his instrument, the instrument being merely a vehicle. Therefore it seems logical that any sound a performer can make may be used in a musical composition.[2]

1. Bruno Bartolozzi, *New Sounds for Woodwind* (New York: Oxford University Press, 1967), p. 1.
2. Bertram Turetzky, "Vocal and Speech Sounds—A Technique of Contemporary writing for the Contrabass," *The Composer* 1, no. 3 (December 1969):169.

Figure 3.1.   Donald Erb

Strings

Four major additions to string techniques have evolved:

1. percussive effects such as knocking, rapping, tapping, or slapping the strings or body of the instrument (especially in the works of Meyer Kupferman, Eugene Kurtz, and Sydney Hodkinson);
2. singing, speaking, or humming while playing (particularly apparent in the works of Russell Peck, Jacob Druckman, Charles Whittenberg, and Richard Felciano);
3. unusual bowings inclusive of circular bowing, bowing on or across the bridge, bowing between the bridge and tailpiece, bowing directly on the tailpiece, and *undertones* (subharmonics) created by bowing with great pressure on a harmonic node (actually creating notes well below the lowest open string of the instrument): these devices are used extensively in the works of Krzysztof Penderecki, Karlheinz Stockhausen, Mauricio Kagel, and George Crumb, among others.
4. combinations and extensions of traditional techniques (e.g., harmonics, glissandi, fingering without bowing, pizzicati, etc.), especially notable in the works of Krzysztof Penderecki, György Ligeti, Donald Erb, and Mauricio Kagel.

Figure 3.2 shows Krzysztof Penderecki's use of playing between the bridge and tailpiece (↑ and ⃥⃥⃥), highest note pizzicato (↟) and

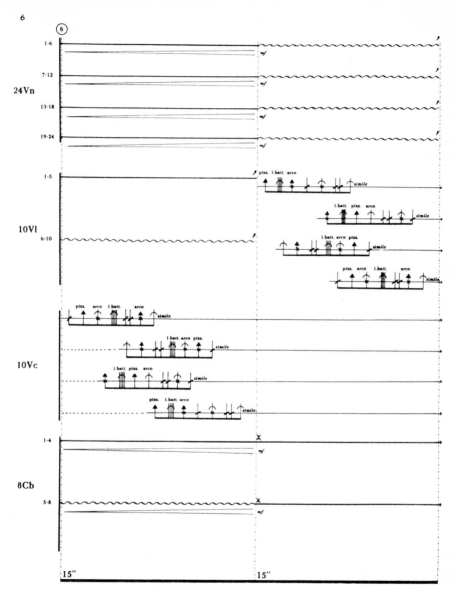

Figure 3.2.   Krzysztof Penderecki:
Threnody for the Victims of Hiroshima.
Copyright © 1961 Deshon Music,
Inc., & PWM Editions. Used with per-
mission. All rights reserved.

irregular tremolo (⨎) among others in his *Threnody for the Victims of Hiroshima* (for explanation of the proportional notation see Appendix 3).[3]

Notable among performers of innovative works for strings are Paul Zukofsky and Max Pollikov (violin), Walter Trampler (viola), Siegfried

Figure 3.3. Krzysztof Penderecki.

Palm ('cello), and Bertram Turetzky and Alvin Brehm (contrabass). String groups particularly dedicated to new music and techniques include the Fine Arts Quartet and the Composers' Quartet, among others.[4]

Winds

Innovative techniques for wind instruments are extremely numerous and, though there is a difference between the ways in which they are applied to sections (brass and woodwind) and to individual instruments

3. For a more detailed discussion of new string techniques, see Bertram Turetzky's articles "The Bass as a Drum," *The Composer* 1, no. 2 (September 1969):92-107; and "Vocal and Speech Sounds: A Technique of Contemporary Writing for the Contrabass," *The Composer*, 1, no. 3 (December 1969):118-34; and his book: *The Contemporary Contrabass* (Berkeley: University of California Press, 1974).

4. It should be noted that throughout the course of this chapter the mentioning of performer's names is necessarily incomplete due to space limitations. Apologies to those many highly dedicated and talented performers who perform contemporary music, yet whose names are not included here; it was just not possible to include the entire list.

Figure 3.4.   Bertram Turetzsky,
bassist.

(particularly between the various single-reed, the double-reed, and non-
reed instruments of the woodwind section), they are combined here for
purposes of space and basic similarities. The author has grouped similar
effects within six major categories:

1. multiphonics (or the creation of more than one pitch simultaneously on one instrument) created by either of two basic methods
   singing along with playing and/or forcing the strong overtone
   content of a given fundamental to become audible (inclusive of
   altering embouchure, fingerings, overblowing, dynamics, and a
   combination of these). Figure 3.5 shows Toru Takamitsu's use
   and notation (in terms of open and closed holes for fingering) in
   his *Voice* (1971) for solo flute (also found in works of Donald
   Erb, Roger Reynolds, Russell Peck, and Jacob Druckman, among
   others);
2. color fingerings involving pitch and timbre fluctuations by changing the available fingerings on the instrument for the same note
   (particularly notable in the works of George Crumb);

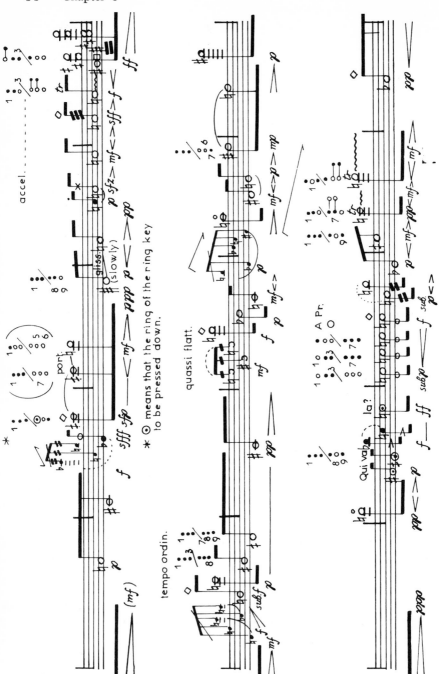

Figure 3.5.   Toru Takemitsu: *Voice*. Permission granted by Editions Salabert. All rights reserved.

3. jazz effects which include a large variety of hitherto avoided sounds often employed in jazz, such as *rips, fall offs, bends,* etc. (see particularly the brass works of William Sydeman, Phil Winsor, Donald Erb, and David Cope);

4. percussive effects such as rapping, tapping, fingering without blowing, fingernails on the bell tremolo, and hand-pops (the palm of the hand slapping the open bore of the mouthpiece) as noted in the works of Aurelio De la Vega, Iannis Xenakis, and many others;

5. use of mouthpiece alone or instrument without mouthpiece, both performable with actual or approximate pitch (see works by Donald Erb, Krzysztof Penderecki, and György Ligeti, among others);

6. extension of traditional techniques such as glissandi, harmonics, speed rates of vibrato, pedal tones, flutter tongue, circular breathing, and many others (see works by composers listed under 1-5 as well as works by Luciano Berio, Lukas Foss, and Gunther Schuller).

Notable performers of woodwind and brass works of the *avant-garde* include: Aurèle Nicolet, Pierluigi Mencarelli, Savarino Gazzeloni, and Harvey Sollberger—flute; Joseph Celli, Lawrence Singer, and Heinz Holliger—oboe; Phillip Rehfeldt, Detalmo Corneti, and William O. Smith—clarinet; William Scribner, Sergio Penazzi, and Bruno Bartolozzi—bassoon; Ken Dorn, and James Houlik—saxophone; Gerard Schwarz, Robert Levy, and Marice Stith—trumpet; James Fulkerson, Stu Dempster, and Vinko Globokar—trombone; and Barton Cummings and Roger Bobo—tuba.

Percussion

The percussion section has been the area in which the maximum degree of enlargement and experimentation has taken place. The more traditional instruments (timpani, snare drum, xylophone, etc.) developed a wide variety of unusual techniques, and especially experiments with various sizes and types of beaters (metal, wood, cloth, glass), to increase timbra resources. Exotic or foreign folk instruments were added mostly for particular effects, and used sparingly. It is surprising to note that, in considering the "noise" many percussion instruments (particularly the "whip") emit, so many mainstream composers who use them nevertheless still refuse to consider the musical potentiality of other often less "noisy" instruments, including the oscillator. For a number of years, the most unusual and philosophically significant of these additions to the percussion section was the brake drum. The fact that a part of a car (or truck) had found its way into the standard percussion section of the symphony orchestra seemed to go unnoticed, clearly implying that any object could act as a usable sound source.[5] Early experimenters in percussion music include John Cage, Edgard Varèse, Carlos Chavez, and especially John Becker, whose *Abongo* (1933) marks one of the first serious efforts in true percussion music. It was the percussion section as well that, since the late nineteenth century, has required new notation systems, necessitated by the fact that performers must read as many as five or six instrumental parts simultaneously, and five-line staves are often impractical (see fig. 3.6).

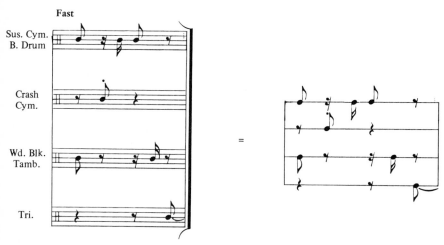

Figure 3.6

    The increasing need for explicit performance directions by the composer indicating the type of mallet to be used, the action of the mallet, and especially, its exact placement on the instrument, has required vastly new and different notations, more explicit and effectively communicative than traditional notation. Figure 3.7A shows the exact movement of the mallet across the timpani head within a certain period of time; figure 3.7B, the exact direction and striking surface of the crash cymbals; and figure 3.7C, the sweep action of wire brushes on a bass drum. Since widely variable timbres can result from mallet direction and placement on each of these three percussion instruments, and as they can also result from direction and amount of crash for cymbals, new notation becomes inevitable and increasingly more graphic.

    An actual listing and numbering of percussion effects would create

5. The brake drum is described and pictured in a number of contemporary orchestration books (e.g., Reed and Leach, *Scoring for Percussion* [New York: Prentice-Hall, Inc., 1969]).

A

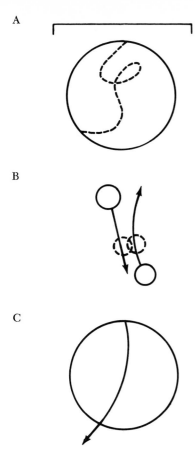

B

C

Figures 3.7A, 3.7B, 3.7C

a book twice the size of this volume for just the unusual uses of the "standard" orchestral percussion instruments. The codification of the percussion section is now such that any instrument, no matter whether strings (e.g., piano), air columns (e.g., slide whistle) or others similar in kind to the orchestra "staples," is given "percussion" classification (this is particularly true when non-Western instruments are used with an orchestra: no matter what the context, the nature of the instrument, or the method of producing sound, it somehow finds its way into the percussion section.)

Notable *avant-garde* composers for percussion include Larry Austin, Karlheinz Stockhausen, Frederic Rzewski, Harry Partch, Edward Miller, Mario Bertoncini, Peter Garland, William Kraft, and many, many others. Performers include Max Neuhaus, Christoph Caskel, and William Kraft. Often, as here indicated (and more often than in any other section of the orchestra), percussionists tend to be composers as well. William Kraft is not only percussionist with the Los Angeles Philharmonic Orchestra, but

Figure 3.8.   William Kraft. Photo
by A. A. Friedman.

is also a gifted and well-known composer for all instruments (which includes his extensive percussion solo and ensemble literature). Among ensembles doing *avant-garde* music exclusively is the well-known Blackearth
Percussion Group (see fig. 3.9).

Vocal

The voice, both in solo and choral situations, has in recent years become a focal point of innovative development realized both in terms of
dramatic emphasis of text and as an instrument separate from verbal
associations. Its ability to be a "percussively stringed wind instrument"
gives it nearly all of the timbre potentials of all the aforementioned instruments. Only the physical limitations of the individual performers become obstacles to the composer's available resources (few can equal Roy
Hart's eight-octave range and multiphonic abilities).
Most vocal experimentation has taken place in three basic areas:

1.   effects, such as panting, whistling, sucking, kissing, hissing, cluck-
ing, laughing, talking, whispering, etc. (especially in the works

of Hans Werner Henze, Krzysztof Penderecki, György Ligeti, Karlheinz Stockhausen, Mauricio Kagel, Pauline Oliveros, Folke Rabe, Richard Felciano, and David Cope);

2. multiphonics (especially notable in the *Versuch über Schweine* by Hans Werner Henze);

3. muting in the forms of humming, hands over the mouth and slowly opening and closing the mouth (employed well in works by Donald Erb and Robert Morris).

Figure 3.10, the *Aventures* of György Ligeti, shows firstly the breathing in and out (measures 1-5 shown by symbols ▶ = inhale and ◀ = exhale) as well as muting (closed mouth *m* in second brace). The work is notable for its many other effects, its lack of text (replaced by a 112-letter alphabet for creating sounds), and the exchanging metric and proportional notations (shown clearly here between braces one and two). Hans Werner Henze's *Versuch über Schweine* (1969) for voice and orchestra is equally impressive in its incredible use of dramatic vocal gymnastics.

Among singers who are known for their performances of new music are Cathy Berberian, Roy Hart, Catherine Rowe, Jan DeGaetani, Bethany Beardslee, Elaine Bonazzi, and Neva Pilgrim. The New Music Choral Ensemble (NMCE) was founded by its director (Kenneth Gaburo) in 1966

Figure 3.9. Blackearth Percussion Group.

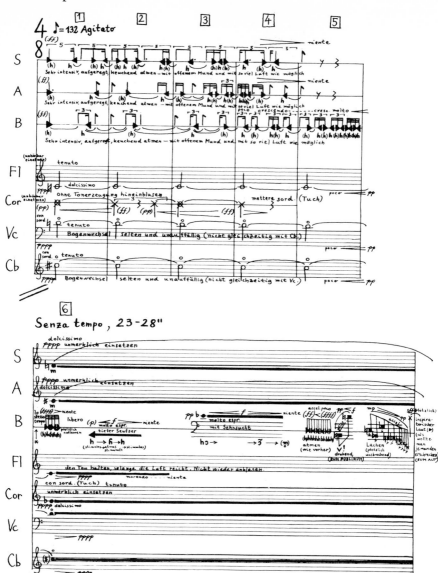

Figure 3.10.   *Aventures* by György
Ligeti (page 1). Copyright © 1964 by
Henry Litolff Verlag. Sole selling
agents in the Western Hemisphere,
C. F. Peters Corporation, 373 Park
Avenue South, New York, N. Y.
10016.
Reprint permission granted by the
publisher.

and stands as one of the world's foremost choral ensembles dedicated to the performance of new music.

Keyboard Instruments

The early experiments and compositions for piano by Henry Cowell (e.g., 1925, *The Banshee,* which involved plucking and stroking the strings inside the instrument) and John Cage (e.g., 1938, *Bacchanale,* and 1946-48, *Sonatas and Interludes* for prepared piano[6]) aroused great interest among at least a few performers that a fantastic array of new sound resources was available on all existing instruments, and that these resources, combined with variable performance techniques, were a compositional material just as viable as those more traditional ones.

Aside from preparation and striking or stroking the strings inside of the piano, the following new techniques are currently being used and explored:

1. muting (usually done by placing the right hand on the string inside the piano between the pin and the dampers and playing the notes on the keyboard with the left hand) is notated with an + above the note (used particularly in the works of George Crumb and David Cope);
2. harmonics (produced by touching a node of the string inside the piano with one hand and striking the keyboard with the other) are employed much like those of string instruments (used in works by George Crumb, Larry Barnes, and many others);
3. using other parts of the instrument by knocking, tapping, rapping, etc., particularly on the wood of the lid and body, the metal of the internal crossbars and soundboard, etc., with mallets, hands, and various other objects (notable in works like *Knocking Piece* by Ben Johnston, and works by John Cage, George Crumb, Donald Erb, and many others).

Pianists who are actively involved in new *avant-garde* works include David Tudor, David Burge, Richard Bunger, and Aloys Kontarsky. David Tudor, William Albright, and Martha Folts have been active in the development of the organ, as has Antoinette Vischer with the cembalo. At present these experiments with organ and cembalo have been more theatrical (organ) and formal (cembalo) than real in terms of sonic exploration (note especially works by Mauricio Kagel, Gordon Mumma,

---

6. That is, the placement of objects such as nuts, bolts, and nails on, around, and between the strings, thus converting the piano into an instrument with an almost limitless variety of new timbres.

Christian Wolff, and William Albright for organ and György Ligeti for cembalo).

Harp

Carlos Salzedo (1885-1961) developed an extremely wide range of possible effects, as well as highly original notations and names for this versatile instrument ("gushing aeolian chords," etc.). Most of these have become standard for the harpist and need not be considered *avant-garde*, though they may sound like it to the uninitiated (composers utilizing these numerous effects include Salzedo himself, Luciano Berio, and George Crumb, in particular).

The harp is indeed unique in that it had, fortunately, a genius as an innovator in Carlos Salzedo as a part of its "growing and developing" period, and that it, more than any other single instrument, is capable of sounds of incredible variety virtually unexplored by the *avant-garde* composer. It is not much of a gamble to predict that the harp will in future years become a foremost attraction for the contemporary composer.

Mixed Ensembles and Unique Works

George Crumb's *Songs, Drones, and Refrains of Death* (1969) for baritone, electric guitar, electric contrabass, electric piano, harpsichord, and two percussionists, contain a great many of the effects discussed above (see fig. 3.11). Crumb's *Black Angels* (1970) for string quartet employs amplification of the instruments both for balance and for the unique timbre alteration which electronics adds to the ensemble. This procedure, employing the use of both contact and acoustic microphones, has within the past ten years become increasingly popular (discussed at greater length under "electronic music," see chap. 4).

It is a fact, however, that even the instrumentalists themselves do not recognize sounds from fellow performers, posing a problem contributory to the extreme difficulty of ensemble rhythmic performance. That problem is here solved by a procedure of notating *events*, in which exact timing is not as important as exact performance of the event itself. A broad spectrum of tone colors and "noise" is thus made available to the composer as musical material usable by even the smallest ensemble of performers.

Barney Childs' *Mr. T. His Fancy* (1967) for solo contrabass is a work which draws upon the extensive sound resources of the instrument. The work involves many aspects of the aforementioned new string techniques, creating a vast new reservoir of sonic material for the composer to draw upon.

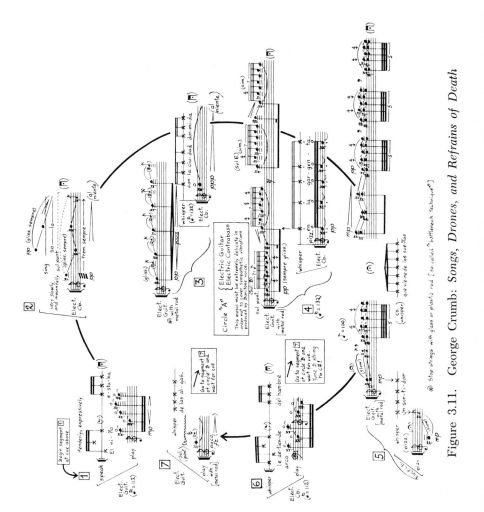

Figure 3.11. George Crumb: *Songs, Drones, and Refrains of Death*

Iannis Xenakis, long interested in preserving live and traditional instruments of the orchestra through creation of new techniques, proves convincingly in Metastasis (1953-54) that sixty-one traditional instruments can compete successfully with electronic sound sources.

Roman Haubenstock-Ramati was one of the first, in his *Interpolation* (1958), to utilize a prerecorded tape made by the performer and not manipulated in any way, together with the live performer, thereby enabling even a single instrumentalist to create a large number of effects using only his instrument and himself as source. His 1961 *Liaisons* for vibraphone includes provisions for a previously prepared tape to be started six to ten seconds after the performer begins. In this instance the tape serves not as an electronic device, but as a tool which enables both composer and performer to elicit more combinations of tones and effects, without losing the inherent instrumental timbre to electronically-derived materials.

George Green's *Perihelion for Concert Band* (1974) employs an incredible array of new and effective timbres often similar in nature (becoming clusters of like textures), though at times contrasted for means of form and direction.

David Cope's *Margins* (1972) ('cello, trumpet, percussion, and two pianos) emphasizes the "marginal" aspects of each instrument in a single movement structure. "The composer equally explores the contrast and developmental possibilities of dynamics and contrapuntal articulations. The tempo remains very slow throughout and the beat is divided into multifold groupings of often very quick and pointillistic integrations from instrument to instrument."[7]

The previously discussed effects have also been used in combination or in conjunction with extracurricular performer activity, from finger-snapping and music stand-tapping to such dramatic effects as costumes, theatrical staging, and substitution of the original with other instruments. Often composers use whispers, speaking, and shouting (as in the aforementioned Crumb example, figure 3.11) along with the performance of additional instruments such as triangles hung from music stands, maracas, and a large variety of other percussion instruments.

Whether in solo or chamber ensembles, it is obvious that the complete realization of all possible sonoric events creates an entirely new performance situation with virtually endless combinational possibilities. The audience can no longer attend a string quartet performance, expecting that a traditional string quartet is what will be heard. New materials have created of orchestral and multiorchestral combinations an almost

---

7. From liner notes on recording: ORION ORS=75169.

endless number of possibilities equal to that of tape. Indeed, recordings of these works, without the visual confirmation, distort beyond recognition the imagination's comprehension of the sound source. It would seem more appropriate not to label instrumentation in the program at all, unless this problem of expectation is a realizable and controllable theatrical element of the work (or, of course, to contribute to the realization of the composer's and performers' genius).

Ensembles of mixed instrumentation have contributed greatly to the development of instrument exploration. Such active groups commission, perform, and record new music and include the Contemporary Chamber Ensemble, The Aeolian Chamber Players, Die Reihe Ensemble, The Philadelphia Composers Forum, Cologne New Music Ensemble, The MW 2 Ensemble, and the Melos Ensemble, to name but a few. There also exists a large number of school-affiliated new music ensembles made up of faculty and students possessing both a high degree of professional ability and large repertoires.

Timbre Modulation

The expansion of possibilities in the area of timbre modulation has proved to be a significant development resulting from instrument exploration. With the composer's increasing awareness of the subtle timbre alterations available in various instruments' different registers—muting, dynamics, attacks, and decays—came the realization that a wealth of timbre overlap existed between instruments. Figure 3.12 shows three such overlaps with the evolving timbre changes inherent in the combinations. In the first example the piccolo is initially covered by the triangle. Its slow crescendo gradually modulates the sound to solo piccolo through the decay of the triangle sound. In the second example the trumpet (with straight mute) slowly dies away as the like-timbred oboe crescendos, and so takes over. The effect is demonstrated by the intersecting vertical dotted line wherein at the beginning we find only the trumpet, at the line we find a subtle combination of the two ("obet" or "trumboe" are often employed by composers to emphasize the significance of the truly "new" sound created by the modulation) and finally we find that the oboe is alone. The third example demonstrates less subtlety in its direct approach to dynamics (the bass drum clouding the piano attack completely) but a unique effect is achieved in the "ringing" of the piano coming out of the bass drum (as the piano chord slowly decays out of the hand-stopped percussion attack).

Works employing timbre modulation effectively include, among others *Sinfonia* (1968) by Luciano Berio, *Lontano* (1967) by György Ligeti,

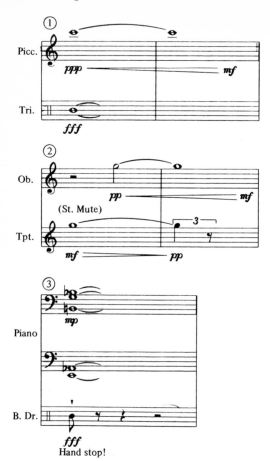

Figure 3.12. Timbre-
modulations.

Ancient Voices of Children (1970) by George Crumb, and *Apotheosis of This Earth* (1971) by Karel Husa.

Antiphonal and Spatial Modulation

Spacing and placement have also played an important role in the struggle for new directional sonorities from traditional instruments, especially in the works of Henry Brant and Karlheinz Stockhausen. Brant's experiments with the vast potential of vertical, horizontal, and circular arrangements have brought meaningful solutions to problems of acoustics and have given, in effect, a new dynamic force to even the most traditional of musical sounds. Surprisingly enough, few previous similar experiments have taken place, aside from Ives's *The Unanswered Question* (1908) for string orchestra, four flutes, and trumpet, isolated, and Gabrieli's eight- and twelve-part canzonas. In his "Space as an Essential Aspect of Musical Composition," Brant describes many of his successful experiments in performer arrangement for optimum directional, acoustical, and balance effectiveness.[8] The spatial composing technique of one of his examples (*Voyage Four*, 1964) involves percussion and brass on stage, violins on one side balcony, violas and 'cellos on the other, basses on floor level at the rear of the auditorium, with various woodwind instruments and a few strings on the two rear balconies. Three conductors combine to direct the performers (including tuba, timpani, and chimes in the audience). Brant contends that, if the composer indeed intends to control his performance, each work should contain specific instructions as to performer placement and, because every work is different in both structure and instrumentation, rehearsal experimentation is necessary for exact results, with no *right* schematic existing except in individual terms for each work or movement of a work.

Spatial modulation, aided largely by developments in timbre modulation discussed earlier, involves the active motion of a sound from one point to another. An extreme example of this would be a large number of violins surrounding the audience, the sound beginning with one violin then slowly moving with the same pitch to each violin in turn until the first was encountered again. Works by Henry Brant, Donald Erb (*Fanfare for Brass Ensemble and Percussion*, 1971), Cliff Crego (*Implosions*, 1971), and many others employ this technique.

Elliott Schwartz's *Elevator Music* (1967) employs the vast acoustical, directional, and movement possibilities which a multi-story building provides. Twelve floors of a building become the performing areas for twenty-four performers (stationary) while the audience rides an elevator up and down through the constantly-changing environment of sound. The small spaces around the elevators make for a leakage of sound between the floors, thus providing an overlay of sounding materials; there is no really distinct concept of twelve individual entities (except when the conductor, who is also the elevator operator, stops at a certain floor and opens the elevator doors, while the performers on *all* floors are continuing to play regardless of elevator position). Dramatic change is available when the elevator stops at certain empty floors (empty in the sense of visual activity, but completely filled with sound due to the above-mentioned leakage from other floors), as explicitly outlined in the score.[9] Recording of this and many of Brant's works become virtually impossible, inasmuch

8. Elliott Schwartz and Barney Childs, eds., *Contemporary Composers on Contemporary Music* (New York: Holt, Rinehart, and Winston, 1967), pp. 223-42.
9. For a complete description and score of this work, see *The Composer* 2, no. 2 (September 1970).

as the aspects of space, movement, direction, and theater are inherent in the structure of the works and their concept, to the point that live performing situations are required.

Stockhausen's *Ensemble* arrangement shows the theatrical and acoustical placement of performers as an inherent part of the work. Recent experiments have developed along lines of audience placement and intermingling of audience with performers for greater communication. All these prove realistically valuable as timbre and line prove increasingly susceptible to change when direction and spacing enter into consideration.

New Instruments

Enlargement and transformation of sounds on traditional instruments represents only a part of new, non-electronic sound sources for the composer. Harry Partch, unlike Cage and Cowell, began early to create new instruments rather than to transform existing ones (though his first such instrument was an adapted viola). His division of the octave into forty-three tones instead of twelve brought home to him very early the need to create instruments capable of realizing his theoretical concepts (see his *Genesis of A New Music*). Except for his use of the human voice, almost all of his works employ original instruments (primarily percussion and struck string). Partch's *U.S. Highball: Account of Hobo Trip* (1943) and *Account of the Normandy Invasion by an American Glider Pilot* (both early works) reflect more than his interest in the breakdown of the octave into more than seven notes, or his fascination with instruments; they attempt at music becoming no longer imitative but part of nature. In his later *Revelation in the Courthouse Square* (1961), the visual (theatrical) elements—the performers and their instruments—become an integral part of the work. *And on the Seventh Day Petals Fell in Petaluma* (a 1964 work comprising studies, in the form of twenty-three duets, for *Delusion of the Fury*, a larger 1967 work) explores the possibilities of harmonic and melodic uses of microtones based on his tonal and polytonal theories of intonation (his word for major is Otonality, for minor, Utonality).

I. A. MacKenzie too set out to create new instruments—instruments that played themselves (wind sound sculptures), thus actually becoming the works. More recent compositions have extended instrumental possibilities to anything which can be beaten, blown, or bowed, with each work demanding a new instrument for realization—cars, brake drums, even a jet engine, for example. Few of these "instruments" enter any standardized orchestra, as their intrinsic theatrical value lies in their being recognized as having a direct relationship to one work or composer.

It becomes immediately apparent that these new instruments require "new" performers, the virtuosity of whom must certainly be questioned: one could hardly expect as practiced and polished a performance on an instrument created or adapted for one work alone as he could expect from a violinist after intense study of a Beethoven concerto. One of two alternatives is suggested: (1) a simple but fully notated score, or (2) a more free improvisational structure whereby the performer could substitute freedom and creativity for familiarity. Douglas Leedy chooses the latter in *Usable Music I* (1968), for very small instruments with holes. This work depends almost completely on graphic representation of activities (i.e., the use of symbols to indicate such general directions as "blow" or "draw"), with less emphasis on exact rhythmic and pitch notation. Robert Moran, in *Titus* (1968), has the score projected on the stage upon an automobile, showing pictorially the performers' area and amount of activity (see fig. 3.13). Each of from five to fifteen performers, using contact microphones, files, hammers, and the like, move around and within the car, guided by the score.

In such works, there is an increasing availability of performer creativity. Once the composer has admitted that the act of composition is a partially shared responsibility (for whatever reason), it is not difficult to understand the motivation inherent in graphic or less exact notational systems. New instruments and techniques have evolved from concepts of new sounds, but have as a result also created new implications and philosophies of composer-performer relationships much more significant in their ramifications than the mere searching for different timbres.

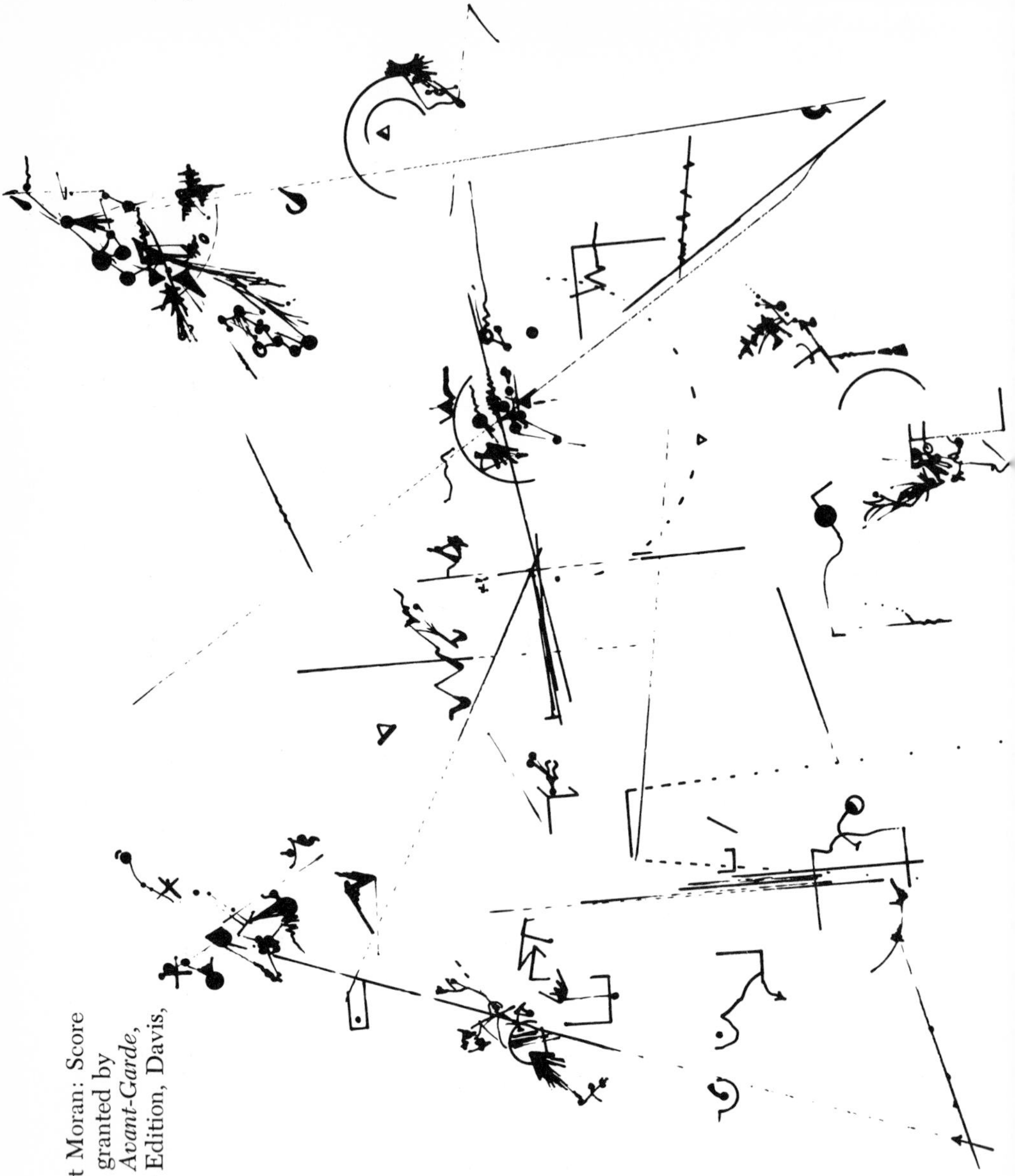

Figure 3.13.   Robert Moran: Score to *Titus*. (Permission granted by *Source: Music of the Avant-Garde,* Composer/Performer Edition, Davis, California.)

Bibliography

*Further Readings**

Bartolozzi, Bruno. *New Sounds for Woodwind.* London: Oxford University Press, 1967. Excellent source for new techniques on woodwind instruments.

Backus, John. *The Acoustical Foundation of Music.* New York: W. W. Norton & Co., 1969. A must for those seeking expert knowledge in this area for spatial and timbre modulation.

Becker, John. "Finding a Personal Orchestral Idiom." *Musical America,* (February 1950). Much insight and subjective information from a man very much an innovator, especially in his use of percussion.

von Bekesy, Georg. "Musical Dynamics by Variation of Apparent Size of Sound Source." *Journal of Music Theory* 14, no. 1 (Winter, 1970):141. A fascinating study of traditional instruments and their acoustic variability in both psychological and spatial terms.

Brant, Henry. "Space as an Essential Aspect of Musical Composition." In *Contemporary Composers on Contemporary Music.* Edited by Elliott Schwartz and Barney Childs. New York: Holt, Rinehart and Winston, 1967. An important contribution to thinking in terms of spatial modulation and acoustics regarding structuring composition.

Brindle, Reginald Smith. *Contemporary Percussion.* London: Oxford University Press, 1970. A superb book devoted to the growing aspects of this section of instruments. It also includes a rather complete and detailed account of special effects, visual symbology of percussion instruments and mallets, and special performing techniques along with many examples from current literature.

Bunger, Richard. *The Well-Prepared Piano.* Colorado Springs: The Colorado Music Press, 1973. Superb book dealing with the essentials and potentials of this ever-increasingly-used "instrument."

Cope, David. "Chronicles of a Cause." *The Composer* 1, no. 1 (June 1969). An interview with I. A. MacKenzie featuring his lucid though incredible accounts of his "sculptures."

Cowell, Henry. *American Composers on American Music.* New York: Frederick Unger Publishing Co., 1933. Contains a brief but interesting article on Carlos Salzedo (p. 101).

Cummings, Barton. "A Brief Summary of New Techniques for Tuba." *Numus West* 5:62. A very good introduction to new sounds for this instrument interest is gaing rapidly among composers of new music.

*Addresses for record companies, periodicals, and music publishers mentioned in this Bibliography can be found in Appendix 4.

Erickson, Robert. *Sound Structure in Music*. Berkeley: University of California Press, 1975. A superb book whose title is bit misleading in that it deals with timbre and texture primarily in new and *avant-garde* music. Highly recommend reading.

Goldstein, Malcom. "Texture." In *Dictionary of Contemporary Music*, edited by John Vinton (New York: E. P. Dutton & Co., 1974.) A fine study of works in depth, often with concentration on both timbre and spatial modulation, though they are not so designated.

Heiss, John C. "For the Flute: A List of Double-stops, Triple-stops, Quadruple-stops and Shakes." *Perspectives of New Music* 5, no. 1:189.

–––. "Some Multiple Sonorities for Flute, Oboe, Clarinet and Bassoon." *Perspectives of New Music* 7, no. 1 (Fall-Winter, 1968):136.

Howell, Thomas. *The Avant-Garde Flute*. Berkeley: The University of California Press, 1974. An excellent book containing the fingerings for an incredible number of multiphonics. Along with the Turetzky book mentioned later, it is the beginning of a most important series of books on new techniques for every orchestral instrument. (This series, edited by Barney Childs and Bertram Turetzky, is at this writing soon to come from the University of California Press.)

The Instrumentalist vol. 28, no. 10 (May 1974). Entire issue dedicated to new directions in instrumental music. Articles feature: strings, by Pat Strange; woodwinds, by Frank McCarty; percussion, by Dennis Kahle; band music, by Larry Livingston; and electronics, by Allen Strange.

Johnston, Ben. "Harry Partch." In *Dictionary of Contemporary Music*. Edited by John Vinton. New York: E. P. Dutton & Co., 1974. Exceptional article; a useful tool in understanding this man and his personal instruments.

Kaufman, Harald. "Ligeti's Zweites Streichquartet." *Melos* 37 (1970):391. A good study of Ligeti's techniques.

Kostelanetz, Richard. *John Cage*. New York: Praeger Publishers, 1968. An excellent source of information of all kinds about this revolutionary figure in world musics, especially on his piano preparation techniques and his ideas about new instrumental techniques in general.

Livingston, Larry, and McCarty, Frank. "Expanding Woodwind Sound Potential." *The Composer* 3, no. 1 (1971):39. A good broad introduction to the area of using woodwind instruments for new sounds.

Musical America vol. 24, no. 4 (April 1974). Contains a most interesting article on Jan DeGaetani, one of the most important of avant-garde singers (p. MA-6).

Palm, Siegfried. "Notation for String Instruments." *The Composer* 3, no. 2 (1972):63. A very good cross section of effects in current use for string instruments.

Partch, Harry. "And On the Seventh Day Petals Fell in Petaluma." *Source* 2, no. 1 (January 1968). Includes description of instruments and score.

–––. *Genesis of a New Music*. Madison: University of Wisconsin Press, 1949.

Pooler, Frank, and Pierce, Brent. *New Choral Notation*. New York: Walton Music, 1973. Fascinating source of various examples of new techniques for writing for the voice.

Read, Gardner. *Thesaurus of Orchestral Devices*. London: Sir Isaac Pitman & Sons, 1953. Huge and extremely useful volume.

Reed, H. Owen, and Leach, Joel T. *Scoring for Percussion*. New York: Prentice-Hall, 1969.

Rehfeldt, Phillip. "Clarinet Resources and Performance." *Proceedings* 7, no. 8 (1974). Fine article on the multiphonic and other aspects of new clarinet performance.

Rossi, Nick, and Choate, Robert. *Music of Our Time*. Boston: Crescendo Publishing Co., 1969. Contains two excellent sections on personages involved with instrument exploration: Edgard Varèse (p. 220) and Henry Cowell (p. 339).

Salzedo, Carlos. "Considerations on the Piano and the Harp." *Harp News* vol. 3, no. 4 (Fall 1961). A fascinating article which originally appeared in 1923. The issue of *Harp News* cited here is dedicated to this innovative genius in memoriam, and is well worth studying.

————. *Modern Study of the Harp*. New York: G. Schirmer, 1921.

————. *Method for the Harp*. New York: G. Schirmer, 1929. With the above, a classic in new techniques for this instrument which seem far in advance of their time.

Schuller, Gunther. "Conversation with Varèse." *Perspectives of New Music*, 3, no. 2:32 and idem, "American Performance and New Music," Ibid. 1, no. 2:1. Two general but very good articles.

Schwartz, Elliott. "Elevator Music." *The Composer* 2, no. 2 (1970):49.

Soundings 2 (April 1972). Half the issue is devoted to Harry Partch and his work, and includes a brief biographical sketch, the score to *Barstow*, and a short article by Partch, "A Somewhat Spoof."

Source: Music of the Avant Garde (Davis, California). Has included numerous articles and descriptions of new instruments. See especially Robert Erickson in vol. 3, no. 1 (January 1969), and Harry Partch in vol. 2, no. 1 January 1968).

Steinberg, Michael. "Some Observations on the Harpsichord in Twentieth Century Music." *Perspectives of New Music* 1, no. 2:189. A good introduction to this instrument's potential.

Turetzky, Bertram. "The Bass as a Drum," *The Composer* 1, no. 2 and idem, "A Technique of Contemporary Writing for the Contrabass," ibid. 1, no. 3.

————. *The Contemporary Contrabass*. Berkeley: University of California Press, 1974. Superb book dealing with this man's original work on his instrument, as well as the many works written for him; contains chapters covering almost every conceivable aspect of the new instrumental techniques for this instrument.

Verkoeyen, Jos. "String Players and New Music," *Sonorum Speculum* 45 (Winter 1970). Short but interesting look into this subject.

Vinton, John, ed. *Dictionary of Contemporary Music*. New York: E. P. Dutton & Co., 1974. Contains numerous articles pertinent to the subject matter of this chapter, including contributions by William Brooks (s.v. "Instrumental and Vocal Resources"), and Henry Brant (s.v. "Orchestration").

Wen-chung, Chou. "A Varèse Chronology." *Perspectives of New Music* 5, no. 1:1 See also Henry Cowell, "The Music of Edgard Varèse," *Modern Music* 5.

Yates, Peter. "Lou Harrison." *ACA Bulletin* 9, no. 2:2. Provides a good bibliography of his works; special note should be taken of those for percussion orchestra.

Recordings and Publishers

Albright, William. *Organbook* (1967). Jobert. Recorded on CRI S-277.

Austin, Larry. *The Maze* (1965). CPE-*Source*. For three percussionists, tape, and projection; performers move from one group of instruments to another.

Bamert, Matthias. *Septuria Lunaris*. Recorded on London S-725. Very effective use of mass orchestral effects.

Becker, John. *Abongo* (1933). Autograph Editions. For percussion orchestra, two solo dancers, dance group.

Berio, Luciano. *Sinfonia*. Universal Edition. Recorded on Columbia MS-7268.

Blank, Allan. *Esther's Monologue*. Recorded on Orion ORS-75169.

Brant, Henry. *Fourth Millennium* (1963). MCA. Recorded on Nonesuch 71222. For brass quintet.

———. *Hieroglyphics* 3 (1957). MCA. Recorded on CRI S-260. For chamber group.

———. *Voyage Four* (1963). MCA. For three orchestral groups; real spatial separation.

Cage, John. *Amores*. Peters. Recorded on Mainstream 5011.

———. *Bacchanale*. Peters. Recorded on Columbia M2S-819.

———. *Concerto for Prepared Piano and Chamber Orchestra* (1951). Peters. Recorded on Nonesuch 71202.

———. *Perilous Night, Suite for Prepared Piano*. Peters. Recorded on Avant 1008.

———. *Sonatas and Interludes* (1948). Peters. Recorded on Columbia M2S-819.

Chavez, Carlos. *Toccata for Percussion* (1942). Mills Music. Recorded on Columbia CMS-6447. A standard for the literature.

Chihara, Paul. *Logs* and other works. Recorded on CRI S-269. Very subtle effects.

Childs, Barney. *Mr. T. His Fancy*. CPE-*Source*.

Cope, David. *Iceberg Meadow* (1969). Carl Fischer. Recorded on Capra 1201. Use of partially prepared piano.

———. *Margins* (1972). Carl Fischer. Recorded on Orion ORS-75169.

Cowell, Henry. *The Banshee* (1925). AMP. Recorded on Folkways FX 6160.

Crumb, George. *Ancient Voices of Children*. Peters. Recorded on Nonesuch 71255.

———. *Songs, Drones, and Refrains of Death*. Peters. Recorded on Desto 7155.

———. *Black Angels* (1970). Peters. Recorded on CRI S-283. For amplified string quartet.

Dahl, Ingolf. *Concerto for Saxophone* (1949). MCA. Recorded on Brewster 1203. Brilliant work by a master craftsman; a work for a much-maligned instrument.

Dlugoszewski, Lucia. *Space is a Diamond* (1970). Recorded on Nonesuch 71275. For trumpet and piano.

Druckman, Jacob. *Incenters* (1968). MCA Music. Recorded on Nonesuch 71221.

Erb, Donald. *Fanfare for Brass and Percussion*. Merion Music. Instrumentalists scattered on stage, balcony, etc., for spatial effects.

———. *The Seventh Trumpet* (1969). Merion Music. Recorded on Turnabout 34433. Interesting use of rapping, tapping, etc., effects from orchestra.

Foss, Lukas. *Elytres* (1964). Fischer and Schott. Recorded on Turnabout 34514. For flute, violin, piano, harp, and percussion.

Globokar, Vinko. *Discours 11* for solo trombone. Peters. Recorded on DG 137005. This is a fascinating record of other works as well.

Green, George. *Perihelion for Concert Band* (1974). Recorded by Cornell University Wind Ensemble, Record No. 15.

Harrison, Lou. *Canticle No. 1 for Percussion* (1940). Recorded by Mainstream 5011.

Haubenstock-Ramati, Roman. *Interpolations: a "Mobile" for Flute* (1, 2, 3) (1958). Universal Edition. Recorded on RCA VICS-1312.

———. *Tableau 1* (1967). Universal Edition. Recorded on Wergo 60049.

Hodkinson, Sydney. *Imagine Quarter* (1967). BMIC.

Henze, Hans Werner. *Versuch uber Schweine*. Schott. Recorded on DG 139456.

Husa, Karel. *Apotheosis of this Earth* (1971). AMP. Recorded on Golden Crest 4134.

Johnston, Ben. *Knocking Piece*. CPE-*Source*. Unconventional use of piano, with knocking on lid, sides, etc., and avoidance of keyboard.

Korte, Karl. *Matrix*. Recorded on CRI S-249. For woodwind quintet.

Kraft, William. *Triangles*, a concerto for percussion, ten instruments (1968). MCA. Recorded on Crystal S-104. Very effective use of percussion by a professional percussionist/composer.

Kupferman, Meyer. *Infinities 22* for trumpet and piano. General Music. Recorded on Serenus 12000. Part of a cycle of infinities, all based on the same twelve-tone row.

Leedy, Douglas. *Usable Music I*. CPE-*Source*.

Ligeti, György. *Aventures* (1962). Peters. Recorded on Candide 31009.

———. *Atmospheres* (1961). Universal Edition. Recorded on Wergo 305.

———. *Lontano* (1967). Schott. Recorded on Wergo 322.

Mayuzumi, Toshiro. *Concerto for Percussion*. Peters. Recorded on Point 101.

Messiaen, Oliver. *Oiseaux Exotiques* (1955). Universal Edition. Recorded on Candide 31002. Notable for its effects.

Meytuss, Julius. *Dnieper Dam*. Recorded on Folkways FX 6160.

Moran, Robert. *Titus*. CPE-*Source*.

Moryl, Richard. *Chroma for Chamber Ensemble* (1972). Recorded on Desto 7143.

Mossolov, Alexander. *Steel Foundry* (1928). Recorded on Folkways FX 6160.

Norgard, Per. *Waves* for percussion. Wilhelm Hansen. Recorded on Cambridge 2824.

Partch, Harry. *Daphne of the Dunes* (1958). Recorded on Columbia MQ-31227, which includes other works as well, e.g., *Barstow*, which is published in *Soundings* 2. Features his own unique instruments.

———. *And on the Seventh Day Petals Fell in Petaluma. Source.* Recorded on CRI S-213.

Penderecki, Krzysztof. *De Natura Sonoris,* for orchestra (1966). Moeck. Recorded on Nonesuch 71201.

———. *Threnody for the Victims of Hiroshima.* PWM. Recorded on RCA VICS-1239. Extraordinary special effects.

Reynolds, ·Roger. *Ping. CPE-Source.* Recorded on CRI S-285.

———. *Quick are the Mouths of the Earth.* Peters. Recorded on Nonesuch 71219.

Salzedo, Carlos. *Chanson dans la Nuit.* Recorded on DG 139419. Not so much a composer as a master genius of invention.

Schoenberg, Arnold. *Five Pieces for Orchestra* (1909). Peters. Recorded on Columbia M2S-709 and Mercury. A masterpiece of orchestration.

Schubel, Max. *Insected Surfaces,* a concerto for five instruments (1966). Recorded on Opus One S-1.

Schuller, Gunther. *Seven Studies on Themes of Paul Klee.* Universal Edition. Recorded on RCA LSC-2879.

Smith-Brindle, Reginald. *Pollfemo de oro,* four fragments for guitar. Peters. Recorded on RCA LSC-2964.

Stockhausen, Karlheinz. *Zyklus* (1950). Universal Edition. Recorded on Mainstream 5003. For one percussionist.

———. *Gruppen.* Universal Edition. Recorded on DG-137002. For three orchestras, which surround audience.

Sydeman, William. *Texture Studies for Orchestra.* Okra Music.

Varèse, Edgard. *Hyperprism.* G. Schirmer. Recorded on Candide 31028 and Columbia MS-31078.

———. *Ionisation* (1933). G. Schirmer. Recorded on Columbia MS-6146. One of the first full percussion orchestra works.

———. *Integrales* (1925). G. Schirmer. Recorded on London 6752.

Whittenberg, Charles. *Games of Five for Woodwind Quintet.* Joshua Publishers. Recorded on Advance 11 and Serenus 12028.

Xenakis, Iannis. *Metastasis* (1954). Boosey & Hawkes. Recorded on Vanguard C-10030.

Timbral Variations (UBRES CS-301) is an album of works by Franz Furrer, Edwin London, Stuart Smith and Paul Zonn which, as the title implies, are very much involved with instrument exploration. Opus One No. 22 recording has the Blackearth Percussion Group performing works by Lou Harrison, Ed Miller, Mario Bertoncini, Peter Garland, John Cage, and William Albright.

4 Electronic and Computer Music

Brief Background

Electronic music,[1] or that music composed from or altered by electronic apparatus, has a long and involved history: from early experimental instruments (such as the "Clavecin Electrique" or "Electric Harpsichord" of Delaborde in Paris, 1761; and Elisha Gray's "Electroharmonic Piano" in Chicago, 1876),[2] mostly intent upon imitating styles and materials of their times, to fascinating predictions of this new sound source. In 1936, Edgard Varèse said: "I am sure that the time will come when the composer, after he has graphically realized his score, will see this score automatically put on a machine that will faithfully transmit the musical content to the listener. . . ."[3] A year later, John Cage remarked: "To make music . . . will continue to increase until we reach a music produced through the aid of electrical instruments."[4] Concomitant with these was the desire of many composers to develop a new aesthetic wherein *all* sounds could act as material for composition (e.g., E.T.A. Hoffman's *The Automaton* in the early nineteenth century, and *The Art of Noises*, 1913, by the Italian futurist Luigi Russolo). Around 1920, experiments with electronic instruments to create infinite sound resources took place with Otto Luening, Norman McLaren, Pierre Schaeffer, Leon Theremin (who in 1923 invented the Theremin), Friederich Trautwein, Paul Hindemith, Ernst Toch, and many others. In 1948 Pierre Schaeffer presented a "Concert of Noises" over French radio; this *musique concrète* involved manipulation of both natural and instrumental sound sources. Thereafter, and

1. It must be made abundantly clear that the author does not seek to imply, by the use of the term *electronic music,* any stylistic or material similarity among composers who employ this medium. The term as used here does not connote an inherent style, something which is in fact nonexistent. In a lecture given in Los Angeles, Milton Babbitt argued that a recording of a Tschaikovsky Symphony is actually electronic music, in that all the sound actually heard is electronically produced. The term as used by the author here refers *only* to that music composed from or altered by electronic apparatus, and as such is as limitless stylistically as music for *string quartet* or *symphony* orchestra.

2. For more detailed history, see Otto Luening, "Some Random Remarks on Electronic Music," *Journal of Music Theory* 8, no. 1 (Spring 1964):89-98.

3. From a lecture given at Mary Austin House, Santa Fe, New Mexico, 1936.

4. John Cage, *Silence* (Cambridge, Mass.: The M.I.T. Press, 1961), p. 3.

particularly in 1951 (with Vladimir Ussachevsky, John Cage, Otto Luening, Karlheinz Stockhausen, Bruno Maderna, Herbert Eimert), music involving electronic sound sources, both with and without live instrumentalists, became increasingly popular. Within the past few years, due to the availability of ready-built studios (especially from Buchla Associates and R. A. Moog), a great many universities as well as individuals have electronic studios, and it is difficult to treat the results as experimental any longer!

Aesthetics

It is undeniable that with the advent of tape and unlimited resources of sound and rhythm, such concepts as "noise," "consonance-dissonance," and "live performance" become increasingly indefinable. Synthesizers have enabled composers to control all the elements of production (dynamics, envelope duration, etc.), except performance acoustics and audience receptivity. This philosophy, if one is implied, has not gained a universal acceptance. Igor Stravinsky said:

What about the much publicized "infinity of possibilities" in connection with the new art material of electronically produced sound? With few exceptions "infinite possibilities" has meant collages of organ burbling, rubber suction (indecent, this), machine-gunning, and other—this is curious—representational and associative noises more appropriate to Mr. Disney's musical mimicries.[5]

Ernst Krenek seems almost to answer Stravinsky's objection in his article "A Glance over the Shoulders of the Young":

To the superficial observer, it appears that the phenomena demonstrated so far in electronic music: levels of colour, texture, density, consistency and mass of sound material, are of a considerably lower intellectual level of musical consciousness than the aspirations which were associated with the demanding music of the past. Perhaps this only represents a beginning; history cites us many examples of the way in which creative energy has been expended on the achievement of progress of one dimension while temporarily impoverishing the other dimensions of the subject.[6]

The ability of the composer to place on tape material which exceeds the limits of audience perception is a new problem born of electronic music. *Psycho-acoustics,* the study of listener discrimination and receptivity of these complexities, has become a real and vital tool of the com-

5. Igor Stravinsky and Robert Craft, *Dialogues and A Diary* (Garden City, New York: Doubleday & Co., Inc., 1963), p. 25.
6. Ernst Krenek, "A Glance over the Shoulders of the Young," *Die Reihe I* (Bryn Mawr, Pennsylvania: Theodore Presser Co., in association with Universal Edition, c. 1958), p. 16.

poser attempting to communicate. This necessarily self-imposed composer restriction redefines the "newfound freedom" of electronic music.[7]

Likewise, the inexperienced electronic music composer can very often be "hypnotized" by his complex patch-cord setup and the time required to make the exact sound he needs, to the point where visual studies of "spaghettied" patch cords seem as necessary to the work as the sound itself.

Fundamentals

There exist two basic sound sources: electronic, including the oscillators and generators; and nonelectronic, or *musique concrète* (e.g., instrumental sounds, sounds of nature). There seems to have been, at least in the early fifties, a definite desire by composers to make a choice between one or the other. However, even by 1960 (especially in Stockhausen's *Gesang der Jünglinge*), both sources were considered of equal potentiality. Certainly the latter of the two involves less control and determinability. Experimentation with the sources themselves has evolved with tape loops (continuous lengths of tape looped so as to pass and repass the playback head, creating rhythmic ostinati or continuous sound flow), and current experimentation with gluing bits of recorded magnetic tape to white leader tape results in either a very controlled and measurable (in fractions of inches) rhythmic base or a random flux of sounds, depending on the composer's wishes.

The second step, after choice of sound materials, and as shown in the following extremely simplified schematic (fig. 4.1), is the manipulation of material. At this point, it is only raw in form and now available for altering in the form of combining sounds (with mixer, ring modulator), eliminating certain sounds with the use of various filters such as low-pass, high-pass, band-pass and band reject and filter banks (the effect of band-pass and band-reject filters is shown in figure 4.2), or distorting sounds (by reverberation and/or various types of modulations: frequency, amplitude, and ring; along with speed changes of the tape recorder, etc.).

Finally synchronization, or the placing of all events into a composed order (by means of such devices as splicing, rerecording, mixing, speed alteration), results in the final tape being ready for playback. *Classic* electronic music is that composed by recording sounds (or short groups of sounds) individually, and then splicing them together. While most electronic music involves a certain amount of splicing, *classic* electronic

7. See especially: Fritz Winckel," "The Psycho-Acoustical Analysis of Structure as Applied to Electronic Music," *Journal of Music Theory* 7, no. 2:194; and Milton Babbitt, "An Introduction to the R.C.A. Synthesizer," *Journal of Music Theory* 8, no. 2: 251.

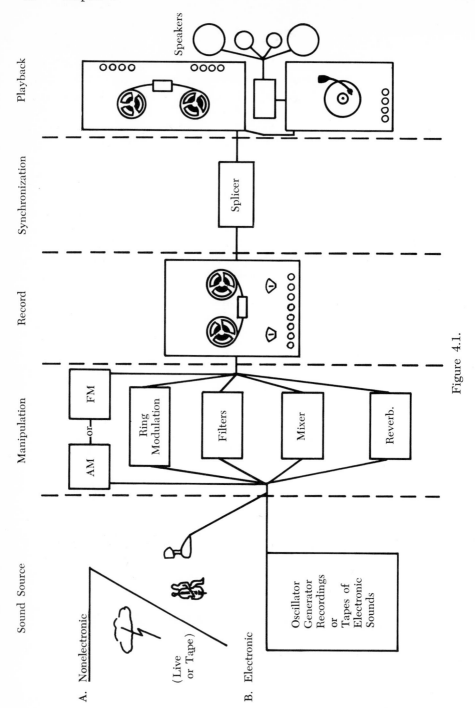

Figure 4.1.

music is a basic construct of the genre with timing, order, etc., of sounds and silences composed by splicing. The introduction of voltage control (keyboards, sequencers, etc.) and multitrack recorders, making "live" production on tape of as many consecutive sounds as the composer wishes without splicing, has eliminated many such *classical* approaches. The *classic* approach (used for example in the *Poème Électronique* (1958) by Edgard Varèse by virtue of necessity, since voltage control was not yet in use) is still retained by a number of composers, including Mario Davidovsky and Vladimir Ussachevsky. One possible point to this prolongation of a tedious and time-consuming approach is that if one is constantly confronted by the splicing block for each new sound he will surely "think twice" about its being compositionally viable and musical. Certainly keyboards, sample-holds, sequencers, etc., make near "real-time" performance possible, a performance which some feel more easily leads to sonic masturbation than to great music. No doubt, *classic* and "live" electronic means can both serve the talented composer well, each having its share of advantages and drawbacks. The playback stage cannot be underestimated in its importance, as the viability of a majority of compositions on tape require specific placement of loudspeakers, and some have even stated proper placement of the tape machine itself for theatrical or dramatic

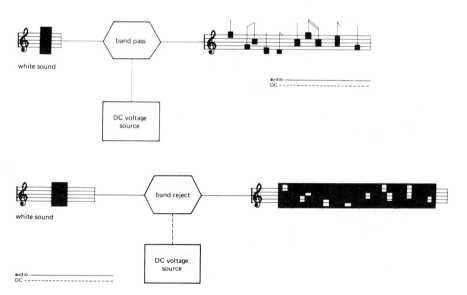

Figure 4.2.   Band-pass and band-reject filtering. From *Electronic Music*, by Allen Strange. © Copyright 1972. Wm. C. Brown Company Publishers, Dubuque, Iowa. Permission granted.

effect. In *Musik für ein Haus* (1968) by Karlheinz Stockhausen, exact locations of all electronic materials in a two-story house with patio are inherent to the "real" performance of the tape work. Acoustical considerations likewise become extremely important for the composer and/or performer in the placement of loudspeakers. Stockhausen discusses this:

. . . I should like to explain . . . just how loudspeakers are properly placed in an auditorium (a procedure which is becoming better and better known to me and which demands the greatest care in the particular place in question, as well as often up to four hours of time from me and several other collaborators sitting in various parts of the hall; in Madrid, for example, Kontarsky, Fritsch, Gehlhaar, Alings, Boje, and I took several hours to set the loudspeakers up; some of them were even lying on their backs up in the balcony, and others were on stands on the stage, and we had put pieces of wood under the front edge of each speaker so that they were pointed up at the ceiling and the sound was only reflected into the house at an angle at a greater distance; we set up two loudspeakers contrary to the usual way with their diaphragm sides at an acute angle directly toward the wooden walls in order to prevent hiss and to enable the people sitting right in front of these loudspeakers—at a distance of about 5-7 meters (16½ to 23 feet)—to hear also the loudspeakers standing on the opposite side, as well as those which were diagonally opposite; in principle we try to send the sound of the loudspeakers, particularly when instrumentalists are playing at the same time, as *high* as possible into the house and to achieve a smooth acoustic match, especially in four-track reproduction).[8]

Synthesizers

Sophistication and generalization in studio equipment are still important missing elements in production of music on tape. So-called "studios" vary from a single tape recorder and splicing machine to the R.C.A. Synthesizer valued at $250,000.[9] Unlike instrumental music, in which the performance may vary with both the instrument and performer, tape music generally has *one* performing version, that made by the composer himself and under his studio conditions.

Electronic music synthesizers, such as the three shown in figure 4.3, provide a wide range of sound materials (oscillators, generators, white sound generators) and manipulation instruments (ring modulators, filter banks, mixers, envelope control, etc.), combined with "real-time" keyboard synchronization possibilities. Their construction is basically modular; that is, each unit fits a certain size or multiples of that size, so that

8. Karlheinz Stockhausen, "Not A Special Day," *The Composer* 1, no. 2 (September 1969):65-66.

9. *Music Educators Journal* 55, no. 3 (November 1968). A number of kits and guides to electronic music are currently available, including *Electronic Music* (with pictures and leaflets, from Keyboard Jr. Publications); *Exploring Music: Grade Six* (Holt, Rinehart, and Winston); and *Nonesuch Guide to Electronic Music* (Nonesuch HC-73018, a two-record set).

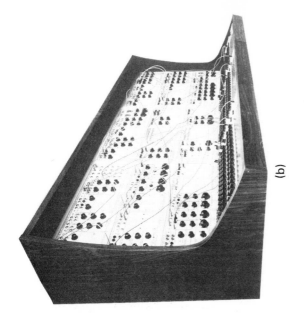

(b)

(a)

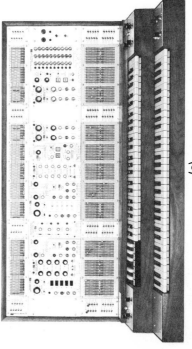

(c)

Figure 4.3.   (a) The Moog Synthe-
sizer (produced by R. A. Moog Co.,
Williamsville, N. Y. 14221); (b) The
Buchla Electronic Music System
(Buchla and Associates, Box 5051,
Berkeley, Calif. 94705); (c) The ARP
Synthesizer (Tonus Inc., 45 Kenneth
St., Newton Highlands, Mass. 02161).

the purchaser may choose the exact complement of instruments he wishes, with any remaining space metal-covered or used for "pots" (potentiometers: voltage-measuring devices). A standard unit might contain the following equipment: one or two voltage-controlled oscillators; three to five oscillators; one random signal generator (white and pink sound possibilities); one filter bank; one voltage-controlled low-pass filter; one voltage-controlled high-pass filter; two envelope generators; two voltage controlled amplifiers; one reverberation unit; one power supply; one keyboard controller; one ribbon controller. Such a unit would cost from $3,000 to $6,000 depending on the numbers of each unit present as well as the manufacturer involved. These synthesizers can come in either portable or console models. Larger models which include sample-hold units, sequencers, ring modulators, and built-in linear mixers may cost upwards of $8,000, again depending on make and model.[10]

Studios

Pierre Boulez, in an interview with the author, offered the following observations:

I think that you cannot do good work in this area until you have teams working together. You must have composer and technician alike. Four things, really: composer, technician, good equipment, and a company or factory with money to back the operation, as well as performers in some cases, and as long as these elements cannot work together you will have small laboratories without any outstanding results.[11]

Highly sophisticated studios do exist, among them the Institute of Sonology at Utrecht State University in Holland (which contains four studios, six scientific staff members, four technical staff members, and two secretaries, with computer, *classic*, "live" and DC/AC patch panels and combination availabilities);[12] the EMS studio in Putney, England (see fig. 4.4) and a host of advanced studios based at American universities, including the aforementioned Columbia-Princeton Laboratory, studios at the University of Illinois, North Texas State University, University of California at San Diego, the Cleveland Institute of Music, and many, many others. The RCA Mark II Synthesizer, located at the Columbia-Princeton Center since 1959, has served as the source of a large

10. As of April, 1969. Prices subject to change; this sample from the Moog catalog gives the reader an idea of price ranges. Up-to-date catalogs can be obtained by writing to the individual companies (see figure 4.3 for addresses).

11. Galen Wilson and David Cope, "An Interview with Pierre Boulez," *The Composer* 1, no. 2 (September 1969):84-85.

12. For a more detailed and complete description of the Institute of Sonology with photos and block diagrams see *Sonorum Speculum #52* (Donemus, 51 Jacob Obrechtstraat, Amsterdam, Netherlands).

Figure 4.4. The SYNTHI 100 of
Electronic Music Studios (London)
Limited, 277 Putney Bridge Road,
London SW 15 2pt, England. By per-
mission.

number of important compositions by Babbitt, Ussachevsky, and Luening—
especially the first totally synthesized extended work, *Composition for
Synthesizer* (1961) by Milton Babbitt.[13]

The last eight years or so have seen an increasing interest among
educators in creating small electronic laboratories or "tape manipulation
centers." Small studios, relatively inexpensive and designed primarily for
classroom use, have been developed by Ionic Industries of Morristown,
New Jersey (the Putney, VCS 3), and Electronic Music Laboratory, Inc.
of Vernon, Connecticut (the "ElectroComp," EML-101) to help meet
the music educators' increasing demand for equipment to implement their
need to fulfill the blossoming student interest in experimental music. Likewise, R. A. Moog Company has developed classroom synthesizer (the

13. Unlike the *analog* synthesizers previously mentioned, the RCA Mark II uses
punched paper tape relatively the size of a player-piano roll instead of a keyboard.
Though computer-like in appearance (with the *digital* input), the Mark II is not a
computer: for computer information see subheading later in this chapter.

Mini-Moog) capable of acting as graphic demonstration unit, instruments for live performance and tools for tape composition. Each year new instruments in this category are put on the market: these include the Moog *Sonic VI*, the Buchla *Music Easel*, the ARP *2600*, and numerous others.

Other Developments

Experiments in 1940 by Norman McLaren with film sound tracks (especially dots and loops) have created a unique and less expensive approach to electronic "notation." By cutting notches in the film, and by scratching and painting on the sound track portion of the film, McLaren was able to produce a wide variety of "electronic" sounds from the projector (the performer). Lejaren Hiller who with Leonard Isaacson wrote *Experimental Music* (McGraw-Hill, 1959), has more recently described situations in which the composer, with a pen filled with magnetic dyes, could sit at his desk and compose on unmagnetized tape without the aid of any electronic equipment, except possibly a tape recorder for experimentation and synchronization. Though at first these experiments seem farfetched, in actuality such necessary experimentation to discover what "notation" would produce what sounds need be no more extensive than that required of an electronic setup, wherein the composer is faced with a maze of complicated possibilities.

The major body of electronic music has come into existence within the past twenty years. Prior to 1954 composers were primarily interested in experimentation, personal technical understanding, research and upgrading of the physical conditions of their equipment and materials.

Notable Composers and Works

Unquestionably one of the most popular of early tape pieces is Stockhausen's *Gesang der Jünglinge* (1955-56), which combines sounds of singing with electronically produced sounds. Stockhausen controls the *musique concrète* sounds electronically to produce variable comprehensibility of the text (Daniel 3, "Song of the Men in the Fiery Furnace"). The score calls for five groups of loudspeakers to surround the audience. Stockhausen uses the spatial direction and movement of the sounds to create form, avoiding the traditional melodic or timbre repetitions.

Stockhausen's numerous other electronic works, especially *Kontakte* (1960), *Telemusik* (1966), and *Hymnen* (1969)—the latter a collage of electronically altered hymns and *concrète sounds*—has made him one of the most widely known of Europe's electronic composers.

In 1958, an historic performance of Edgard Varèse's *Poème électronique* took place at the Brussels World's Fair. There, in the Philips Radio Corporation pavilion, Varèse, together with architect LeCorbusier, placed four hundred loudspeakers (along with paintings and projections) to provide an almost constantly repeated performance (with 15,000-16,000 people daily for six months as audience). Similar to the Stockhausen in respect to its use of both *concrète* and electronic materials (such as voice, bells, oscillators), it is most assuredly different in respect to organization. Built primarily of motives, both rhythmic and timbric, the basic form becomes easily apparent even during a first listening. Varèse's favorite definition of music, that by Hoene Wronsky ("the corporealization of the intelligence that is in sound") is very apparent in this highly organized work.

Figure 4.5.   Karlheinz Stockhausen. (Copyright: Werner Scholz.)

Luciano Berio's *Thema: Omaggio a Joyce* (1958) is a variations form using the human voice (completely *concrète*) speaking first recognizably and then being slowly transformed into a fantastic array of sounds (by means of splicing and tape speed variation), and is a good example of what can be achieved with the use of an absolute minimum of materials. Berio's *Visage* is a "classic" of electronic music (1961); an imaginative vocal-electronic treatment in a strikingly dramatic form (originally composed as a radio program). The voice (Cathy Berberian) speaks only one word (*parole:* Italian for "words"), but through an intense variety of emoting (crying, whispering, laughing, etc.) is able, combined with the collaborating electronic sounds, to evoke an emotional gamut almost without peer in the history of music.

John Cage was among the first of the Americans to employ tape techniques. His *Imaginary Landscape No. 5* (1951-52) uses a prepared score for making a recording on tape. All of Cage's works must, however, be considered in the light of his *indeterminate* concepts of musical technique (see chap. 7) and as such must be considered for the most part a cooperative effort between himself and the performer. Therefore, the bulk of his electronic music is found scattered throughout this entire book, especially under the subject headings of chapters 7 and 8.

A large percentage of Vladimir Ussachevsky's early works (from 1951 to 1954), including *Sonic Contours, Transposition, Reverberation,* and *Composition* (all on Folkways FX 6160), were experiments only, mostly based on sounds of piano and flute. His *A Piece for Tape Recorder* (1955) is less of an experiment, yet obvious enough in construction to serve well as a good educational or introductory tool in electronic music. His longtime associates Otto Luening and Milton Babbitt have produced, especially at the Columbia-Princeton Electronic Music Center, a large number of works, particularly tape in combination with live instrumentalists.

Figure 4.6.   Vladimir Ussachevsky.
BMI Archives. Used by permission.

Ussachevsky's *Of Wood and Brass* (1965) is a unique work employing tape loops of varying lengths (on which are recorded *concrète* sounds "of wood and brass") fed through a ring modulator (which collects the sidebands and nullifies the original inputs, creating neoelectronic effects). This and others of Ussachevsky's later works are highly sophisticated examples of electronic music—quite individualistic and advanced from the early embryonic years.

Mario Davidovsky's *Study No. II* (1966) for tape is a truly incredible creation in that each of the extremely quick-moving electronic sounds were placed in order by splicing (*classic* electronic music). The straight-forward ABA form and the use of more or less "pure" electronic material (sine and square waves) marks another unusual feature of this work: the "limitless possibilities" are almost completely unexplored and, except for the obvious performance limitations, one could easily imagine the work as a string quartet. It is most apparent that the drive for new sounds is not the sole reason for the increasing popularity of this medium.

Figure 4.7.   Mario Davidovsky

More recently, Morton Subotnick (one of the founders of the San Francisco Tape Center) achieved much success with *Silver Apples of the Moon* (1967), commissioned to fit the two sides of an LP recording (Nonesuch H-71174), and *The Wild Bull* (1968). Both works employ contrasts in texture and timbre as organizational principles, and the composer has distinctly abandoned the "pure" electronic sounds (e.g., sine waves, traditionally the most "hostile" of the new materials) for more instrumental- and natural-like sounds with heavy overtone series production.

Milton Babbitt's *Ensembles for Synthesizer* (1961-63) is a highly organized and structured work which, unlike a large number of other electronic musics, does not attempt a display of timbre varieties but concentrates on compact rhythmic texture, and formal aspects of the tape medium.

Charles Wourinen's *Time's Encomium* (1968-69) was realized on the RCA Mark II Synthesizer at the Columbia-Princeton Center. The work evidences the composer's instrumental style in both its clear composer control (twelve-tone often in sound) as well as its extremely complicated rhythmic passages. The work contrasts what the composer calls "synthesized" (clarity of pitch) with "processed synthesized sound" (processing here primarily in the form of reverberation).

Figure 4.8.   Milton Babbitt. By permission.

It is interesting to note that a number of "rock" groups have employed electronic sound materials in their music. The Beatles (especially in *Sgt. Pepper's Lonely Hearts Club Band*, Capitol MAS-2653), Jimi Hendrix Experience (Reprise 6261), and The United States of America (Columbia CS-9614) use electronically produced or altered sound but, for the most part, these have remained on the experimental level, exploiting such sounds for shock or text emphasis rather than actual musical or sound development. Walter Carlos, on the other hand, developed electronic "orchestrations" of works by Bach (e.g., *Switched-on Bach*) which represent an interesting application of the Moog instrument. These performances demonstrate particularly the tape medium's ability to perform at levels of speed and accuracy far beyond human capability. These records have

Figure 4.9.   Charles Wuorinen

provided the stimulus for some of the ever-increasing manifestations of popularity of electronic sounds among the general public.[14]

Tape and . . .

The obvious loss (to the audience) of more or less theatrical or visual activity during performance of works on tape has brought about three solutions to this problem: (1) combination of live performer with tape; (2) live electronic music: from the Syn-Ket (a complex, compact live electronic instrument invented and developed by Paul Ketoff in 1963) to extremely complex situations involving recording and playback in numerous arrangements in concert, and performers or audience intercepting light beams to set off oscillators; (3) tape used in conjunction with projections and/or theatrical events. In fact, as will be discussed in a later chapter, the need of electronic music for auxiliary action played a large part in the need for developing mixed-media presentations.

Works for live performer(s) and tape have become increasingly popular in the past several years. Henri Pousseur (b. 1929), in *Rimes pour*

14. A large number of new realizations in this area have appeared in the last five years including works by Erik Satie (Deram 18066: *Electronic Spirit of Erik Satie*), Debussy, and others (see under "Electronic Music" in the Schwann Catalog).

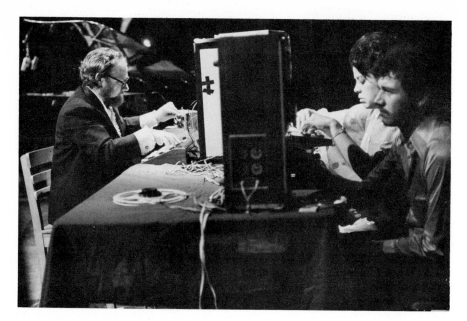

Figure 4.10.   John Eaton playing
the Synket. Photo used by permission.

Différentes Sources Sonores (1959), treats orchestra and sounds on tape
as antiphonal bodies, contrasting the available materials of each (the tape
in this instance is constructed entirely from electronically originated
sounds). The speakers are placed on stage, in "live" performance, in such
a way as to accentuate visually the contrast. Otto Luening (b. 1900) and
Vladimir Ussachevsky, who worked together on *Rhapsodic Variations for
Tape Recorder and Orchestra* (1954), were among the first to realize
and experiment with live and prerecorded sound sources in America, while
Bruno Maderna (in *Musica su due Dimensioni*) had begun studies in
this area in 1952 at the NW German Radio in Cologne. These earliest
examples, like the Pousseur, extended the contrast possibilities of live and
recorded sources.

Mario Davidovsky has composed a number of *Synchronisms* for a
variety of traditional instruments and tape. The first, third, and sixth of
these are for solo instruments and tape (flute, cello, and piano respectively, with the latter winning a Pulitzer Prize)—intense compositions
requiring a great deal of "synchronized" rhythmic interchange from "live"
to recorded source (all the *Synchronisms* are recorded; see chapter Bibliography for record numbers).

Kenneth Gaburo's 1962 work *Antiphony III* (*Pearl-white Moments*)
combines sixteen soloists in four groups performing live with tape (through

Figure 4.11.   Otto Luening. By permission of the composer.

two speaker systems), incorporating the antiphonal interplay possible between live and tape sounds both acoustically and visually. *Antiphony III*'s tape material includes both purely electronic sound sources and those more imitative of the live performers, expanding the echo and reiterative effects inherently restricted in totally live performances.

As it became apparent that instruments were capable of a large variety of sonic materials, complementary possibilities of electronic and instrumental sounds became a reality. Donald Erb (b. 1927), in *In No Strange Land* (1968) for trombone, double bass, and tape, reflects more imitative techniques, employing the instruments in neoelectronic sound effects, thus minimizing the musical and sonic disparities between electronic and instrumental materials. Recently composers like Robert Erickson have used prerecorded instrumental sounds with live performance. In *Ricercar á 3* (1967), Erickson (b. 1917) employs two prerecorded contrabass with one live contrabass, allowing the performer to play along with and against himself, using the tape as a source of unusual combinative effects.

David Cope's *Arena*, 1974 ('cello and tape), is a *classical* studio composition which reflects both a dialogue between live instrument and tape, and contrasting cohesion. Figure 4.12 shows a passage in which the tape "takes over" each pitch begun by the 'cello, in turn creating vertical sonorities from the horizontal line. The rhythm and pitch of the 'cello must be precisely in "sync" for the passage to work (including the quarter-tone inflections indicated by the arrows attached to the accidentals). The bottom staff reflects more interplay—the harmonics on the

Figure 4.12. David Cope: *Arena* ('cello and tape), page 7. © Copyright 1974 by David Cope. All rights reserved.

Figure 4.12 (continued)

tape only symbolically represented—answered by the artificial harmonics on the 'cello. This page reflects the often necessary, exact, and graphic notations used by composers for tape with "live" instruments.

Richard Felciano has written many works for a wide variety of combinations of traditional instruments and tape. *God of the Expanding Universe* and *Litany* are excellent examples of works for organ and tape. His *Crasis* and *Lamentations for Jani Christou* are good examples of chamber music with tape.

John Watts' *WARP* (1972) includes ARP-created electronic sounds on tape with brass quintet. The four-channel quadraphonic speaker setup heightens both the balance and the effective humor and drama of this work. Combinations of large ensembles with tape occupy an increasing bulk of current tape music composition. Works for tape and band include

Donald Erb's *Reticulation* (1965), and Herbert Bielawa's *Spectrum.* Vladimir Ussachevsky's *Creation-Prologue* (1961) is for tape and choir.[15]

John Eaton has combined the compact "live performance" *Syn-Ket* and full orchestra in his *Concert Piece for Synket and Symphony Orchestra,*

Figure 4.13.   Richard Felciano.
Photo © Michelle Vignes. By permission.

effectively utilizing the visual "concerto" performance technique with specially designed electronic equipment. Merrill Ellis includes soprano, live synthesizer, and orchestra in his *Kaleidoscope.* These last two works concentrate on the "live" performability of synthesizers or *live electronic music.*

15. For a more complete listing, see *Music Educators Journal* 55, no. 3 (November 1968):73. Also consult publishers' listings.

Live Electronic Music

John Cage (b. 1912) was the first to employ entirely live electronic techniques in his *Imaginary Landscape No. 4* (c. 1949, performed in 1951) in which twelve radios are performed by two performers each (twenty-four performers in all). His *Imaginary Landscape No. 1* (1939), which used recordings of constant and variable pitch frequencies in combination with more conventional percussion instruments, was the first real example of tape ("record" is synonymous here), nonimitative of "electronic music."

A number of groups have been formed, dedicated to the live performance of electronic music: The Sonic Arts Group (formed in 1966), with Gordon Mumma, Robert Ashley, Alvin Lucier, and David Behrman; *Musica Elettronica Viva* (1967, in Italy), with Frederic Rzewski, Allan Bryant, and Alvin Curran; the Once Group (Michigan), with Robert Ashley, Gordon Mumma, and others (many continue to flourish). Festivals of live electronic music at Davis, California (1967), Buffalo (1968), and Los Angeles (1968 and 1969), among others, have proved this concept of lasting significance. A live electronics group ("It takes a yar one earth to go around the sun," formed in 1970 by David Rosenboom, originator and director of New York's Electric Circus until 1969, with Jon Hassell, Gerald Shapiro, and Terry Riley) spent the summer of that year performing on electronic instruments designed by the members themselves, on "mesas in Wyoming, ghosts towns in Death Valley, and lava caves in New Mexico." The works performed (see later descriptions) are by the composer/performers and for the most part are extremely loose in construction, serving rather as "lauching pads" for the performers' rehearsed interplay.

Alvin Lucier's *North American Time Capsule 1967* involves usage of the vocoder (Sylvania design), an instrument designed to encode speech sounds into digital information. The results of the speech of the performers as coded material acts as the electronic source material in "live" performance. Likewise, electronic sound modification is the technique in Gordon Mumma's *Mesa* (1966). In this case, a Bandoneon (an accordion-like instrument) is used instead of voices. Work with tape-delay techniques (in effect, echoes and canon) in live performance have been used particularly by Pauline Oliveros (*I of IV*, 1966, and *Lightpiece for David Tudor*, 1965).[16] By separation of record and playback heads, cross-coupling, and so on, a large number of reiterative compositional techniques can be employed.

16. See Pauline Oliveros, "Tape Delay Techniques for Electronic Music Composition," *The Composer* 1, no. 3 (December 1969):135-42.

In *Reconnaissance* (1967) Donald Erb employs a Moog synthesizer performed live with a group of other live instrumentalists (viola, piano, bass, percussion), achieving both the visual complement of total performance and the available sonic resources of electronic equipment. The work also utilizes a Moog polyphonic instrument (live, also): a keyboard instrument of four octaves each divided into forty-three tones, and capable of producing polyphony in a live performance situation (the synthesizer can only produce chords of the same ratio in live performance).

Notation

Notation of electronic music becomes a unique problem. U.S. Public Law 92-140 made it possible to copyright certain sound recordings if published with the notice after Feb. 15, 1972. At the same time this did not really solve the problem of unpublished tape compositions. Composers have reacted to these problems in a variety of ways.

Figure 4.14 is from Stockhausen's *Studie II* (1956, Universal Edition). The left portion is notation of dynamics (envelope); the right portion denotes pitch (100 to 17,200 Hertz, or cycles per second) based on a scale of 81 steps "equal-tempered" at a constant interval ratio of $\sqrt{5}$ (piano at $\sqrt{2}$) and timbre; the middle portion indicates centimeters of tape at 76.2 centimeters per second. This score represents less than seven seconds of performing time. It is not a score in the traditional sense, but rather instructions for re-creation of the score on tape.

Another reason for electronic notation is that of synchronization in tape and traditional instrument performances (see fig. 4.12, David Cope's *Arena*, for example). Except for the Mark II digital synthesizer (the notation here rests in punched paper rolls to be fed into the instrument), notation for the most part has come after the composition rather than before. Notation differs in exactness and form to the same degree as composers and works differ. Standardization will come when an exact method for oscilloscope graphic representations can be produced on paper.

If a "system" exists even in the rough that is somewhat consistently used it is that of Paul Beaver's in the *Nonesuch Guide to Electronic Music* booklet. It is very inexact, however, and indicates only the bare essentials of necessities for re-creation of sound on tape. Unusual instruments such as the *Mellotron* (a keyboard instrument with a large number of prerecorded tape loops of traditional sounds enclosed, activated by depressing the keys and producing neotraditional sounds of violins, etc.) create just that much more confusion to the scene of notation.

The close association of live electronic music performance and aleatoric procedures has caused most composers to rely on graphs and dia-

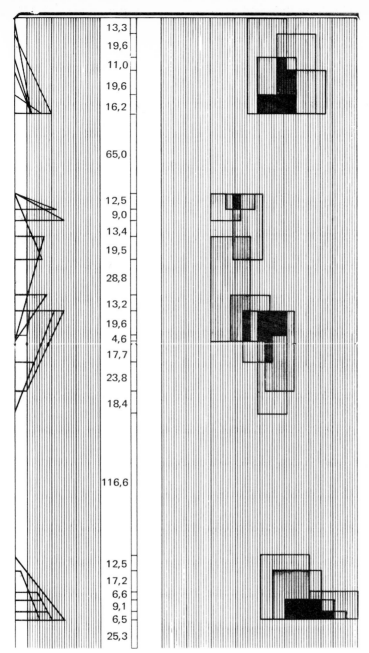

Figure 4.14.   Karlheinz Stockhausen:
Studie II. (Reprinted by permission
of Universal Edition; as it appeared
in the English edition of *Die Reihe*
No. 1, copyright 1958 by Theodore
Presser Company, Bryn Mawr, Pa.)

grams as "before the fact" scores (if indeed any score or directions are used at all). The extremely complicated notation necessary for performance on electronic instruments destroys "real" possibilities of live performance with exact composer control.

Computer Music

The computer is often referred to as an object which can quickly perform a sequence of calculations without human aid, based on the retrieval of stored information. From this definition one can see the beginnings of the misconceptions encountered in terms of the realities of computer-generated sound. Both "sequence" and "without human aid" easily lend themselves to the inevitable interpretation of *sequencers* being computers in the first example and the *loss of human control* in the second (neither of which is necessarily true or false: some sequencers do indeed bridge the tenuous gap to computer definition as well as some computer programs being designed to provide the bulk of compositional control; these are less often the case but adequately demonstrate the continual confusions surrounding the computer and the composer).

This author has divided composer use of the computer into five basic categories:

1. computer-composed music in terms of "human-imposed parameters" (computer selection from programmed styles);
2. computer-generated sound wherein the composer has possibly the most control over his materials;
3. computer aid for random or probability theory constructs;
4. direct control of synthesizer functions by the computer;
5. visual (CRT) notation for direct analog output.

In a sense, then, the computer serves five functions: composes, performs, aids, stores for retrieval, and reacts. The following subheadings parallel these concepts describing briefly their history, composers, works, and materials.

Computer Composition

Actual "computer composition" experiments began (primarily by Lejaren Hiller and Leonard Isaacson) in 1955-56 at the University of Illinois with the Illiac automatic high-speed digital computer and involved programming of basic material and stylistic parameters within which the computer could operate. The first work to make its appearance was the *Illiac Suite for String Quartet* (1957) composed by the computer but transposed to traditional music notation by the composers for "live" non-electronic performance. The score of this work and the experiments leading to its composition are described in *Experimental Music*.[17] Though these directions in "computer control" have not proved to be great artistic successes, the experiments were extraordinarily important, for they indeed opened the door to new vistas in the expansion of the computer's development as an instrument with high potential for a variety of uses by the composer.

Figure 4.15.   Lejaren Hiller. By permission.

Computer-Generated Sound

Computer-generated sound (sometimes referred to as "computer sound synthesis") indeed contrasts "computer composition" in that it affords the composer as near to complete control over his composition as is currently possible. This development began at the Bell Telephone Laboratories in 1959 with Max Matthews and James Tenney. J. K. Randall and Hubert Howe, among others at Princeton, collaborated with the Bell Laboratories to produce the first effective computer program for sound generation: MUSIC IVB. MUSIC IVB, as well as the host of programs designed since, allow the composer extensive control over all the elements of his composition (MUSIC IVB was a culmination of MUSIC IV designed by Matthews using the IBM 7090 computer; it eventually became MUSIC V for the GE 645 computer). Figure 4.16 shows in very basic terms some of the early work done by James Tenney—firstly the

17.   Lejaren Hiller and Leonard Isaacson, *Experimental Music* (New York: McGraw-Hill, 1959).

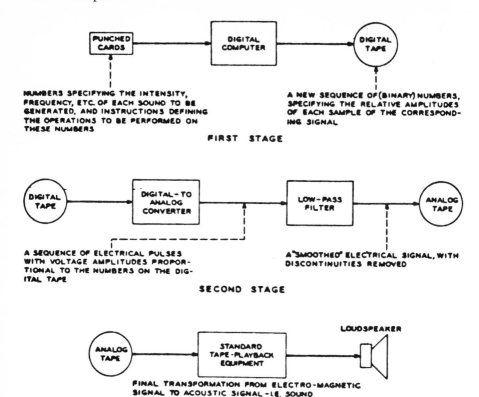

Figure 4.16.   Stages of *computer-generated sound.* J. Tenney (Permission granted by the *Journal of Music Theory,* New Haven, Conn.)

card to digital-tape conversion, secondly the digital to analog conversion, and thirdly the tape-recorder performance.[18] Figure 4.17 shows the outline of a series of functions in terms of vibrato, envelope, and timbre.

Other programs include the Music Simulator-Interpreter for Compositional Procedure (Musicomp) developed for the IBM 7090 by Hiller and Robert Baker, MUSIGOL developed by Donald MacInnis for the Burroughs 5500, and the Transformational Electronic Music Process Organizer (TEMPO) developed by John Clough at Oberlin College. All of these programs deal explicitly with composer control of all the avail-

---

18. *Digital* as used here refers to "on-off" states usually found as input in terms of punched-hole or lack of such in a card or roll of paper; *analog* refers to a continuous directional flow of information as found in the electromagnetic arrangements of "domains" on magnetic recording tape.

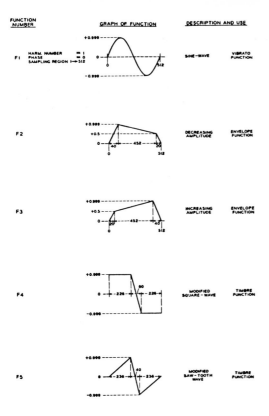

Figure 4.17.   Outline of a series of functions. J. Tenney. (Permission granted by the *Journal of Music Theory*, New Haven, Conn.)

able parameters of sound and *use* the computer (with digital input) as a high-speed "performer" to achieve a magnetic tape recording of their works as output (analog voltage on tape). It is important to note here that, while control is a most important feature of *computer-generated sound,* this control need not in any sense be a "row"-controlled process as described in chapter 1; indeed, any style can be served accurately by the computer and no dodecaphonic imposition is implied.

Excellent examples of current computer uses with computer-generated sound are described in *Proceedings* 7/8, American Society of University Composers. A complete recording of the works referred to by their respective composers or programmers is included (Hubert S. Howe, Jr.: *Freeze;* David Cohen: seven examples including a Bach fugue original studies, and computer-generated fragments; John Melby: *Forandrer;* and Donald MacInnis: *Quadrilith*). These, with their verbal annotations, prove invaluable to the uninitiated as well as to the initiated. Computer-generated sound has proved to be a most prolific and fertile area of computer directions in music. Yet even this area has just begun the process of discovery. An area just beginning at this writing is the concept of reversing the digital to analog (D/A) function of the computer. The D/A interface, necessary for the actual creation of sound on tape, can be arranged in such a way that an A/D concept is derived. In this way, it becomes possible for the computer to convert tapes (e.g., recordings of traditional instruments) to digital information and storage. The potential of this system becomes enormous when one discovers that the *real* obstacle in computer-generated sound is not the computer or its language but the programmer. By high sampling rates (thus high fidelity) of a multitude of *concrète* and electronic sounds of high complexities, the composer/programmer (not always one and the same person) can call on a vast storehouse of accumulated information, having then a near infinity of possibilities at hand (rather than having to rely upon the slow process of experimental programming with which he is, more often than not, now faced).

Computer Aid

Computers are being used as an aid to making composition-related computations in a number of ways. Iannis Xenakis, using FORTRAN IV programming with the IBM-7090, has produced data for his free *stochastic music* (detailed in his *Formalized Music,* Indiana University Press, 1971, pp. 131-54). A number of his works (all realized by traditional instruments) have been composed aided by the high-speed computations of probability theory made accessible by computer application. These works include *ST/10-1, 080262* (1962, with first performance on May 24 of that year at the headquarters of IBM in France), *ST/48-1, 240162* (for large orchestra), *Atrées* (for ten soloists, 1962) and *Morisma-Amorisima* (for four soloists, 1962). In 1969, Lejaren Hiller and John Cage teamed to produce *HPSCHD* and, through the use of computer printout sheets of "highly sophisticated random numbers," created the first available recording of which each performance (the listener performing on his record player knobs), and each copy of the recording, is different and indeterminate. Each printout sheet contains a different set of numbers for loudness and treble/bass control on each speaker. With both Xenakis and Cage, the computer has served as an aid (though to different ends) to achieve results otherwise completely impossible. In neither case has the computer actually produced the resultant sound; it has only aided the composer by virtue of its high-speed computations.

Computer Control of Synthesizer Functions

Research and composition in the area of direct computer control over synthesizer modules (oscillators, filters, etc.) has become very impressive in the past few years. In a sense, the sequencer referred to at the beginning of this computer section is a mini-analog-computer in that by various potentiometer settings (usually three to five per note) on a sequence of notes (variable number depending on the make and model of the sequencer) one can "program" a *series* of notes rather than one or two at a time.

New developments, such as the Synthi 100's Digital Sequencer 256 (E.M.S.), with solid-state storage capacity of 10,240 bits of information capable of precisely controlling six different simultaneous parameters over a sequence of 256 successive events, has brought neo-computer availability within the reach of even the most modest of electronic music laboratories. Through several modes of operation any or all of the 256 stored items and their time relationships can be retrieved and even varied without difficulty. This Sequencer 256 is indeed a small special-purpose digital computer, complete with analog-to-digital and digital-to-analog converters. Surprisingly compact (about the length of a five-octave piano keyboard, with depth and width about one-third of that), the 256 is indeed a mini-computer with high-speed operation and full information retrieval. Buchla Associates (see under *Synthesizer* subheading in this chapter for addresses of this and the E.M.S. studios) has a *Music Easel* which in many respects has full potential of analog retrieval especially designed for storage of live traditional instrument sounds. Though not a computer in the full sense it is a device aimed at aiding the composer through storage and control over synthesizer functions.

Salvatore Martirano has constructed a semiportable "live-performance" computer with retrieval and storage capabilities: the *Sal-Mar Construction* (1973). His performances and tours with this instrument have brought much attention to the "live" potential of the computer-synthesizer combination.

MUSYS, developed by Peter Zinovieff, Peter Grogono, and David Cockerell, uses PDP8/L and PDP8/S computers to control special-purpose electronic equipment.

Visual Notation and Control

New concepts and applications of the computer for the composer continue to be explored. Visual input is an increasingly viable source for future experimentations. One method is to *draw*, using a special light pen, directly on a cathode-ray tube (CRT-television-like computer input) the graph representations of wave forms. The computer then translates such to digital information, processes it and through a D/A converter produces an electromagnetic force on tape (and/or "live" through studio speakers as the composer may wish). Printed graphs can now be assimilated by computer functions through adaption of *Graphos I* and it seems merely a matter of time before optical recognition by computers of a traditionally notated score results in actual performance of the work by the computer. This would make possible the performance of incredibly difficult music without the composer having any knowledge of computer languages. It would likewise present the composer with an incredible experimental laboratory: immediate performance of his works (with any degree of complexity included) for experimentation, revision, and/or re-orchestration.

Future

As one can readily see, the umbrella term "computer music" embraces a vast number of musics and potentials just now beginning to be actualized. Equally important are the many other computer functions outside the realm of composition. Analysis, for example, has benefited from style programming with the results being nearly instantaneous—highly accurate analysis of given works within the parameters fed the computer.

As with all instruments, systems, and styles it should be noted that there is no more guarantee of good music with the computer than without; good music rests as always with the talent and craftsmanship of the composer. The computer has, however, opened a large number of doors for realization of works hitherto unperformable or uncomposable due to the vast amount of time required for devotion to them, or to the physical limitations of composer and performer alike.

Bibliography

*Further Readings**

Appleton, Jon, and Perera, Ronald, eds. *The Development and Practice of Electronic Music.* Englewood Cliffs, N. J.: Prentice-Hall, 1974. Another in the growing list of excellent textbooks on electronic music.

Babbitt, Milton. "An Introduction to the RCA Synthesizer." *Journal of Music Theory* 8 (Winter-Spring 1964):251. Excellent survey and introduction to this instrument.

Baker, Robert A. *Musicomp.* Champaign, Illinois: University of Illinois School of Music, 1963.

Beckwith, John, and Kasemets, Udo, eds. *The Modern Composer and His World.* Toronto: University of Toronto Press, 1961. Has a group of articles and discussion (p. 109) by a number of active composers and physicists dealing with electronic music: Hugh LeCaine, Josef Tal, Vladimir Ussachevsky, among others.

Berio, Luciano. "The Studio di Fonologia Musicale of the Milan Radio." *Score* 15 (March 1956). Fascinating view of this, one of the early studios of electronic music in Europe.

Cage, John. *Silence.* Cambridge, Mass.: The M.I.T. Press, paperback edition, 1961. Provides many insights into the early experiments in electronics by this innovator in the field.

Ceely, Robert. "Thoughts about Electronic Music." *Composer* 5, no. 1 (1973): 11. A most fascinating and direct view of this Boston composer.

Chowning, John. "The Stanford Computer Music Project." *Numus West* 1:12. Thoroughly fascinating article on this developing project.

Christiansen, Louis. "A Visit to the Electronic Music Studios in Moscow." *Numus West* 5:34. Interesting look at this country's progress in the art form.

Cohen, David. "Composer-Generated Music." *Southeastern Composers League Newsletter* 66. Fascinating early account of the origins and study of this growing area of music.

Cole, Hugo. *Sounds and Signs.* London: Oxford University Press, 1974. Has some interesting information on the notation of electronic music (p. 112).

Cope, David. "A View on Electronic Music." *db The Sound Engineering Magazine* (August 1975). This is a broad article covering the problems currently encountered in the electronic music studio as relevant to the sound engineer.

---

*Addresses for record companies, periodicals, and music publishers mentioned in this Bibliography can be found in Appendix 4.

Cope, David. "An Approach to Electronic Music Composition." *Composer* 6, no. 1 (1975):14. One composer's view on the creation of electronic music.

Cott, Jonathan. *Stockhausen*. New York: Simon & Schuster, 1973. A fascinating view of the composer if your tastes run to studies of egocentric composers.

Cross, Lowell M., ed. *A Bibliography of Electronic Music*. Toronto: University of Toronto Press, 1967. A thorough source from one of the capitals of experimental music.

Dallin, Leon. *Techniques of Twentieth Century Composition*. 3rd ed. Dubuque, Iowa: Wm. C. Brown Company Publishers, 1974. Has a very good section covering electronic music.

Davies, Hugh. "A Discography of Electronic Music and Musique Concrete." *Recorded Sound* 14 (April 1964):205. An excellent source, though in need of updating.

Davies, Hugh, ed. *International Electronic Music Catalog*. Cambridge, Mass.: M.I.T. Press, 1968. Presents a wealth of material including an international list of electronic music studies, both public and private.

Divilbiss, J. L. "Real-time Generation of Music with a Digital Computer." *Journal of Music Theory* 8:99. Good treatment of its subject matter.

Dockstader, Tod. "Inside-Out: Electronic Rock." *Electronic Music Review* 5 (January 1968):15.

Douglas, Alan. *Electronic Music Production*. London: Pitman Publishing, 1973. An interesting book, though very much slanted towards British equipment and its usage.

Eimert, Herbert, and Stockhausen, Karlheinz, eds. *Die Reihe* 1 (Theodore Presser Co., 1965; original German edition, 1955). Presents articles by the editors and Krenek, Klebe, Stuckenschmidt, Pousseur, Boulez, and Meyer-Eppler; a most fascinating general text in the European middle-fifties concept of the development and structuring of electronic music.

Eimert, Herbert; Enkel, F.; and Stockhausen, Karlheinz. *Problems of Electronic Music Notation*. Translated by D. A. Sinclair. Ottawa, Canada: 1956.

Electronotes (see Appendix 4). A veritable "tome" of information for the serious and knowledgeable electronic music buff.

Ellis, Merrill. "Musique Concrète at Home." *Music Educators Journal* 55, no. 3 (November 1968):94. Offers suggestions concerning small "tape manipulation centers."

Everett, Tom. "Five Questions: Forty Answers." *Composer* 3, no. 1 (1971):30. Questions dealing with electronic music with varied answers from N. K. Brown, Barney Childs, Sydney Hodkinson, Donald Martino, Richard Moryl, Pauline Oliveros, Elie Siegmeister, and John Watts.

von Foerster, Heinz, and Beauchamp, James W., eds. *Music by Computers*. New York: John Wiley & Sons, 1969.

"Four Views of the Music Department of the University of San Diego." *Synthesis* 1, no. 2 (July 1971). Diverse study of this school dedicated to new music, and of its electronic studios.

Fulkerson, James. "What Defines a Piece of Music." *Composer* 5, no. 1:15. An interview with Joel Chadabe, and good insight into new constructs and ideas for electronic music.

Hiller, Lejaren and Isaacson, Leonard. *Experimental Music*. New York: McGraw-Hill, 1959.

Howe, Hubert S., Jr. *Electronic Music Synthesis.* New York: W. W. Norton & Co., 1975. Most informative.

Interface 2, no. 2 (December 1973). Contains a number of articles relating to computer music, including Steven Smoliar's "Basic Research in Computer-Music Studies"; "A Data Structure for an Interactive Music System"; and Barry Truax's "Some Programs for Real-Time Computer Synthesis and Composition."

Judd, F. C. *Electronic Music and Musique Concrète.* Neville Spearman, 1961. Interesting but outdated.

Luening, Otto. "Some Random Remarks about Electronic Music." *Journal of Music Theory* 8 (Winter-Spring 1964).

———. "An Unfinished History of Electronic Music." *Music Educators Journal* 55 (November 1968):35. Superb study of the long history of electronic music.

"The Many Worlds of Music." *BMI.* (Summer 1970). Entire issue devoted to electronic music, with an excellent discography by Peter Frank and articles by Carter Harman and Louis Chapin.

Mathews, M. V., and Miller, Joan E. *Music IV Programmer's Manual.* Murray Hill, N. J.: Bell Telephone Laboratories. An important source for those interested in pursuing detailed information on computer programming.

Mathews, Max. *The Technology of Computer Music.* Cambridge, Mass.: M.I.T. Press, 1969. A superb book and the first major edition in its field; now suffers from outdatedness, but still a landmark in the subject.

Mellotron: information available from Dallas Music Industries, 301 Island Rd., Mahwah, N.J. 07430.

Meyer, Robert G. "Technical Basis of Electronic Music." *Journal of Music Theory* 8. An interesting, mathematical and electronically oriented introduction (in four parts) to the basic mechanics of electronic sound production for those interested in their scientific foundation.

Numus West 4. Entire issue devoted to computer music, with articles by Bruce Rogers, Otto Laske, Barry Truax, Leland Smith, Louis Christiansen, Herbert Brün, and Pauline Oliveros; a very good study in the variety of uses of the computer.

Oliveros, Pauline. "Tape Delay Techniques for Electronic Music." *Composer* 1, no. 3 (1969):135. Excellent source of information on "live" performance possibilities of electronic music.

Olsen, Harry F. *Music, Physics and Engineering.* New York: Dover, 1967. Short on electronic music but quite long on extremely important facts pertaining to acoustics, makeup, operation of instruments, etc.

Oram, Daphne. *An Individual Note.* London: Galliard Ltd., 1972. Most provocative, even bizarre book on "Oramics equipment" for electronic synthesis which, despite the "Cagean" writing, is far more significant than it at first appears.

Pousseur, Henri. "Calculation and Imagination in Electronic Music." *Electronic Music Review* 5 (January 1968):21.

Proceedings (American Society of University Composers). Vol. 1 has a series of articles by J.K. Randall, Herbert Brün, Ercolino Ferretti, Godfrey Winham, Lejaren Hiller, David Lewin, and Harold Shapero, relating to computer music; also excellent reference material and diverse comments. Vol. 4 (1969) includes an excellent panel discussion on recent developments in electronic music: Hubert S. Howe, John Clough, David Cohen, Emmanuel Ghent, Max Mathews, and Robert Moog are the contributors. Vol. 5 (1970) has a number of articles pertaining to electronic music (beginning on page 37) by Jean Eichelberger Ivey, Ronald Pellegrino, David Rosenboom, Joel Chadabe, Benjamin Boretz, Francois Bayle, Gordon Mumma, and Alvin Lucier. They are diverse and most interesting.

Rossi, Nick, and Choate, Robert, eds. *Music of Our Time*. Boston: Crescendo Publishing Co., 1969. Has a number of excellent studies of composers involved in the electronic medium (biographical as well as informative for study of works): Stockhausen, p. 181; Ussachevsky, p. 326; Babbitt, p. 348; Subotnick and Wourinen, p. 380.

Russcol, Herbert. *The Liberation of Sound*. Englewood Cliffs, N. J.: Prentice-Hall, 1972. Good book on electronic music but suffers from erratic organization.

Schaeffer, Pierre. *A la Recherche d'une Musique Concrète*. Paris: Editions du Seuil, 1952. Valuable and incredibly fascinating study of Schaeffer's early work in *musique concrète*.

Schwartz, Elliott. *Electronic Music: A Listener's Guide*. New York: Praeger Publishers, 1972. Fine book on the subject with accurate materials on all aspects of the art from "live electronic to computer" sources.

"Setting Up Your Moog Synthesizer." Issued by Moog Music (P.O. Box 131, Academy St., Williamsville, N.Y. 14221) and valuable to those interested in this equipment.

Slawson, Wayne. "A Speech-Oriented Synthesizer of Computer Music." *Journal of Music Theory* 13, no. 1 (1969):94. A most important article and, though a bit technical for the layman, highly original.

Smith, Stuart. "Communications." *Perspectives of New Music*. (Spring-Summer, 1973). Fascinating but highly mathematical study of some of Xenakis's remarks in *Formalized Music*.

"Sound Generation by Means of a Digital Computer." *Journal of Music Theory* 7, no. 1 (Spring 1963):24. An excellent general source for coverage of printout cards, programming, digital tape, etc.

Stockhausen, Karlheinz. "The Concept of Unity in Electronic Music." In *Perspectives on Contemporary Music Theory*. Edited by Benjamin Boretz and Edward T. Cone. New York: W. W. Norton & Co., 1972. Excellent article on this subject but a bit egocentric in relating to the author-composer's own works.

———. "Mikrophonie I and II." *Melos* 33:144. Fascinating and revealing study of these works by the composer himself.

Strange, Allen. *Electronic Music*. Dubuque, Iowa: Wm. C. Brown Company Publishers, 1972. Fine textbook for use in electronic music classes.

———. "Tape Piece." *Composer* 2, no. 1 (1970):12. Explains correct care and use of the most important element of electronic music: the tape itself.

Tenney, James. "Computer Music Experiences 1961-64." *Electronic Music Reports* 1:23. Account of this composer's work in the studio at Utrecht State University.

Trythall, Gilbert. *Electronic Music*. New York: Grosset & Dunlap, 1973. Brief but very good textbook on the subject.

Ussachevsky, Vladimir. "Notes on a Piece for Tape Recorder." In *Problems of Modern Music*. Edited by Paul Henry Lang. New York: W. W. Norton & Co., 1960. Excellent personal analysis of this historic work by its composer.

———. "Sound Materials in the Experimental Media of Musique Concrète, Tape Music and Electronic Music." *Journal of the Acoustical Society of America* 29: 768. Quite interesting and informative.

de la Vega, Aurelio. "Electronic Music, Tool of Creativity." *Music Journal* 23 (September, October, November 1965). A defensive and more philosophical reflection on electronic music in general.

Vercoe, Barry. "Electronic Sounds and the Sensitive Performer." *Music Educators Journal* 55, no. 3 (November 1968).

———. "The Music 360 Language for Sound Synthesis." *Computer Music Newsletter* 2 (June 1971).

Vinton, John, ed. *Dictionary of Contemporary Music*. New York: E. P. Dutton, & Co., 1974. See in particular the following, dealing with electronic music: "Apparatus and Technology," p. 205; "History and Development," p. 212; "Notation," p. 216. Volume also contains biographies of a great many of the composers listed in this chapter.

Weilland, Fritz. "The Institute of Sonology at Utrecht State University." *Sonorum Speculum*. A fascinating article on what is possibly one of the world's finest electronic laboratories.

Weinland, John David. "An Electronic Music Primer," *Journal of Music Theory* 13, no. 1 (1969).

Wörner, Karl. *Stockhausen, Life and Work*. Translated by Bill Hopkins. Berkeley: University of California Press, 1973. A good view of this composer's work to date, but like Cott's book, a bit premature in its gamble on this composer's automatic "greatness."

Zinovieff, Peter. "A Computerized Electronic Music Studio." *Electronic Music Reports* 1:5.

Recordings and Publishers

Albright, William. *Organbook II*. Jobert. Recorded on Nonesuch 71260. Uses organ and tape.

AMM "live electronic" improvisation group is featured on Mainstream's 5002, which also has the Musica Electtronica Viva.

Ashley, Robert. *Purposeful Lady, Slow Afternoon* (1968). Recorded on Mainstream 5010. This nearly pornographic "lady" highlights a collection of works performed by the Sonic Arts Union, including works by David Behrman, Alvin Lucier, and Gordon Mumma.

Babbitt, Milton. *Composition for Synthesizer* (1963). Columbia MS-6566.

———. *Ensemble for Synthesizer* (1967). Recorded on Columbia MS-7051.

Beerman, Burton. *Sensations for Clarinet and Tape*. ACA. Recorded on Advance Recordings FGR 15S.

Berio, Luciano. *Thema: Omaggio a Joyce* (1958). Zerboni Editions. Recorded on Turnabout 34177.

———. *Visage* (1961). Turnabout 34046.

Bielawa, Herbert. *Spectrum.* Recorded by Cornell University Wind Ensemble, CUWE-1.

Blacher, Boris. *Electronic Impulses.* Recorded on Mace S-9097.

Bolcom, William. *Black Host* (1967). Recorded on Nonesuch 71260.

Borden, David. *Variations on America by Charles Ives* (1970). Recorded by Cornell Wind Ensemble, CUWE 7. For tape and wind ensemble.

Cage, John. *Aria with Fontana Mix* (1958). Recorded on Mainstream 5005.

———. *Imaginary Landscape No. 4.* Peters.

———. *Imaginary Landscape No. 5.* Peters.

———. *Variations IV* (continuation). Recorded on Everest 3230.

Chadabe, Joel. *Street Scene* (1967), and *Daisy.* Recorded on Opus One 16.

Cope, David. *Arena.* Carl Fischer. Recorded on Orion ORS-75169. For cello and tape.

———. *K* and *Weeds* (1971). Recorded on Discant 1297.

Davidovsky, Mario. *Synchronisms 1, 2* and *3.* Edward B. Marks Corp. Recorded on CRI S-204.

———. *Synchronisms 4, 5,* and *6.* Edward B. Marks Corp. Recorded on Turnabout 34487.

Dockstader, Tod. *Quartermass* (1964), and other works. Recorded on Owl Records 6, 7 and 8.

Dodge, Charles. *Earth's Magnetic Field* (1970). Recorded on Nonesuch 71250. A computer-generated work.

Druckman, Jacob. *Animus II* (1969). MCA Music. Recorded on CRI S-255. For mezzo soprano, two percussionists, and tape.

———. *Animus III* (1969). MCA Music. Recorded on Nonesuch 71253. For clarinet and tape.

Duckworth, William. *Gambit* (1967). Recorded on Capra 1201. For tape and percussion.

Eaton, John. *Concert Piece for Synket and Orchestra.* Recorded on Turnabout 34428.

Ellis, Merrill. *Kaleidoscope.* Recorded on Louisville S-711.

Erb, Donald. *In No Strange Land.* Merion Music. Recorded on Nonesuch 71223.

———. *Reconnaissance.* Recorded on Nonesuch 71223.

———. *Reticulation.* Merion Music.

Felciano, Richard. *God of the Expanding Universe.* E. C. Schirmer.

———. *Litany.* E. C. Schirmer.

———. *Crasis.* E. C. Schirmer.

———. *Lamentations for Jani Christou.* E. C. Schirmer.

Gaburo, Kenneth. *Antiphony III* (*Pearl White Moments*). Recorded on Nonesuch 71199.

Hiller, L. and Baker. *Computer Cantata* (1963). Recorded on CRI S-310.

Hiller, L. and John Cage. *HPSCHD* (1968). Peters. Recorded on Nonesuch H-71224.

Hiller, Lejaren. *Machine Music* (1964). Presser. Recorded on Turnabout 34536. For piano, percussion, and tape.

Kagel, Mauricio. *Acoustica* (1970). Recorded on DG-2707059. For Experimental Sound Generators and Loudspeakers.

Korte, Karl. *Remembrances.* Recorded on Nonesuch 71289. For flute and tape.

Kupferman, Meyer. *Superflute.* Recorded on Nonesuch 71289.

Ligeti, György. *Articulation* (1958). Recorded on Wergo 60059.

Lucier, Alvin. *North American Time Capsule* (1967). Recorded on Odyssey 32-160156.

Luening, Otto. *Synthesis* (1960). Peters. Recorded on CRI S-219. For orchestra and tape.

MacInnis, Donald. *Collide-a-Scope* (1968). Recorded on Golden Crest S-4085. For twelve brass instruments and tape.

McLean, Barton. *Genesis.* Recorded on Orion ORS 75192. This album also contains two other electronic works by this composer: *The Sorcerer Revisited* and *Dimensions II* (the latter for piano and tape).

McLean, Priscilla. *Dance of Dawn.* Recorded on CRI SD 335. This album also contains an electronic work by her composer husband Barton McLean: *Spirals.*

Miller, Edward. *Piece for Clarinet and Tape* (1967). Recorded on Advance Recordings FGR 17S.

Mimaroglu, Ilhan. WINGS *of the Delirious Demon,* and other works. Recorded on Fin. 9001.

Mumma, Gordon. *Mesa* (1966). Recorded on Odyssey 32-160158.

Nonesuch Guide to Electronic Music. Recorded on Nonesuch HC-73018.

Oliveros, Pauline. *I of IV* (1966). Recorded on Odyssey 32-160160.

Randall, J. K. *Lyric Variations for Violin and Computer* (1967). Recorded on Vanguard C-10057.

———. *Quartets in Pairs* (1964). Recorded on Nonesuch 71245, which also includes works by Charles Dodge and Barry Vercoe. *Quartets in Pairs* is computer-generated.

Stockhausen, Karlheinz. *Gesang der Jünglinge.* Recorded on DG-138811.

———. *Hymnen.* Universal Edition. Recorded on DG-2707039.

———. *Kontakte.* Universal Edition. Recorded on DG-138811.

———. *Telemusik.* Universal Edition. Recorded on DG-137012.

Strange, Allen. *Two x Two* (1968). Recorded on Capra 1201.

Subotnick, Morton. *4 Butterflies.* Recorded on Columbia M-32741. Includes his other "music box" works written for a record.

———. *Sidewinder.* Recorded on Columbia M-30683.

———. *Silver Apples of the Moon.* Recorded on Nonesuch 71174.

———. *The Wild Bull.* Recorded on Nonesuch 71208.

Taylor, Dub. *Lumière.* Recorded on Varèse 81001. For synthesized and concrete sounds.

Ussachevsky, Vladimir. *Creation-Prologue.* Recorded on Columbia MS-6566.

———. *A Piece for Tape Recorder.* Recorded on CRI-122.

———. *Of Wood and Brass.* Recorded on CRI S-227.

Varese, Edgard. *Poeme électronique.* Recorded on Columbia MS-6146.

Watts, John. *WARP*. Composers' Autograph Publications.

Wilson, Galen. *Applications*. Recorded on Capra 1201.

Wilson, George Blach. *Exigencies*. Recorded on CRI S-271.

Wuorinen, Charles. *Times Encomium* (1969). Recorded on Nonesuch 71225.

Xenakis, Iannis. His electronic music is featured on Nonesuch 71246.

Folkways 6301 and 33436 include collections of a variety of electronic musics. Folkways FX 6160 contains some early electronic experiments including Ussachevsky's *Sonic Contours, Transposition, Reverberation,* and *Composition,* and Otto Luening's *Fantasy in Space*. Luening's and Ussachevsky's *Concerted Piece for Tape Recorder and Orchestra,* made at the Columbia-Princeton Music Center, is available on CRI S-227, along with works by Mel Powell, and another Ussachevsky work.

Milton Babbitt's *Vision and Prayer* (1961) for soprano and tape (AMP) is part of CRI-268, a large two-disc collection, which includes also Varèse's *Deserts,* 1961 (AMP); Luening's *In the Beginning* (1956); Ussachevsky's *Computer Piece No. 1* (1968), and *Two Sketches* (1971); together with works by Smiley, Shields, and Davidovsky.

Orion 7021 features electronic works by Swickard and Heller. DG 137011 features four works composed at the Utrecht Institute of Sonology. Desto 6466 has works by Luening and Ussachevsky as well as *Incantation,* on which they collaborated.

The Schwann Record Catalog has a separate listing of electronic music records which is of value even though a number of European discs are not included (especially Wergo). A short list of works and records is listed in the *Music Educators Journal,* November 1968. The *Repertoire International des Musiques Electroacoustiques* (Electronic Music Catalog) which appeared as *Electronic Music Review* No. 2/3 (April/July 1967), compiled by Hugh Davies is, though out-of-date, still the best source for information on available nonrecorded electronic music.

5 Media Forms

Definitions, Aesthetics, and Origins

The term *multimedia* is often used synonymously with a number of terms, most often *inter-media* and *mixed-media*. Adding to the confusion are the terms *theatre pieces, merged-medium, environmental works, happenings,* etc. To avoid continuing this terminology explosion, the author has attempted to define three major categories of *media forms* in the following manner:

a. Multimedia: this form is a loose structure in which the various media do not depend on each other for meaning (*happenings* are excellent examples of *multimedia* events, in that usually each element is significant and structured of itself in such a way that were it necessary it could stand on its own merits);

b. Mixed-media: this form tends "toward equalization of the elements," though "any hierarchial order is possible" (*environments* more often than not fit this media form in that, though the elements are dependent on each other, "they are mixed, but not truly integrated.");[1]

c. Inter-media: this form has all of its elements in equal balance and integrated to the fullest degree (*merged-medium* fits this category well in that ". . . all elements are equal and integrated").[2]

Within these three main categories are a number of terms which the author has listed (some are listed in more than one category as they may or may not attain balance or integration):

Multimedia	*Mixed-media*	*Inter-media*
(loosely knit composite forms)	(more integrated with varied degree of importance of elements)	(very integrated, each element depending on the other for the work to hold together)

1. Stanley Gibb, "Understanding Terminology and Concepts Related to Media Art Forms," *The American Music Teacher*, April-May, 1973, pp. 23-25. This is possibly the most well thought-out and formulated writing on this subject and is highly recommended to those seeking real insight into media art forms. This author is highly indebted to Mr. Gibb.
2. Ibid.

Multimedia	*Mixed-media*	*Inter-media*
happenings	environments	merged-medium
collage	opera	environments
theatre pieces	film and TV	films
opera	kinetic theatre	meditations
ballet		
light-show		
film and TV		

Two important factors must be considered carefully in observing the above listings:

1. Composers have been very flexible in their usage of the above terms. Indeed, their use of certain of the terminology may not fit the above chart (the author's own *Deadliest Angel Revision* [1971] is a good example: it is billed as *multimedia* or a *theatre piece* when in fact it is *inter-media*). Therefore one cannot always accurately judge the composition by its "nomer."

2. None of the above classifications implies a quality judgment. Each is merely a starting point from which one can discuss the forms with some degree of consistency (the fact that one can often listen to an opera over the radio without seeing the action and still enjoy the quality of the music is witness to the fact that indeed great works exist in each of the categories).

With this in mind it is necessary to note that the author has attempted to choose works which emphasize in particular each of the above categories (realizing that the author's term may conflict with the composer/artist's term for his own work—a matter of semantics, and not to be considered in any way as a value implication imposed by the author on either the work or the composer/artist).

The aesthetics of media forms are indeed wide in scope at this writing, and though coming to grips with the definitions and categorization of varieties of intentions involved may help in the conciliation of some antagonists, these forms remain targets at which many an active as well as passive participant or bystander seem to take special aim. Two composers, Robert Ceely and Paul Goldstaub, tend to sum up the points of view quite succinctly:

Ceely: " . . . it [multimedia] is most interesting in that it usually fails."

Goldstaub: "The first time I conducted [Toshiro] Mayazumi's *Metamusic* (certainly a multimedia work of classic stature) it brought home the simple truth that people have overlooked for centuries: concert going is partially a visual and social experience, as well as musical. If composers can *use* this to enrich the quality of the experience of their music, every-one gains."[3]

Media forms are both the rational extension of composite forms such as ballet and opera, and the result of the need for visual activity in connection with tape music. Many of the multimedia forms grew from experiments with "chance" relationships between simultaneously produced art forms (e.g., *happenings*).

The Dadaists and those who worked in the Bauhaus were among the first to openly confront the concepts of media compositions (that is, try to *integrate* all the art forms available; certainly one can trace other attempts through Wagner's *gesamtkunstwerk* back to Greek concepts, but to do so would both go beyond the scope of this book and thereby neglect the unique attributes of the "audience participation" aspects of today's media forms).[4] Aside from early commercial "shows" which employed perfumes (*The Song of Solomon* was performed in Paris in 1891 with sound, light, and perfumes, for example) and Scriabin's aforementioned *Poem of Fire* (see chap. 1) which was not truly realized, Erik Satie's *Relâche* (1924) was one of the first landmarks in media forms. René Clair's film (also a landmark in cinematography for 1924), the understated Satie music, the ballet, the surrealistic scenery—all combined to create a vessel of often interplaying, often contradicting images.

Multimedia

The summer of 1952 marked some of the first multimedia "happenings" when Cage, Tudor, Rauschenberg, and Cunningham teamed to play records, read lectures from stepladders, dance, use projections, and display "white paintings" at Black Mountain College. The concept was random sequence of nonrandom materials; that is, the order and combinations were chance, but the lectures, projections, and paintings in themselves were not. Consequently, the resultant "theater" of events allowed each art form to remain isolated, contributing to the whole only as each performer reacted to another's event or personality

April 17, 1958 saw the introduction of *Poème èlectronique* by Edgard Varèse at the Brussels World's Fair (see chap. 4). This multimedia presentation by Varèse, in collaboration with architect Le Corbusier, took place within a pavilion which was shaped externally like a three-peaked

---

3. Tom Everett, "Questions and Answers," *Composer Magazine* 4, no. 1 (Fall-Winter 1972):20-21.

4. The Bauhaus, founded by Walter Gropius in 1919, included very basic interdisciplinary media by including art, architecture, and design. Though short-lived (until 1933) it has served as an example in the arts that has founded very solid ground in the American university and media forms in general.

circus tent and internally like a cow's stomach. The composition, 480 seconds in length, was accompanied by projected images of paintings, written script, and montages. Neither of the artists made attempts at correlation between visual and aural images, the result being occasional simultaneity of rhythm or spatial relationships, but more often separation of concepts. Rhythm remains the one cohesive element of aural and visual correlation, and the result of this experiment *could* have been equal to the "cheap" movie house with its change of recordings in the middle of the love scene. The intense organization of each artist's approach to his own material, however, was so apparent that correlation seemed almost inappropriate. The performance, attended by nearly three million people, remains as the most culturally significant representation of multimedia in history.

Multimedia as an offshoot of the American experimental school has also developed along lines more indeterminate than structured. The thread of separation lies in the area of "theater": the necessity of partial indeterminacy for a play to "happen." Roger Reynolds's *Ping* (1968), based on a text by Samuel Beckett, is an excellent example of a somewhat improvisatory work which explores "theater." Three performers (flute, piano, and harmonium-bowed, cymbal-bowed tam-tam) create the "live" situation, augmented by a 25-minute tape, using amplification and contact microphones, of recurrent materials. A 22-minute film and 160 slides (projected alternately to the left and right) of Beckett's story add visual material. Effects in the environment and around the performance area are created by matrixed mirrors projecting secondary images, blurs, and colors: a cohesive factor enjoining sight and sound experience. The score[5] is explicit as to materials, duration, pitches (for the most part), and dynamics, yet allows improvisation from *all* performers, including the projectionists. For example, the projectionists may, within certain limitations, alter images through the use of such devices as filters and prisms. Reynolds's *The Emperor of Ice Cream* (1962) includes the projection of the score (both graphic and traditional in notation) for the performers (eight singers, piano, percussion, and bass). Each projection, or score page, represents twenty seconds of time, and the position, movement, and "choreography" of each performer is indicated by dotted lines and the positioning of the sound-symbol. Theatrical effects are written on the score in words, some as performance cues, others to be spoken, and performers truly become actors and dancers as well as sound producers.

Morton Subotnick's *Ritual Electronic Chamber Music* involves four performers at "game boards" (lighted buttons for channel or amplitude

5. Roger Reynolds, *Ping*, as published in *Source: Music of the Avant-Garde* (Composer/Performer Edition) 3, no. 2 (July 1969):70-86.

Figure 5.1.   Morton Subotnick

of the electronic tape or one of four projections). Each performer's choice of which button to press will set up choices for other of the "players." In the center, a "High Priestess" moves about, playing lights on her body and moving the sound throughout the room. The work may be performed without an audience or in a very small chamber group of interested persons.

"Relevant action is theatrical (music [imaginary separation of hearing from the other senses] does not exist) . . ."[6] speaks John Cage of, among other things, the audience's ability to see and hear other sounds outside the performance area. Feelings, smells, and even tastes seem somehow neglected by most composers in the superficially imposed and irresponsible restriction of their creativity to sound alone. More often than not, Cage's approach to multimedia is philosophical: accept *all* sounds, sights, and other sensory experiences which occur in and around a performance situation, *equally,* regardless of their origin (this would include such things as car noises, coughs, the structure of the auditorium). Some other of his works involve "stage" multimedia. *Water Walk,* for example (first performed over Milan television in 1958 by Cage, who was a quiz show contestant), includes banging a rubber fish inside a piano on

6. John Cage, *Silence* (Cambridge, Mass.: The M.I.T. Press, paperback edition, 1961), p. 15.

the strings, Cage watering a vase of roses, and a pressure cooker spurting steam, among other "props."

Whether initiated by determinate or indeterminate procedures, multimedia is the result of a natural concern by the composer and artist alike to allow and/or control *all* the aspects of the human sensory system within the framework of the performance situation. It is the preoccupation with enlarging the field of communication and effect for the audience (not antagonism) which has led the creative mind to multimedia.

Figure 5.2.   Peter Maxwell Davies. Photography by Keith McMillan. Permission by Boosey & Hawkes, Ltd., London.

Peter Maxwell Davies's *Eight Songs for a Mad King* (premiered in April, 1969 in London) has the flute, clarinet, violin and 'cello players sitting in cages "representing, on one level, the bullfinches the King (George III) was trying to teach to sing . . . the percussion player . . . the King's brutal keeper, who plays him off stage at the end, beating a bass drum with a cat-o'-nine-tails. The climax of the work is the end of Song 7 where the King snatches the violin through the bars of the player's cage and breaks it."[7] While the visual forms of drama and setting contribute to live performance intensity, the significance of this highly acclaimed work is caught aurally on the recording (and interestingly enough

7. Liner notes on the recording (Nonesuch H-71285) by Peter Maxwell Davies.

the media form is born in the listener's mind with the multimedia information in hand while listening to the record).

Boguslaw Schäffer is a very active composer of theatre music and happenings. His *Audiences No. 1-5* (1964) for actors (see fig. 5.3) is "music for actors" with the texts by the composer, and involve projections, drama, and musical events. His happenings include *Non-Stop* (1960) for piano (with a duration varying from six to four hundred and eighty hours), and *Incident* (1966) for the "ensemble" of *audience* (lasting four hours).

Figure 5.3. Boguslaw Schäffer:
Audiences No. 4.

George Crumb's *Voice of the Whale* (*Vox Balaenae*) (1971), like Davies's work, has multimedia aspects which are related to live performance only, and which in no real way deter from the music by their absence (i.e., when the music is on a record). The work has the performers wearing black half masks (or visor masks) and the stage bathed in deep blue light. It is clear here that the music can easily stand alone and the visual aspects, though interesting in performance, are by no means absolutely essential to the work (i.e., the music retains its artistic identity with or without the visual complement).

Mixed-media

In any event in which the superficially (man-made) imposed art definitions (e.g., music, painting, sculpture) exist psychologically within the audience, the problem of domination of one art form can exist. Projected scores or performer-interpreted projections share equally the difficulty of misinterpretation; "music seen" or "paintings as sound" represent displacement of traditional dogmatic categorization of the arts. Daniel Lentz's *Sermon* (1970) for string quartet modified by electronic filters, reverberation, ring modulation, and gate device, involves score projection. Once a score is visible to the audience it becomes obvious that it must be made visually interesting and artistic. Lentz has solved this problem by creating an artistic score in color and creating thereby more notational significance: red = played, blue = sung, green = hummed, yellow = whistled, violet = spoken, brown = whispered, with an orange line surrounding the score page referring to time (at ten-by-twelve-inch projection, each half-inch representing one second). The result is greater visual excitement *and* more meaningful notation for the performers.

Allen Strange's *No Dead Horses on the Moon* requires seven 16mm projectors so placed as to surround the audience with visual images (see fig. 5.4). The recorded sound is projected from the four corners of the room to truly create an environmental situation. Correlation between visual and aural materials is obtained by written instructions to the performers (in this case the projectionists). In No. 6, for example, the projectionist is instructed to move his projector. The films to be shown are created by scraping the emulsion from 16mm black leader film and then constructing loops by which a seven-fold visual ostinato is created (see example). The resulting flashing dots, lines, and "strobe" effects, along with the sound, engulf the audience in an imaginative "light-show" and the essence of multimedia.

At the same time, these concepts alter a basic concert ritual of audience-performer separation. If all senses of the audience are to be a part of the work, then their control of these aspects enables them too to become composer/performer *and* audience, and "total theater" becomes possible. Robert Ashley's *Public Opinion Descends Upon the Demonstrators* (1961) embraces this ideal. Specific prerecorded sounds are produced by a single performer on electronic playback equipment only when a member of the audience acts or reacts in a certain manner (e.g., by speaking, glancing, looking about, gesturing, looking toward a loudspeaker, or leaving). Whether or not performance precludes knowledge on the part of the audience of the compositional concept, it soon becomes obvious that all participants (composer, performer, audience) share equal responsibility in creating the "total theater."

Barton McLean's *Identity* series of compositions deals directly with man and his relation to his surroundings, perception of a work in a complete environmental setting, and the audience exercising real and sig-

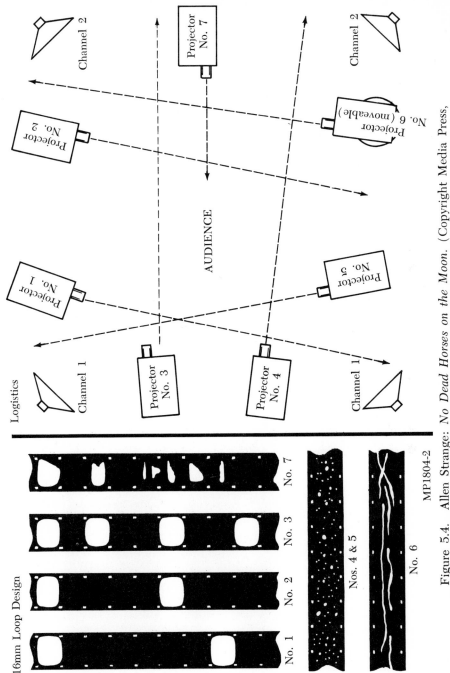

Figure 5.4.   Allen Strange: *No Dead Horses on the Moon.* (Copyright Media Press, Champaign, Ill., 1969. Used by permission. All rights reserved.)

nificant control over sounds. More complete and detailed than Stock-hausen's *Musik für ein Haus* or Sigmund Krauze's experiments with environmental music in Poland and Germany, McLean's *Identity* series implies specific works for specific buildings and situations. One of these, (for the Cultural Center in South Bend, Indiana) is, in the composer's words:

> . . . a true environmental experience in that the hearer who walks through
> it reacts to the sounds both passively and actively. This latter aspect, perhaps
> the most unique in its conception, although allowing for the overall direction
> and control of the work to remain in the hands of the composer, never-
> theless provides to the listener the opportunity to participate in smaller, but
> highly meaningful choices. Thus, the hearer, in exercising creative choices
> of his own which shape the smaller details of the work, enters into the actual
> creative experience. Furthermore, no musical training is necessary for this
> interaction, since it is set up so that all choices made by the hearer on this
> smaller structural level are equally valid. On the other hand, for those
> who have more time and intuitive ability, it is possible to grow with the work
> and, upon repeated hearings, to exercise intelligent choices on gradually
> higher and higher planes.[8]

The work (building) is controlled in terms of lighting, speaker activity, etc., by the audience motion which triggers a wide variety of sounds. By movement and by the audience's discovery of the planned placement of photoelectric cells, microphones, and various visual control devices, the building becomes for the hearers a self-contained environment.

Figures 5.5 and 5.6 show the extent to which media techniques have become sophisticated during the past few years. These represent two of the media aspects of the recently completed (late 1974) Learning Re-sources Center at Middle Tennessee State University in Murfreesboro. The figures speak for themselves of the incredible future, and the poten-tials of media in education, the sciences, and communications, as well as in the arts.[9]

Composers, lacking somewhat in legitimate theater models, have con-sequently improvised techniques beyond the "time-honored" Grecian con-cepts of dramatic ritual. The physical aspect of any sensual act no longer distinctly separates one artistic ideal from another. Paul Ignace's *Feast* (1964) culminates all possible environmental encounters within the frame-work of a totally composed multimedia work. The performers (even the composer) no longer exist except in concept. The audience is fed all as-

8. The quote from the composer is from materials about the work made available to the author. Other environmental works and studies are included in chapter 8, as they imply significant *antimusic* message content.

9. More information on this most interesting media center is available from Dr. Marshall Gunselman, Director of Learning Resources Center at Middle Tennessee State University.

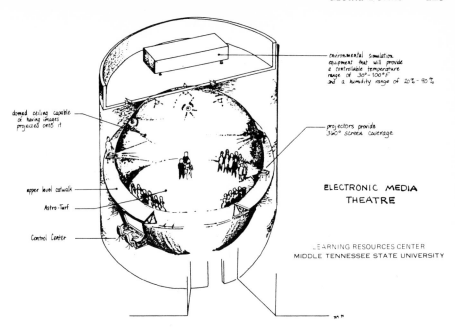

environmental simulation equipment that will provide a controllable temperature range of 30°-100°F and a humidity range of 20%-90%

domed ceiling capable of having images projected onto it

projectors provide 360° screen coverage

ELECTRONIC MEDIA
THEATRE

upper level catwalk

Astro-Turf

Control Center

LEARNING RESOURCES CENTER
MIDDLE TENNESSEE STATE UNIVERSITY

Figure 5.5. Permission granted by the Learning Resources Center, Dr. Marshall Gunselman, Director; Middle Tennessee State University.

pects of sensual experience, the menu requiring only individual choice within reason. Preferably for two people, *Feast* enacts the "last request" prerogative of the death victim, making choices available on most levels of immediate desire, including choices of sounds, smells, tastes, touches, and sights. The duty of the composer now is not to evoke *certain* responses, but to make available as many responses as possible. In *Feast,* mixed-media achieves the ideal philosophically implied and inherent within its thesis: no action (relevant or not) can be considered unimportant to the total aspect of a composition. The activants of *Feast* no longer escape the projection of their actions, from heartburn to divorce! Total theater environments cannot avoid the direction toward complete involvement and what traditionally has been called life. All the categories between "theater" and "reality" must eventually be exterminated if even the simplest of media concepts be projected rationally to its ultimate end: the theater of life!

Mauricio Kagel's *Match* (for two violoncellos and percussion) is a dramatic game which unfolded to the composer in a dream in full-blown detail. The work is characterized by visual humor (which met with immediate applause at its premiere in Berlin in October of 1965), yet strik-

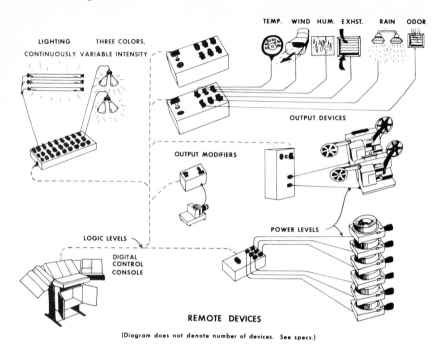

Figure 5.6. Permission granted by
The Learning Resources Center,
Dr. Marshall Gunselman, Director;
Middle Tennessee State University.

Figure 5.7.   Mauricio Kagel

ingly serious music (leading to what the composer has called a "shaking concert of derision" at the end of the first live performance).[10] The music, by itself, is intense and dramatic but when fused with the visual wittiness results in a complicated *collage* of constantly varying grades of emotional polarities. Regarding a portion of *Match* the composer has noted:

During the first rehearsal of these uncertain measures I was told by the inter-preters that the passage in question reminded them of the most memorable of the *circene* scenes: the death leap.
Such an appreciation was already known to me; the similarity between this situation with what was dreamed a few weeks previously left no room for doubt: both musicians were suspended in mid-air with their cellos on top of their heads and by means of slow pirouettes they produced very sharp, brilliant sounds. The roll of the drum, that from some point in space resounded over the entire environment, maintained the spectators in pure tension until leading to an aggressive attack on the cymbal. Thus was overcome the first of the mortal leap with good fortune.[11]

Possibly one of the most prolific and well-known mixed-media com-posers is Robert Moran. His *Hallelujah* (for twenty marching bands, forty church choirs and organs, carrillons, rock groups, a gospel group, and the entire city of Bethlehem, Pennsylvania) was first performed in 1971 and is truly a landmark in mixed-media performance. His earlier *39 Minutes for 39 Autos* (for thirty-nine amplified auto horns, auto lights, Moog Syn-thesizer, thirty skyscrapers, radio stations, a television station, dancers, etc.—first performed on August 29, 1969 in San Francisco) is another work of equally staggering proportions. Of these the composer has re-marked (in communication with the author):

In my work, *39 Minutes for 39 Autos*, I attempted to make everyone a musician. One hundred thousand persons participated in the premiere. My *Hallelujah*, commissioned by Lehigh University, used hundreds of musicians. . . . in this composition I tried to make every musician a human being.

Moran's works embrace an incredible variety of mixed-media explora-tions exemplary of which are: *Divertissement No. 1*, 1967 (for popcorn, electric frying pan, and any instrumental soloist), which employs the performer reading popping corn as noteheads on five-lined white-staved dark sunglasses; and *Bombardments No. 4*, 1968 (for trombone and tape, commissioned by Stu Dempster) in which the trombonist, wrapped in a sack, becomes a visual analog gargoyle (legs, slide, arms, and body move-

10. Mauricio Kagel, "On Match for Three Performers," *Composer* 3, no. 2 (Spring 1972); translated from *Sonda #3* (Juventudes Musicales, Madrid) June 1968, pp. 70-78.
11. Ibid., p. 73.

ments all sharing in the vision of struggling shape, lit dimly from both sides, and its aural counterpart).

In general, film music does not as such qualify as a particularly significant exploration of media forms. There are, however, a number of exceptions which should be noted. Aside from the *Relâche* film of 1924 by René Clair mentioned previously, work by composer John Whitney and his painter brother James is particularly significant. Beginning in 1940 they began their experiments with abstract film and infrasonics (in this case, a series of pendulums mechanically connected to a wedge-shaped aperture influencing an optical sound track producing sine wave oscillations with a frequency range of a little more than four octaves). Like the *Three Pieces for Sound Projector* (to be discussed under intermedia) and the sound track notations of Norman McLaren (discussed under *Electronic Music*), the Whitney experiments have provided a vast new source of media materials, one which, however, has not as yet consummated a significant body of artistic achievement.[12] John Whitney speaks to this point:

It is hoped that the partnership of sound and picture will attract the attention it deserves in artistic circles. The problem that confronts the individual consists of a number of difficulties whose acquaintance he may already have made in the course of his experiences in modern music or painting. Whether the necessary technical apparatus will always be placed at the disposal of the artist is a question that touches on an elementary problem, whose solution lies hidden in the darkness of the future.[13]

Salvatore Martirano's *L'sGA* (1968) is a massive and intense mixed-media work overloading the senses with dramatic, visual, and aural messages. *L'sGA*, in the composer's words, is:

Lincoln's *Gettysburg Address* for actor, tape, and film, using a helium "bomb" which the actor breathes from at the end of the piece so that his voice goes up a couple of octaves . . . all you need to do is catch a few words now and then to understand what the meaning is. You hear "government" and you hear "people." And thus I would hope that the person watching would create the framework of specific and exact meaning according to how he sees things. Because I'm not forcing him to catch on to a sequence of events in which each one has to be understood for the next one to make sense. It's almost kind of throwing it in all different places and gradually, I would hope, the conception is built up in the audience.[14]

12. Recent "popular" *visual music* devices wherein strobes or 3-D "color-organs" translate bass, treble, and midrange sounds into visual abstractions, while interesting, prove to be little more than *light-shows* of the most simplistic order.
13. John Whitney, "Moving Pictures and Electronic Music," *Die Reihe* 7 (1960):71.
14. Panel Discussion: *ASUC Proceedings* 3 (1968):43.

Inter-media

It is possible, using many similar materials, to approach media forms in a determinate method. Exploration of some of the possible creative and psychological relationships of aural and visual composition in media art forms demonstrates the increased number of parameters in simultaneous projections and sounds, implying new combinatorial creative procedures resulting from art and music which cannot rely implicitly on either unique approach.

Important is the articulation of those areas in common and those in contrast between aural and visual forms. Both deal in *time* (even the smallest still projection requires it) and all that time perception implies: rhythm, meter (or organized groups of events in time), and especially form. The difference is in control of time: excepting the simplest line image, for instance, in motion picture projections, visual direction in time is uniquely within the perceiver. The manner in which he develops rhythm, meter, and form within the time of perception is not controllable as in music, where these elements remain within almost complete possible direction by the creator and/or performer.

Both deal in *space,* though somewhat differently. All the spatial characteristics of visual perception apply to aural perception, for example, direction of material to the audience by means of physical positioning of sound-producing objects (instruments and loudspeakers, for instance; surprisingly, this has been, until recently, one of the least explored possibilities of control in music), and directions of objects within the material (although in sound, directions such as up, down, and to the right lose physical meaning, these same directions as applied to pitch order, intensity, and frequency are as viable as those in visual perception).

Both deal in *color,* and to both, this is the most completely overlapping quality.

The recognition of space in inter-media is the easiest and most controllable aspect of the overlapping elements. When directions are the same (e.g., sound behind or coming from the visual object) and then are suddenly changed radically (to, for instance, the opposite direction), the perceiver can lose the continuity of both.

It is much more difficult to recognize relationships of direction *within* the material. Though "up" and "down" in music traditionally implies higher or lower frequency, studies have shown that this aspect is learned but rationally not real; that is, it stems from notation, not sound itself. Experiments quickly show that when dots are placed on a screen in such an order as to imply "notes" and corresponding sounds, the effect of up and down is apparent. When dots are placed in unorganized structure with sounds, they do not appear wrong, but just not observably related in any way to the sounds. With any increased complexity of aural and visual materials, the relationships of up, down, right, and left (whether or not these relationships are recognizable) are lost; however, the relationships of simplicity and complexity remain. Experiments here show immediate recognition (see fig. 5.8).

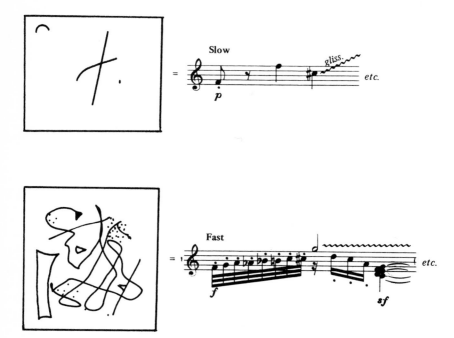

Figure 5.8

Experiments in *time* relationships have evolved a number of separate but related rhythmic concepts:

1. Sound imitation of action ("Mickey-Mousing It," in movie jargon) is possibly the simplest and least significant application.

Two screens set up about ten feet apart and ten feet from the audience, the speakers for the electronic sound track behind the screens. Duplicate projections were run about two inches apart, utilizing duplicate line and dot motion, while an electronic sound track produced a low and high sine wave, the first being a continuous (or line imitation), the latter a pointillistic and variable pattern run one inch behind the first projection or midway between the two projections. The canon effect between aural and visual perception is immediately recognizable.[15]

15. Experiment carried out by the author.

Contrapuntal effects such as the one described above prove more observable than when using one or the other art forms separately. Recognition of imitative elements in rhythm between aural and visual elements seems heightened immeasurably by the combination of the two materials.

2. As in *space* study, rhythmic complexity vs. simplicity provides material for formal considerations.

3. Ostinato and similar rhythmic concepts between aural and visual materials work easily and effectively even when highly complex:

A "light-show" was constructed around flashing projections of green, blue,

and red in repetitive pattern ♩. ♩. ♩ (♪ = 92) with sound

ostinato ♩. ♩. ♩ (♪ = 92). When played beginning at the same

time, recognition was immediate (by third repetition). When played at complex lag intervals, the effect was less immediately recognizable but nonetheless perceived. Even when the tempo of each was changed (visual ♪

= 120, audio ♪ = 76), the counterpoint and effect was observable.[16]

Experiments in *color* relationships prove least effective. Obviously, no standard relationships of color frequency exist; therefore, each work must depend upon explanation of color relationships if they are to be used.

These experiments, though rudimentary in nature, have indicated a vast range of communicable material relationships available to the artist for assimilation into form and style. The following is a short description of the compositional process of *Three Pieces for Sound Projector*:[17]

Piece I (fast) involves three visual and three aural elements. The visual elements (dot, line, and moving blob of rainbow colors) are exposed individually, simultaneously with aural counterparts (high-pitched staccato sounds, low continuous pitch, and blocks of white sound), though no rhythmic relationship is structured (the aural and visual materials appear at approxi-

16. Experiment by the author.
17. The composer believes that his works should "stand alone" and therefore does not sign his name or the date of his works, and does not allow this information to appear on programs. In keeping with his belief, no such information appears here. The analytical information here was derived from conversations with the composer.

mately the same time, but duration and rhythm of appearance is nonstructured):

Figure 5.9

Section B of this piece involves use of two and three elements in combination again, with sight and sound approximating appearance at the beginning; however, as the section progresses (speed of appearance increasing), rhythmic simultaneity increases until, at the end of B, all elements of visual and aural activity are simultaneous:

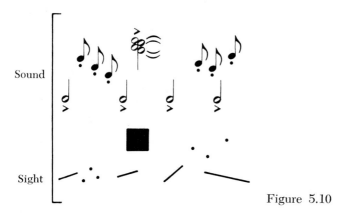

Figure 5.10

The third and final section incorporates overlapping ostinati on established patterns of the previous sections in two ways. First, it is with simultaneous visual/aural materials:

Etc.

Figure 5.11

Secondly, it is with as ostinato canon between sight and sound in pairs, using different pairs in different ostinati.

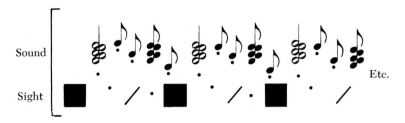

Figure 5.12

Piece II (slow) employs speakers, one in front of and one behind the audience. No correlation between object shown and sound is consciously established except in time. The still projectors are turned on and off, with different material chosen at random from a prepared selection. The first section sets up exact imitation: the sounds come on and off with the projections and from behind the screen. The first variation (aside from the variation in sound and slides in the projectors) involves a slow breakdown and return of order of the rhythmic simultaneity of aural and visual events:

Figure 5.13

The second variation first substitutes speakers at the rear with those in front and then this substitution becomes haphazard and a rhythmic section based on direction is created:

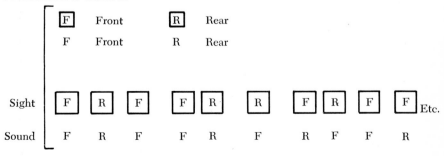

Figure 5.14

After returning briefly to the original organization pattern, the final section accelerates a return to each of the previous variations, culminating in a rapid sum, utilizing all variations at once. Finally the original concept is stated again.

The final piece explores spatial relationships *within* the visual structure in both space and color. Three timbres were chosen at random and attached to three colors in the motion projections, so that whenever a visual color appeared, its appropriate timbre sounded. Even if a continuous pitch was involved, it changed to match the color. Pitches were randomly selected and attached to particular areas of the screen (four in all). Rhythm and dynamics were controlled by the rhythm and size of the color grains appearing on the screen. A continuously variable counterpoint exists throughout between color and direction, changing at highly variable rates of speed:

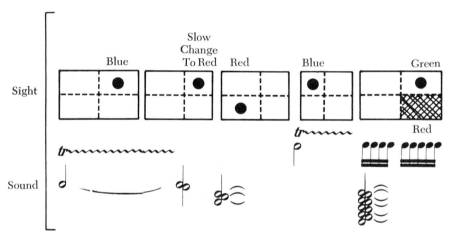

Figure 5.15

The resultant serialization (and combination of sizes, directions, and colors combining in harmony) achieves the desired highly structured effect, with a high degree of variation available (the increased parameters using a minimal amount of material).

While at times *Three Pieces* takes on attributes of all three types of media forms, there is no doubt that the visual and aural elements as a whole are so closely integrated that one without the other would be only half a work and not viable as a complete artistic contribution.

Figure 5.16 is *Metabiosis V: 'A Light, Sound and Audience Environment'* (1972) by Ronald Pellegrino. The total environmental system is explored in this work (to be published as part of a book: *Thinking for the Electronic Music Synthesizer*, chapter 6, as outlined in *ASUC Proceedings*, 7/8) with the incorporation of the given space and natural variables an intrinsic part of the design.

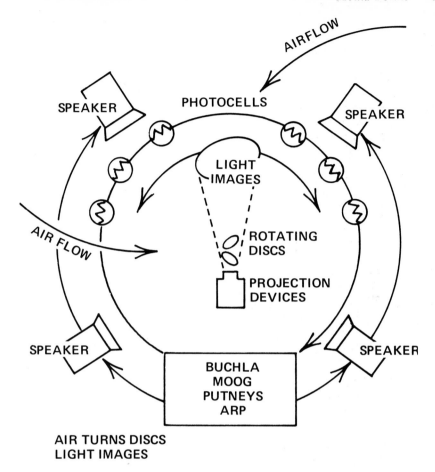

Figure 5.16. Metabiosis V: A light, sound, and audience environment by Ronald Pellegrino. Used by permission of Proceedings of the American Society of University Composers 7/8 (72-73) © ASUC, Inc., c/o American Music Center, 210 Broadway, Suite 15-79, New York, N. Y. 10023.

Private Mirrors by David Mathew (see fig. 5.17) incorporates an integrated approach to the lighting and dancing to tape. The score itself (particularly the tape part notation) is indicative of the composer's aural

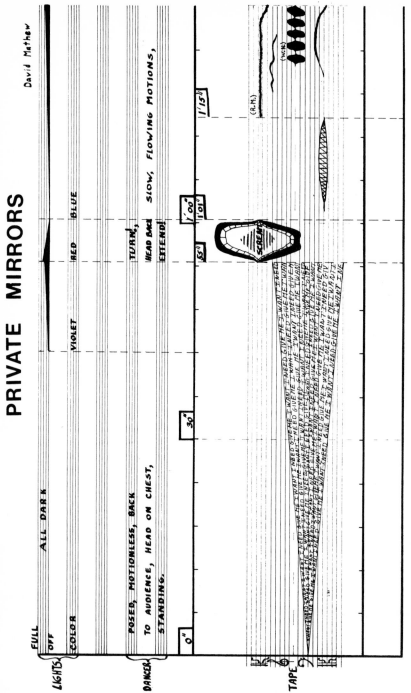

Figure 5.17.   David Mathew: *Private Mirrors*. Published by Composers Autograph Publications. © David Mathew 1973. All rights reserved. Used by permission.

and visual simultaneity with both elements intensely functional upon one another.[18]

Merrill Ellis's *Mutations* for brass choir, electronic tape, and light projections is likewise a dramatic integrated approach to inter-media. The work begins with a standard concert setting. Suddenly the hall is plunged into darkness, the players leave the stage (to make vocal and other unusual sounds) and, with the electronic tape becoming the main aural source, projections (in the form of films, lights, etc.) flash on the stage, ceiling, and walls, engulfing the audience in a "sea" of visual activity. *Mutating* the ABA form (not as simplistic as it may appear here) the

Figure 5.18.   Merrill Ellis
(photo by Ron Bray: North
Texas State University,
Electronic Music Center,
Denton, Texas).

players return to the hall (rear this time) and perform again under a dim flashing light. The work concludes in total darkness and silence.

Landscape Journey (1964) by Donald Scavarda, for clarinet, piano, and film projection, reflects the contrasting elements of aural and visual materials. Sections of sound alone interplay with soundless projections to create a very obvious alternating formal structure. The abstract fast-

18. This six-minute cyclic work involves as well the use of strobe and black lights—
the dancer painted with red fluorescent body paint.

moving shapes and colors on *two* screens balance the contrast and dependence of the *two* instruments in use.

Quotes

A growing dramatic media form is that of quoting a fragment from another composer or style within the framework of one's own creative structures. While it is hardly new (almost every composer has at one time or another quoted other musics, from Bach's borrowed chants to Mahler's quotations of his own music), the use of strikingly different styles in the twentieth-century *avant-garde* has taken a decisively novel direction. The hymn quotes of Charles Ives as well as his free borrowings of any material to suit his message (evident in such works as *Central Park in the Dark* and *Symphony No. 4*) are often starkly presented against highly dissonant textures highlighting the cognizant drama present. While one might easily contest the placement of this singularly aural activity in a *media-forms* chapter, it is argued that the *message* indeed combines to form a "drama," and quite unlike the "theme and variations" quoting of previous centuries, this new actively polarized inclusion of borrowed material is indeed a full-bred "psycho-drama."

Reasons for such quoting vary from composer to composer and often from work to work by the same composer. George Rochberg speaks of his usage:

The centerpiece of my *Music for the Magic Theatre* is a transcription, that is, a completely new version, of a Mozart adagio. I decided to repeat it in my own way because I loved it. People who understand, love it because they know it began with Mozart and ended with me. People who don't understand think it's by Mozart.[19]

Peter Maxwell Davies's use of Handel quotes in the aforementioned *Eight Songs for a Mad King* (1969) results in a strange periodization (George III period) as well as a superimposed *collage* effect (especially in "Comfort Ye, Comfort Ye My People," of Song #7).

Michael Colgrass achieves an Ivesian *montage* in *As Quiet As* (1966) for orchestra by a multitude of effectively varied quotes framed by a background of subtle clouds of modulating chords.

Mauricio Kagel superimposes quote upon quote from Beethoven in his *Ludwig Van* (1970) creating, like Lukas Foss in his *Baroque Variations* (1967) and Stockhausen in his *Opus 1970*, a surrealistic intertwining of raw material stylistically consistent but rhythmically and texturally deranged. Each is contextually dramatic as additive overlays contribute to the increasing cognizant tension of the "composer" intention.

19. George Rochberg, "No Center," *Composer* 2, no. 1 (September 1969):89.

Luciano Berio's *Sinfonia* (1968) (for eight soloists and orchestra), quoting extensively from Mahler and Debussy among others (in movement no. 3), shows dramatic potency in its use of striking text (likewise quoting from a number of sources including Samuel Beckett) and driving musical force.

Certainly more innocent, at least in its length and continuity, is George Crumb's use of a short Bach fragment in his *Ancient Voices of Children,* (1970) (this quote as well as a portion of the Berio are shown in figures in chapter 9). The performance (on a toy piano) complete with Baroque ornaments is possibly one of the most powerful quotes in recent music, though the dynamics of the movement barely rise above *mezzoforte.*

Phil Winsor's *Orgel I* (for pipe organ and prerecorded tape) includes some performer choice (e.g., *which* Bach fugue, prelude, etc.) yet the incredible diversity culminates to create a constant rationale of forged opposites. Figure 5.20 shows page X, a page of directed choices from which at points in the score (not shown) the performer may choose items within a prescribed time limit. The tape, made by the performer, contributes further overlays of the given material resulting in massive densities of crowded triadic clashes dramatically tangible in their recognized identity (each listener will, of course, recognize from his own experience only a percentage of the quotes), their often simultaneous polarized styles, and indeed the listener's inherent quest for message.

Figure 5.19.   Phil Winsor.
Photo by Julia Winsor.

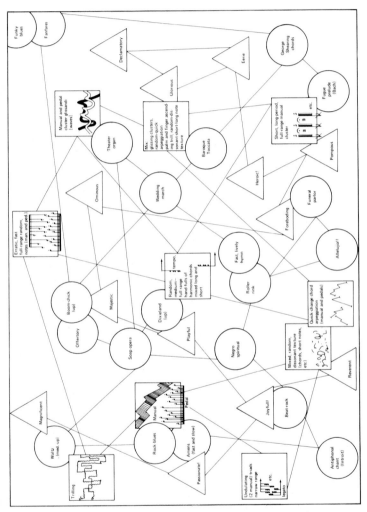

Figure 5.20.   Phil Winsor's *ORGEL 1* (page X). Copyright © 1975 by Pembroke Music Co., Inc., New York. International Copyright Secured. 62 Cooper Square, New York, N. Y. 10003. Copying or reproducing this publication in whole or in part violates the Federal Copyright Law. All rights reserved including public performance for profit. Used by permission.

Bibliography

*Further Readings**

Ashley, Robert. "Notes for *Public Opinion Descends Upon the Demonstrators.*" *Asterisk* 1, no. 1 (1961):49. Presents score and information about performance of this work.

Austin, Larry. "SYCOM—Systems Complex for the Studio and Performing Arts." *Numus West* 5:57. A most interesting article pertaining to the potentials of media research and study of new combinational art forms.

Becker, Jurgen, and Vostell, Wolf, eds. *Happenings.* Hamburg: Rowohlt, 1965. A good source of information on this topic from a European viewpoint.

Beckwith, John, and Kasemets, Udo, eds. *The Modern Composer and His World.* Toronto: University of Toronto Press, 1961.

Cage, John. *M. Writings '67-'72.* Middletown, Conn.: Wesleyan University Press, 1973.

———. *Silence.* Middletown, Conn.: Wesleyan University Press, 1961.

———. *A Year from Monday.* Middletown, Conn.: Wesleyan University Press, 1967. All very useful books and collections of articles, many of which are related to this man's constant efforts at media connections, be they relevant or not. A complete bibliography of Cage articles and interviews exists in Kostelanetz's book on Cage and need not be reprinted here.

Chase, Gilbert. "Toward a Total Musical Theatre." *Arts in Society,* (Spring 1969):25. Good primer in this concept.

Cross, Lowell. "David Tudor," In *Dictionary of Contemporary Music,* edited by John Vinton. New York: E. P. Dutton & Co., 1974. Article ends with a group of works by Tudor who is probably the most prolific, in media forms, of any living composer aside from Cage himself.

Cunningham, Merce. *Changes: Notes on Choreography.* Edited by Frances Starr. New York: Something Else Press, 1969. Fascinating source book not only for the dance contribution to media forms but also for the variety of ways in which it has been included in the past.

Dallin, Leon. *Techniques of Twentieth Century Composition.* 3rd ed. Dubuque: Wm. C. Brown Company Publishers, 1974. Contains a brief but interesting commentary on multimedia.

Gibb, Stanley. "Understanding Terminology and Concepts Related to Media Art Forms." *The American Music Teacher* 22, no. 5:23. Superb article which brought many insights to this author's consideration of the various forms.

*Addresses for record companies, periodicals, and music publishers mentioned in this Bibliography can be found in Appendix 4.

Hansen, Al. *A Primer of Happenings and Time-Space Art.* New York: Something Else Press, 1968. Fascinating contribution to the media-forms literature.

Higgins, Dick. *Postface.* New York: Something Else Press, 1964.

———. *FOEW&OMBWHNW* New York: Something Else Press, 1969.
Both are interesting contributions to the literature, and overlap significantly with materials in chapter 8.

Hiller, Lejaren. "HPSCHD." *Source* 2, no. 2 (1968). Discusses the work of the same name by Hiller and Cage, with photographs of both composers at the computers.

Hoffman, Paul. "An Interview with Robert Moran." *Composer* 4, no. 2 (1973):46.

Kagel, Mauricio. "On *Match* for Three Performers," *Composer* 3, no. 2 (1972):70.
Fascinating account of one very involved in "media" works from the most bizarre to the most conventional.

———. "Über das instrumentale Theater." *Neue Musik* (Munich, 1961).
Interesting study of this man's views on the subject.

Kaprow, Allan. *Assemblage, Environments and Happenings.* New York: Abrams, 1966. Good source, interesting reading.

Kirby, E. T. *Total Theatre.* New York: E. P. Dutton & Co., 1969. Most fascinating and a very good contribution to the literature though it is slanted in the indeterminate direction: multimedia.

Kirby, Michael. *The Art of Time.* New York: E. P. Dutton & Co., 1969. Relevant and interesting "conceptual" study of media-related forms and structures.

———. *Happenings.* New York: E. P. Dutton & Co., 1965. Good insight into the structure and beginnings of this multimedia event.

Kostelanetz, Richard. *The Theatre of Mixed Means.* New York: Dial, 1968. Though out of print, one of the best sources and pieces of writing on the subject yet available.

———, ed. *John Cage.* New York: Praeger Publishers, 1970. Fine book containing photographs and documents of the tradition of experimentalism started with Cage. Also contains excellent bibliographies relating to media presentations.

"Conversation with Robert Moran." *Numus West* 3:30. Fascinating account of this man's work in the area of media.

Mumma, Gordon. "Four Sound Environments for Modern Dance." *Impulse, the Annual of Contemporary Dance,* 1967. Writing particularly on Cage's work.

Pellegrino, Ronald. "Some Thoughts on Thinking for the Electronic Music Synthesizer." *Proceedings* (American Society of University Composers) 7, no. 8 (1972-73):52. Interesting approach to many problems facing the media composer today.

Penn, William. "The Celluloid Image and Mixed Media." *Composer* 1, no. 4 (1970):179. Discusses philosophical aspects of the form.

Proceedings 3. (American Society of University Composers [August 1968].)
Includes two very interesting discussions: "Theatre Music" with Richard

Browne as chairman and a panel of Barney Childs, Ben Johnston, Salvatore Martirano and Roy Travis; and "Mixed-Media Composition" with Ross Lee Finney as moderator and panelists George Cacioppo, Edwin London, and Salvatore Martirano. Both are of value and interest, and show a multiplicity of views toward both media composition and the personalities involved.

Reynolds, Roger. "Happenings in Japan and Elsewhere." *Arts in Society* 5, no. 1 (Spring-Summer, 1968). Short but quite good reference to some very significant activities in the sixties in Japan by a number of visiting American composers as well as by composers from Japan.

Rochberg, George. "No Center." *Composer* 1, no. 2. (1969):86. Most interesting "train of thought" article which includes very fascinating material regarding his ideas of "quoting."

Rossi, Nick, and Choate, Robert. *Music of Our Time*. Boston: Crescendo, 1969. A number of references to multimedia with coverage of Cage (*HPSCHD*, p. 337ff.) and Subotnick (*Play! No. 1*, p. 377).

Salzman, Eric. "Mixed Media." In *Dictionary of Contemporary Music*, edited by John Vinton. New York: E. P. Dutton & Co., 1974. Good introduction to the subject. The *Dictionary* also includes a great many biographies of composers mentioned in this chapter.

Subotnick, Morton. "Extending the Stuff Music is Made of." *Music Educators Journal* 55, no. 3 (November 1968):109. Short but good study in the problems and origins of multimedia.

Tomkins, Calvin. *The Bride and the Bachelors*. New York: Viking Press, 1965. A brilliant book looking into the lives of four extremely important contributors to the media concept: Marcel Duchamp, Jean Tinguely, Robert Rauschenberg, and John Cage.

Whitney, John. "Moving Pictures and Electronic Music." In *Die Reihe* 7. Bryn Mawr, Pa.: Theodore Presser, 1965. Superb study in inter-media and a most important contribution to the literature.

Yates, Peter. *Twentieth Century Music*. New York: Pantheon Books, 1967. Follows the history of the experimental "ideal" in America, including happenings and multimedia developments.

Young, La Monte, and Zazeela, Marian. *Selected Writings*. Munich: Heiner Friedrich, 1969. Referred to in chapter 8; quite apropos here as well. Interesting but centered around the activities of the two authors.

Recordings and Publishers

Ashley, Robert. *Public Opinion Descends Upon the Demonstrators* (1961). *Asterisk* (magazine) 1, no. 1.

Austin, Larry. *Bass* (1967). CPE-*Source*. For bass, tape, and film. Performed over N.E.T. by Bertram Turetzky. Involves exaggerated gestures and mime.

———. *The Maze* (1965). Audience involvement with lights and dramatic actions by the performers. Both these works show the theatrical possibilities of standard performing situations.

Beerman, Burton. *Mixtures*. Media Press. Ensemble, tape, and candlelight procession.

Berio, Luciano. *Laborintus* II (1965). Universal Edition. Recorded on RCA LSC-3267. For voices, instruments, reciter, and tape.

———. *Sinfonia* (1968). Universal Edition. Recorded on Columbia MS-7268.

Cage, John. Media works include:

———. *Theatre Piece* (1960). Peters.

———. *Variations III.* Peters. Recorded on DG-139442.

———. *Water Music* (1952).

Cage, John and Lejaren Hiller. *HPSCHD.* Peters. Recorded on Nonesuch H-71224.' A "happening."

Colgrass, Michael. *As Quiet As* (1966). MCA. Recorded on RCA LSC-3001.

Cope, David. *BTRB* (1970). Brass Press. For any brass player; theatre piece.

———. *Deadliest Angel Revision* (1971). Composers' Autograph Publications.

Crumb, George. *Ancient Voices of Children.* Peters. Recorded on None-such 71255.

———. *Voice of the Whale (Vox Balaenae).* Peters. Recorded on Columbia M-32739.

Davies, Peter Maxwell. *8 Songs for a Mad King.* Boosey & Hawkes. Recorded on Nonesuch H-71285.

Ellis. Merrill. *Mutations.* Available from the composer, North Texas State University, Denton, Texas.

Foss, Lukas. *Baroque Variations* (1967). Carl Fischer. Recorded on Nonesuch 71202.

Ives, Charles. *Central Park in the Dark* (1906). AMP. Recorded on Columbia MS-6843.

Kagel, Mauricio. *Die Himmelsmechanik* (1965). Composition using vivid images of suns, moons, clouds, etc.

———. *Kommentar und Extempore* (1967). For three actors, singer, seven brass instruments.

———. *Ludwig Van.* Recorded on DG-2530014.

———. *Match* (1966). Universal Edition. Recorded on DG-137006.

———. *Variaktionen* (1967). Universal Edition. For four actors, three singers, and tapes.

Kasemets, Udo. *It: Tribute to Buckminster Fuller, Marshall McLuhan and John Cage.* A computer-controlled audio-visual audience participation work.

Kraft, William. *Contextures: Riots—Decade '60.* Recorded on London 6613. For orchestra and projections.

Lentz, Daniel. *Sermon* (1970). Composers' Autograph Publications.

Lunetta, Stanley. Four excellent theater pieces complete with flashing lights, projections, and sets; all available from CPE-*Source: The Wringer, Mr. Machine, A Piece for Bandoneon and Strings, Spider Song.*

Martirano, Salvatore. *L'sGA* (1968). MCA. Recorded on Polidor 245001.

———. *Underworld.* MCA. For four actors, two basses, tenor saxophone, and tape.

Mathew, David. *Private Mirrors.* Composers' Autograph Publications.

Moran, Robert. The following are available only from the composer, who is at this writing Composer-in-Residence for the city of Berlin, 1974-75: *Bombardments No. 4; Divertissement No. 1; Hallelujah; 39 Minutes for 39 Actors.*

de Oliveira, Jocy. *Probabilistic Theater I.* Uses a map projection as score for musicians, actors, dancers, and lights.

Reck, David. *Blues and Screamer.* CPE-*Source.* An excellent aural-visual composite including an antiwar film and dramatic performer remarks (near the end of the score).

Reynolds, Roger. *Emperor of Ice Cream.* Peters.

———. *Ping.* CPE-*Source.* Recorded on CRI-285.

Rochberg, George. *Music for the Magic Theatre.* Theodore Presser. For orchestra.

Satie, Erik. *Reîache* (1924). Salabert. Recorded on Vanguard C-10037/8.

Schäffer, Boguslaw. *Audiences No. 1-5* (1964). PWM.

———. *Non-Stop* (1960). PWM.

———. *Incident* (1966). PWM.

Scriabin, Alexander. *Poem of Fire.* Balawe Publishers. Recorded on London 6732.

Somers, Harry. *Improvisation.* A theater piece for voices and instruments.

Stockhausen, Karlheinz. *Momente* (1963). Recorded on Nonesuch 71157. Begins with players applauding the audience, with rhythmic notations.

———. *Opus 1970.* Recorded on DG-139461.

Strange, Allen. *". . . and still another story concerns . . ."* Composers' Autograph Publications. For tape and six projectors.

———. *No Dead Horses on the Moon.* Media Press.

———. *Palace.* CAP. For violin, tape, projections, and staging.

———. *Vanity Fair.* Another dramatic multimedia work.

Subotnick, Morton. *Mandolin* (1960). MCA. For viola, tape, and film.

———. *Play* (1962). MCA. Woodwind quintet, piano, tape, film.

———. *A Ritual Game Room* (1970). MCA. Without audience.

Tudor, David. See p. 769 of John Vinton's *Dictionary of Contemporary Music* for a compilation by Lowell Cross of Tudor's work in media forms.

von Wrochem, Klaus. *Limelight.* CAP. Performers are conducted by a directional light which presents a light-show at the same time.

———. *Oratorium meum plus Praeperturi.* CAP. Involves performers in costumes and as characters (e.g., Martin Luther, a prostitute, etc.).

6 Improvisation

Aesthetics and Definition

The morphology of any system which segregates its participants as completely as music has done (composer, performer, audience) must immediately become suspect. It has taken centuries for the music world to
develop a set of symbols that serve to carefully isolate the creative mind
from his audience—symbols, the inadequacy of which cannot begin to
represent the significance of a Mozart, a Brahms, or a Beethoven. Improvisation, even in its most simple forms, must result from that realization and immediacy. Improvisation is not irresponsibility; in fact, it may
produce a result more faithfully representative of the composer's intentions than that of standard symbols. The composer who wishes this, for
example:

Figure 6.1

will find realization impractical and the result studied and imperfect. The
notation

Figure 6.2

or the direction "five 32nd notes from B-flat to low C" results in easy
realization and immediate and practical communication of the composer's
intention. Even

146

Figure 6.3

often mistaken as indeterminacy, results in more accurate performance than studied notation.

Improvisation is more a notational than a philosophical challenge to traditional directions. Improvisation must inherently exist to some extent in all music in which exact notation of every detail is not possible: therefore in *all* music. To a lesser degree than many current directions, of course, *even* Beethoven (*even* because, as Lukas Foss has quoted him: "Does he think I have his silly fiddle in mind when the spirit talks to me?"[1]) must, in the last analysis, relent to performer decision. From his piano sonata, opus 106, measures 264-66:

ritardando

Figure 6.4

more accurately represented:

Figure 6.5

His choice of the loose and interpretative word *ritardando* encourages the performer's creative approach (the terms improvisation and interpretation can be said to be generally interchangeable).

The history of music is riddled with the improvising performer (now called composer): Bach, Chopin, and Beethoven, to mention but a few. Improvisation does not *allow*, but insists upon, participation. Indeed, it *requires* it. The distribution of idolatry by the audience can no longer

1. See *Perspectives of New Music* 1, no. 2 (Spring 1963):46.

function adequately; the recipes for the contemporary performers no longer guarantee success and repeated success without the participation of the cook (selection and preparation) and consumer (determination of spices, cooking time, and other variable elements).

The Baroque figured bass and the classical concerto cadenzas are two predominant examples of improvisation in traditional music. The figured bass, giving merely the bass notes and the intervals above them in terms of shorthand numbers below the note, allowed the performer the creative possibility of improvising and developing rhythmic and melodic fragments and motives. Cadenzas, up to the late eighteenth century, were very rarely written out in detail, giving each performer his chance to "show off" in the manner best suited to his own particularly directed talents (merely suggesting motives and harmonic relevance to the movement or the work as a whole). Donald Erb refers to the latter use in his remarks about his own *Concerto for Percussion and Orchestra* (1966):

The work is cast in the traditional concerto format of three movements.
The solo part is in the eighteenth and nineteenth century virtuoso tradition. The cadenzas in the second and, especially, the third movements harken back to the eighteenth century tradition of having the performer improvise much or all of the cadenza. A variation on this idea was used in the first movement, where instead of having the soloist improvise a cadenza I had the entire orchestra, other than the soloist, improvise it.[2]

As with the Erb *Concerto* it would seem logical for the composer, rather than refusing to admit the existence of (or making as insignificant as possible) the necessary improvisational aspects of his music, to use it to both his own and the performer's advantage. If indeed the "silly fiddler" will have opportunities to shape the final meaning of his work, would it not be more intelligent to work with the performer, in hopes of making him (and consequently the work) less "silly," or to resort to magnetic tape and work with the manifest problem of "silly" speakers and variable acoustics?

The emphasis in improvisation is, in fact, *more creativity,* as *re-creation* no longer exists. Too long have audiences been content to quibble over inadequacies in performances of music its hundredth time around; now they can experience those sounds which for the first time, and possibly the last, express themselves without the heroic image of individual idols.

Allan Bryant states that improvisation is "Similar to free jazz, oriental and African music, things which are impossible to write out."[3] and "Free, wild music and ideas that wouldn't come about with single composers

2. Liner notes of the recording: Turnabout TV-S 34433 by the composer. Taken from the program notes of the first performance in 1966.
3. "Groups," *Source: Music of the Avant-Garde,* vol. II, no. 1 (January 1968).

working alone."[4] Foss adds: "Cardew is right to worry about ethics of improvisation. It needs it. *Improvisation:* one plays what one already knows. . . . Improvisation that works is improvisation made safe."[5] Working individually or in a group, improvisation is a form of composition, the communication and exactness of which is as important and explicit as those of traditional rituals of performance.

Immediate Background

The circumstances under which interest in improvisation developed are unclear, though two distinct possibilities exist. First, such interest in this century may be rooted in jazz: a number of composers associated with improvisation are or were actively involved in jazz (especially Gunther Schuller). The relationship, however, is more in concept than in reality or style; performers react to one another while still affected by basic limits of realization. It is more plausible that contemporary improvisation sprang from the performers' inability to realize accurately the complexities of recent music; the composer, perhaps out of frustration, perhaps because the result was the same (or better), chose to allow a certain freedom in the performance of his work. Luciano Berio, for example, in his *Tempi Concertati*, requires the percussionist to hit everything as fast as possible; exact notation would be impractical or even impossible. The effect is predictable and effective even without a note or rhythm being written.

Improvisation differs from indeterminacy, as its meaning in music refers to the aspect of performer interaction, an activity more often than not controllable in rough shape by the composer, and even predictable within limits. Speaking to this point William Hellermann clearly defines that distinction:

It seems to me that there is a fundamental difference between aleatoric and improvisational music. Improvisation is concerned with the realization in real time of defined artistic goals. Aleatory, by its very nature, does not recognize the existence of goals. Both differ from the traditional "classic music" by leaving open to the performer the choice of the specific materials to be used in the piece. They are often lumped together for this reason and, also, because they are both thought to be "free." Actually, freedom is not really the issue. Improvisation, at its highest, seeks meaning through spontaneity. Aleatory declares meaning to be spontaneity. Both of these are very restrictive states. I find that in my own works I am increasingly concerned with improvisation, and never with anything I would call aleatory.[6]

4. Ibid., p. 24.
5. Ibid., p. 17.
6. Tom Everett, "Questions and Answers," *Composer* 2, no. 4 (March 1971):82.

Improvisation Groups

The 1960s accordingly brought about a number of groups dedicated to improvisation: the New Music Ensemble (Austin, Lunetta, Mizelle, Woodbury, Alexander, and Johnson); Sonic Arts Group (Mumma, Ashley, Behrman, and Lucier); the *Musica Elettronica Viva* (Allan Bryant, Alvin Curran, Jon Phetteplace, Carol Plantamura, Frederic Rzewski, Richard Teitelbaum, and Ivan Vandor); and the University of Illinois Chamber Players, directed by Jack McKenzie. Whatever the means of producing sound (electronic or instrumental), the immediate and temporary creations, based solely on the interaction of the performers (most of whom are composers), are personal, original, and structured, but the responsibility for them lies with an ensemble, not a single personality. Lukas Foss remarks: "I thought I had invented a new kind of improvisation. I now know that I was merely the first not to sign my name."[7] The 1957 U.C.L.A.-based Improvisation Chamber Ensemble, under the direction

Figure 6.6. Lukas Foss, Music Director and Conductor, The Buffalo Philharmonic Orchestra. Photo permission by Carnegie Hall, 154 W. 57th St., New York, N. Y. 10019.

7. As quoted in "Groups," *Source: Music of the Avant-Garde* 2, no. 1 (January 1968): 17.

of Foss and consisting of piano, clarinet, 'cello, and percussion (among the first of such groups), worked primarily from charts indicating only initial ideas (e.g., motive, rhythm, pattern) needed to create a work. Many rehearsals yielded a polished result in performances which varied somewhat, but were more crystalline than live improvisation. The group also performed improvised interludes between the movements of Foss's *Time Cycle* (1960) for soprano and orchestra (first version, 1960).

Cornelius Cardew (of AMM, which also includes Lou Gare, Eddie Prevost, and Keith Rowe), in the same article referred to above, adds: "The past always seems intentional, but at the time it appears to be accidental."[8]

The MW 2 Ensemble of Poland uses instruments of more traditional origin, while at the same time employing two dancers and an actor, with tapes, projection, and scenery (see fig. 6.7), performer interaction therefore taking the form of physical as well as musical improvisation.

Group improvisational situations challenge the aesthetic of a "leading personality." Notation or not, the structure and immediate creation resulting from such groups challenges the audience's categorization of individual idols more than they philosophically or aurally alter traditional methods of creative intention.

Figure 6.7.   MW 2 Ensemble of Poland.

8. Ibid., p. 18.

Works

Usage varies from inexact pitch identification to whole sections left to performer interaction bordering on indeterminacy. One or more elements (or limits) is usually provided to act as a vehicle to shape the material more effectively into the context of the work. Roger Harris, for example, in *Kroma II*, provides notes and some relative durational indication (the composer has noted in the score: "fragments or motives may be repeated at any tempo or dynamic level"), while tempo, dynamics, and composite structure are left to the performer's "reaction" to the audience's "reaction" (see fig. 6.8).

Figure 6.8.   *Realization from Wind Sound Sculpture #1 (Kroma II)* by Roger W. Harris. (Published by Composers' Autograph Publications.)

The concept of *time* is an essential element in the contemporary composer's approach. Morton Feldman expresses his ideas as to how objects exist *as* time, not of, in, or about time:

. . . This was not how to make an object . . . but how this object exists *as* Time. Time regained, as Proust referred to his work. Time as an Image, as Aristotle suggested. This is the area which the visual arts later began to explore. This is the area which music, deluded that it was counting out the seconds, has neglected.
  I once had a conversation with Karlheinz Stockhausen, where he . . . began beating on the table and said: "A sound exists either here—or here—

or here." He was convinced that he was demonstrating reality to me. That the beat, and the possible placement of sounds in relation to it, was the only thing the composer could realistically hold on to. The fact that he had reduced it to so much a square foot made him think Time was something he could handle and even parcel out, pretty much as he pleased.

Frankly, this approach to Time bores me. I am not a clockmaker. I am interested in getting Time in its unstructured existence. That is, I am interested in how this wild beast lives in the jungle—not in the zoo. I am interested in how Time exists before we put our paws on it—our minds, our imaginations, into it.

One would think that music more than any other art would be exploratory about Time. But is it? Timing—not Time—has been passed off as the real thing in music. . . .[9]

Realization of the inadequacy of standard notation for performers may lead not only to new notation, but to the lack of notation entirely, the complete destruction of the composer/performer relationship, a hierarchy wholly created by the audience of idolatry. Lukas Foss, in works like *Echo* (1963), hints toward this lack of notation by employing stems without noteheads (though exact indications of rhythm, dynamics, and order are given).

William Duckworth's *Pitch City* (see fig. 6.9) instructs four wind performers to trace pitches from the four corners to the middle; each note's duration is equivalent to the individual performer's ability to sustain his note(s) as long as possible, then breathing between notes. More notes remain unplayed (73) than played (71), while at the same time a twelve-tone row (top line, left to right) is expressed in all versions—original, retrograde (right to left), inversion (top to bottom), and retrograde inversion (bottom to top)—and in every possible transposition. The composer's intention here is unmistakable: to prepare the complete logical and mathematical twelve-tone row structure, and then totally avoid any realization of this organization. This represents a philosophical blast at twelve-tone rationale that must play a distinct part in any educated performer's realization of the score (none of the outlined portions remotely follow twelve-tone direction). Improvisation occurs in rhythm, instrumentation, and resultant octave (depending on the instrument, the choice of which is restricted only to wind instruments) relationship.

In *III for Double Ensemble*, Harold Budd employs boxes located in high, middle, and low approximate pitch areas around the staff, in which numbers appear indicating the number of notes to be played. Such instructions as pizzicato, staccato, and so on often accompany the boxed improvisation areas. In contrast to this (the jazz trio) the quartet (con-

9. Morton Feldman, "Between Categories," *The Composer* 1, no. 2 (September 1969): 75.

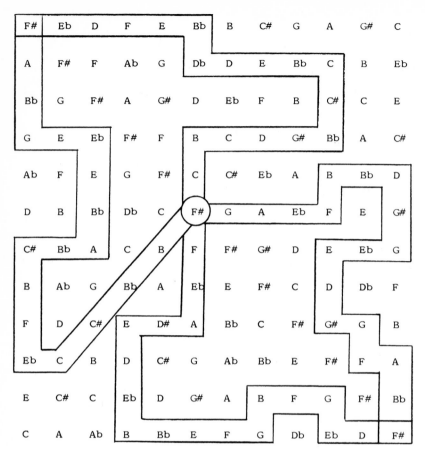

Figure 6.9.   William Duckworth:
Pitch City. (Copyright Media Press,
Champaign, Ill., 1969.) Used by
permission. All rights reserved.

sisting of flute, clarinet, vibes and 'cello, and separated both spatially
and visually from the trio) plays from exact pitch notation but without
real rhythmic directions. Two improvisatory techniques enhance the stylistic distinction between groups, thus limiting improvisatory directions
within the framework of the piece.

Etudes for Organ by Lukas Foss requests four different improvisational techniques, one for each movement. In the first, the performer
varies an exactly-notated motor rhythm single-line melody by repeat-
ing note groups as he desires (no more than twelve score notes should
be played without returning to some group of notes of the performer's
choice). In the second, a large number of groups of notes (right hand)

are scored for which the performer may then choose order, rhythm, octave, and/or number of the notes he desires. Forearm clusters dominate throughout the third, with spontaneous choice of rhythm, white or black key clusters; the form here is more articulate, being verbally presented in four sections: ABA-Coda. Number IV includes performer choice of a four-part "religious or patriotic" hymn around which two secondary performers playing four-note clusters at either end of the keyboard are asked (verbally, again) to interfere, *poco a poco,* with the hymn performance. Foss has used notes (in I, II, and IV), rhythms (in I), timbre (in III), dynamics (in II, III, and IV), each in a somewhat traditional manner, at the same time freeing another aspect of composition and performance for improvisation.

In each of the above discussed works, the composer still claims one or more compositional aspects of his work. Giuseppi Chiari's *Quel Che Volette* is probably more àpropos of Morton Feldman's statement: "Down with the Masterpiece; up with art. . . ."[10] The piece is entirely made up of verbal instructions ranging from indications suggesting materials not be played in a virtuosic manner, to exchanging instruments among performers. However vague the score may appear, close reading reveals a near determinacy, in "word painting" fashion, of composer intention, especially in regard to form (from "you must try and play in a traditional manner" and "play as if playing was a gift" to "We must never overdo"). Likewise, in *Sonant,* Mauricio Kagel employs verbal descriptions of the framework within which the performer may improvise. These many times intricate instructions may be more accurate in terms of performance ease and understanding than traditional notation.

Alvin Curran's *Home-made* employs improvisational freedom effectively in contrast to an exactly notated and rigid composer controlled section. Using boxes within which a minimal number of composer instructions (e.g., *p* to *mf*) are placed, the performer is asked to react to the other performers and/or simultaneous traditionally scored material. Curran alternates the effects of each approach successfully and maximizes the contrast: the more-or-less random effect of improvisation with precise tutti attacks, etc., in the notated material.

Luciano Berio's *Circles* (1960) for female voice, harp, and two percussion players includes a variety of improvisation *boxes.* Figure 6.10 shows the two percussion parts (top and bottom groups of staves) with the voice in the middle (harp out at this point). The "improvisation boxes" are clearly seen here (not to be confused with the small boxes in which the mallets are graphically shown: i.e., the first small box to

10. Morton Feldman, "Conversations without Stravinsky," *Source: Music of the Avant-Garde* 1, no. 2 (July 1967):43.

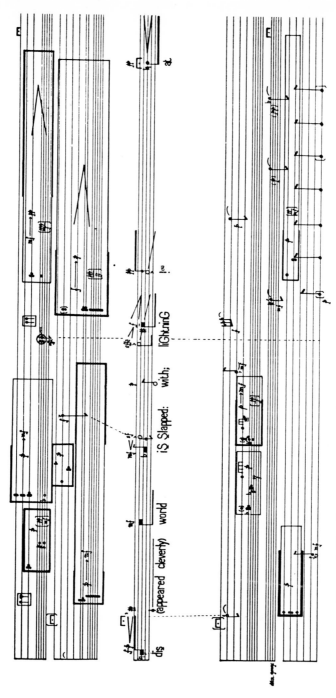

Figure 6.10. Luciano Berio: *Circles*. © Copyright 1961 by Universal Edition. Used by permission.

appear in the two top lines from the left) and the reasoning behind the "improvisation" clear: the percussion parts would become impossible if written out, or tight and "square." Pitches and instrumentation are usually indicated in specific detail. Rhythm is more often than not left to the performer, either with the notes stacked vertically in such a way that the performer can proceed in any order he "feels" (occasionally the pitches are proportionally distributed within the box to indicate the approximate rhythmic placement or to introduce new "stacks" of notes). Dynamics are often notated in terms of *limits* (i.e., mf → pp) with smooth *crescendi* and *diminuendi* indicated by dovetailing notation. It is interesting to note that the score contains no performance directions except those of placement of instruments; the composer, it seems, feels that these performance concepts are obvious. With these methods of improvisation Berio is able to maintain control over a number of elements, while performer flexibility is available with others. With the "boxes" occurring in only one or two parts at a time (there is little flexibility in the vocal line except its proportional non-metered notation) the composer maintains control over the direction and flow of the work, allowing the improvisation to give *life* to each successive performance.

Robert Erickson's *Ricercar à 5* (1966) for five trombones involves a number of improvisational techniques from the performers (the work may be performed with five trombonists or one trombonist and four pre-recorded trombones on tape). The composer varies from complete control to control of only one or two elements (e.g., most often dynamics and pitch or pitch direction are controlled) with the interplay between parts actively calling for sensitive and interpretative improvisatory techniques. The work was written for trombonist Stuart Dempster who, in a recent interview, speaks of these points:

Question (Frank McCarty): "So you began to compile a body of new sounds and techniques through research, practice, and mimicry. I assume you incorporated some of these in the improvisational music that was popular among the San Francisco composers of that era."
Answer (Stu Dempster): "Yes, those pieces gave me the first opportunity to couple my "funny sounds" with other "funny sounds" made by tapes and by other musical instruments such as Pauline's (Oliveros) accordion and Mort's (Subotnick) clarinet. I also became interested in working with composers, I did a demo for Berio in the early 1960's and asked him for a piece, never thinking he'd really do it. Later (1966), when I was working with Bob Erickson on a commission, I decided to resurrect the Berio idea. I wrote him a letter . . . and learned he was already right in the middle of the piece. The *Sequenza* (also involving improvisation techniques) was written in a way for two of us, myself and (Vlinka) Globokar, who had played sketches of what became the B section. But as Berio and I worked together on the final version it became more and more my piece since he saw in me—in my performance—more and more the character of Grock,

the famous European clown, about whom the piece is actually written. In the meantime, Erickson and I were spending many a Tuesday morning developing a vocabulary of sounds and sound-mixes which resulted in his composition of the *Ricercár a 5. . . .*"[11]

Figure 6.11 is from Witold Lutoslawski's *Livre Pour Orchestra* (1968) which contains a number of improvisational sections. These are marked "ad lib" and ". . . all the rhythmic values are approximate. In consequence, the placing of the notes one above the other in the score does not necessarily mean that they are played simultaneously."[12] These "ad libs" take place within each of the four movements and as "interludes" between movements (fig. 6.11 shown is the second such "interlude": i.e., between the second and third movements).

The three initial movements of this work are rather intense. After each of them a moment of relaxation is required. The short interludes are to serve this purpose. . . . I imagine that the attitude of the conductor when he has given the single beat which begins each interlude would be exactly the same as during a pause between movements. An attitude which should suggest that this is the moment for the audience to relax, change position, cough, etc.[13]

As with the Lutoslawski *Livre*, Ivana Loudova's *Chorale* for wind orchestra, percussion, and organ involves "ad lib" sections with notes given (sometimes approximate types of rhythm) which are then followed by an unstaved dotted line (indicating continuance in like manner) until the pattern is to be changed. Often this results in extremely complex composite rhythms unobtainable in any other manner (be it known that while "theoretically" any rhythm is notationally possible in the expanded system in use today, *possible* is not always *playable*).

Phil Winsor's *Orgel* (also discussed in the preceding chapter) includes a sheet of twelve basic improvisatory boxes for organ (and organ recorded on tape). The verbal stylistic indications above each box (see fig. 6.12) plus the timing and overlap directions of the score (not shown) make this "free" improvisation, and not graphic indeterminacy as a quick glance might suggest.

Krzysztof Penderecki combines *sound-mass* with rhythm and pitch improvisation in his *Capriccio for Violin and Orchestra* (1968), shown in figure 6.13. Here the *armonium* ("harmonium": a reed-type organ) and piano (using wire "jazz" brushes on the inside) cover the approximate visual area in the time allowed (2/4 with the quarter note equal to ap-

11. Frank McCarty, "An Interview with Stuart Dempster," *The Instrumentalist* 28, no. 10 (May 1974):36-37. Used by permission of The Instrumentalist Co.

12. From the composer's performance instructions in the score (PWM-Cracow 28.915. Edition Wilhelm Hansen, London).

13. Ibid.

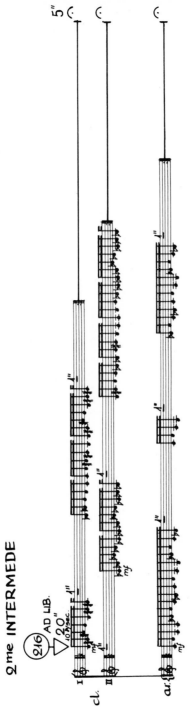

Figure 6.11. Witold Lutoslawski: *Livre Pour Orchestra* (second "interlude"). Permission granted by J. & W. Chester Ltd. London, England. Polskie Wydawnictwo Muzyczne, Cracow, Poland. (PWM)

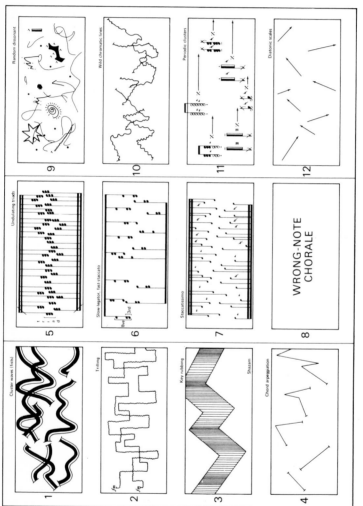

Figure 6.12. Phil Winsor: *ORGEL I.* Copyright © 1975 by Pembroke Music Co., Inc., New York. International Copyright Secured. 62 Cooper Square, New York, N. Y. 10003. Copying or reproducing this publication in whole or in part violates the Federal Copyright Law. All rights reserved including public performance for profit. Used by permission.

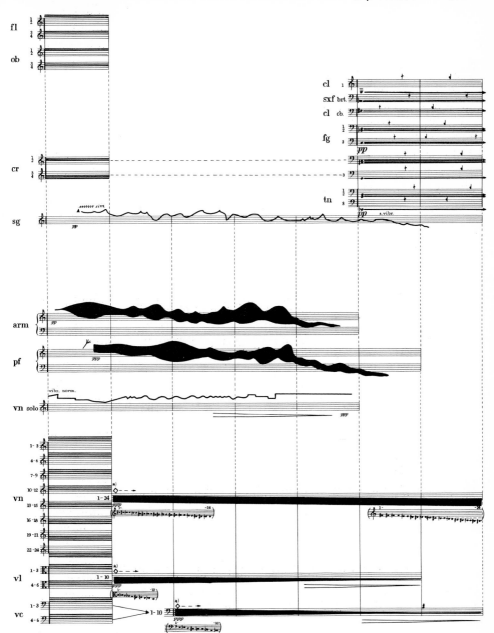

Figure 6.13. Krzysztof Penderecki:
Capriccio for Violin and Orchestra
(p. 29). Copyright © 1968 by Moeck
Verlag. Used with permission. All
rights reserved.

proximately 76mm, though no tempo is given in the score: author derived the tempo by carefully dividing the duration by numbers of measures and combinations of *ritardandi,* etc.). The violin solo as well is improvisatory in terms of actual pitch though the rhythm of approximately 18 sixteenth notes per measure has been continued from a previous page. A great deal of Penderecki's music is necessarily improvisatory as the notation (see Appendix 4) is such that exact rhythmic notation is impossible. Thusly performer sensitivity to other performers, the conductor, and audience is imperative for a successful performance.

Improvisational techniques in the last few years have created a renaissance of live performance situations. Whether as a result of, or a reaction to, the composer isolation of electronic music, the newfound creative collaboration between composers and performers cannot help but enrich the continuum and significance of all of music.

Bibliography

*Further Readings**

Ashley, Robert. His interesting accounts of the ONCE group may be found in both *Arts in Society.* (Spring 1968):86, and *Tulane Drama Review* 10:187.

Boulez, Pierre. "Aléa." *Nouvelle Revue Francaise* 59 (November 1, 1957). The tight comparisons between European concepts of improvisation and so-called "aleatoric" music are drawn herein by the author in regard to his own work *Improvisations sur Mallarmé.*

Chase, Gilbert. "Improvisation and Open Style." In *America's Music.* New York: McGraw-Hill Book Co., 1966. Interesting account of the origins of "American" improvisational style.

Dallin, Leon. *Techniques of Twentieth Century Composition.* 3rd ed. Dubuque, Iowa: Wm. C. Brown Company Publishers. See especially pp. 237-38.

Foss, Lukas. "The Changing Composer-Performer Relationship: a Monologue and a Dialogue." *Perspectives of New Music* 1, no. 2 (Spring 1963).

———. "Work-Notes for *Echoi.*" *Perspectives of New Music* 3, no. 1, (1964).

Hibbard, William. "Some Aspects of Serial Improvisation." *American Guild of Organists Quarterly.* (October 1966), and (January 1967). A fascinating study into this not-too-often-explored area of improvisation.

Hitchcock, H. Wiley. *Music in the United States: A Historical Introduction.* Englewood Cliffs, N. J.: Prentice-Hall, 1969. Contains a number of interesting comments on improvisation (see the index), some relating to its early roots in nineteenth-century America.

Mumma, Gordon. "Creative Aspects of Live Electronic Music Technology." Audio Engineering Society Reprint No. 550. A brief but credible account of how improvisation has been introduced into electronic music.

———. "The ONCE Festival and How it Happened." *Arts in Society* 4, no. 2: 381. A most fascinating account of the origins of this improvisatory group.

Schuller, Gunther. *Early Jazz: Its Roots and Development.* New York: Oxford University Press, 1968. Good source for this stylistic type of improvisation and its inherent roots in today's improvisational concept.

———. See his contribution to *The Modern Composer and His World* (edited by John Beckwith and Udo Kasemets. Toronto: University of Toronto

*Addresses for record companies, periodicals, and music publishers mentioned in this Bibliography can be found in Appendix 4.

Press, 1961) for an excellent and forthright argument favoring the use of improvisation, and his comments about Boulez (especially pp. 38 and 39).

Source 2, no. 1 (January 1968). Contains interviews, remarks, and thoughts of the New Music Ensemble, ONCE Group, Sonic Arts Group, and the *Musica Elettronica Viva* which provide an excellent study of the conflict and interrelation between improvisation and indeterminacy.

Recordings and Publishers

Andriessen, Louis. *Hoe het* (1969). For electronic improvisation group and 52 solo strings.

Ashley, Robert. *In Memoriam Esteban Gomez* (1963). CPE-*Source*.

Austin, Larry. *Improvisations for Orchestra and Jazz Soloists* (1961). Recorded on Columbia MS-6733.

Berio, Luciano. *Circles* (1962). Universal Edition. Recorded on Candide 31027.

Boulez, Pierre. *Improvisations sur Mallarme'* (see Further Readings, above) Universal Edition.

Chiari, Giuseppe. *Quel Che Volete* (1965). CPE-*Source*. Along with the Ashley work cited above, represents borderline improvisation with indeterminacy, depending upon performance circumstances.

Curran, Alvin. *Home-made.* CPE-*Source*.

Douglas, Bill. *Improvisations III* (1969). Recorded on Orion 73125.

Duckworth, William. *Pitch City.* CAP.

Erb, Donald. *Concerto for Percussion and Orchestra.* Merion Music. Recorded on Turnabout TV-S 34433.

Erickson, Robert. *Ricercar à 5* (1966). Okra Music.

Foss, Lukas. *Echoi.* Recorded on Helidon 2549001.

———. *Etudes for Organ.* CPE-*Source*.

———. *Fragments of Archilocos.* Recorded on Helidon 2549001.

———. *Music for Clarinet, Percussion and Piano,* 1961 (out of print). Recorded on RCA LSC-2558.

———. *Time Cycle.* Recorded on Columbia MS-6280.

Harris, Roger. *Kroma II.* CAP.

Hodkinson, Sydney. *Imagined Quarter* (1967). BMI Canada. Described as "an incentive for four percussionists."

Loudova, Ivana. *Chorale* (1971). Peters. Recorded on AWS-102.

Lutoslawski, Witold. *Concerto for Orchestra.* PWM. Recorded on London 6665. Utilizes overlapping improvisation for sound-mass constructs.

———. *Livre Pour Orchestra.* J. & W. Chester Ltd.

Oliveros, Pauline. *Outline for flute, percussion and string bass: an improvisation chart* (1963). Recorded on Nonesuch 71237.

Penderecki, Krzysztof. *Capriccio for Violin and Orchestra* (1967). Moeck. Recorded on Nonesuch 71201.

Reynolds, Roger. *Ping.* Peters. Recorded on CRI S-285. Interesting use of improvisation within limits.

Schafer, R. Murray. *Requiem for a Party Girl* (1966). BMI Canada. Recorded on CRI S-245.

Schuller, Gunther. *Concertino for Jazz Quartet and Orchestra* (1959). Recorded on Atlantic S-1359.

———. *Conversations.* Recorded by the Modern Jazz Quartet, Atlantic S-1345. These two works explicitly locate the influence of jazz on improvisation within traditional techniques, as does the Austin work cited above.

———. *Seven Studies on Themes of Paul Klee* (1959). Universal Edition. Recorded on RCA LSC-2879. Fully defined Third Stream.

———. *Transformation.* Recorded on Columbia WL-127.

Trythall, Gilbert. *Entropy* for Stereo Brass Improvisation Group and Stereo Tape (1967). Recorded on Golden Crest S-4085. Good combination of effects from improvisatory and set sources.

Winsor, Phil. *Orgel.* Carl Fischer.

Woodbury, Arthur. *Remembrances. CPE-Source.* Numerous improvisational sections which represent strong composer control and obvious knowledge of the outcome of their actions.

Mainstream's 5002 includes the live electronic improvisations of the *Musica Elettronica Viva* (Rome) and the AMM (London). Music of the New Music Ensemble is available on two discs from Source Records, Sacramento, Calif. (NME 101 and 102).

7 Indeterminacy

Background

William Hayes' *The Art of Composing Music by a Method Entirely New, Suited to the Meanest Capacity* (1951) describes a technique of composition by spattering notes onto staff paper by running a finger over a stiff brush dipped in ink. Mozart was known to have used dice-throwing to create music (*Musical Dice Game*, K. 294d). Other such indeterminate techniques have been attempted, even as early as eleventh- and twelfth-century treatises, but none with the vigor and philosophical implications of these "discoveries" since the late 1940s.

Beginning in the early fifties an affinity for chance techniques was developed with the operation of the *I Ching*, the English translation of which Christian Wolff had brought to Cage's attention at that time (his father Kurt Wolff being founder of the publishing house, Pantheon Press, which printed it). The *I Ching*, the first written book of wisdom, philosophy, and oracle (attributed to Fu Hsi, 2953-2838 B.C.), expresses directions of action as a result of six tosses of three coins (originally, the tossing of yarrow sticks). The example in figure 7.1 shows all combinations of ——— and — — with six tosses (heads = 2, tails = 3, the addition of points, if even, giving ———, if uneven— —). Having asked the question, "Should I use an example of the *I Ching* in this book?" and performing the required tosses, the author received the following answer (Chun) as a result: "Kun (indicates that in the case which it presupposes) there will be great progress and success, and the advantage will come from being correct and firm. (But) any movement in advance should not be (lightly) undertaken."

Definition

Experimental music, that is, actions the outcome of which are not foreseen, is more a philosophical than an audible phenomenon. Form, intended or not, is inherent in all matter and energy, and is therefore subject to analysis. It is impossible, without prior knowledge of the composer or work, to distinguish the intention or nonintention of the composer, unless the sounds or actions presented are obviously from another source (intentional or unintentional): for example, John Cage's *4'33"* (1952),

THE HEXAGRAMS, in the order in which they appear in the Yî, and were arranged by king Wăn.

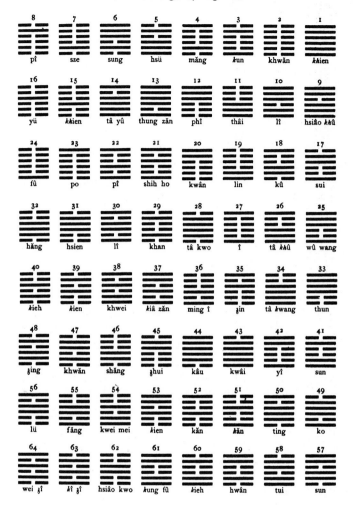

Figure 7.1. The Hexagrams from *I Ching*. (Permission for reprint granted by University Books, Inc., New Hyde Park, New York 11040. Copyright 1964.)

wherein the sounds presented are obviously of another source (nature or the audience itself), and therefore for the most part realizably unintentional except in concept.

It is with this latter idea, this psychoconceptual aspect, that the greatest single musical antagonism has been born. Audiences can be pre-

Figure 7.2.   John Cage. Photo: Dorothy Norman.

sented with highly organized and experimental compositions of the same general genre, instrumentation, and techniques, without reacting adversely. However, when prior knowledge exists, or when a work such as 4'33" is played and the audience *realizes* the unintention involved, the reactions can be much more violent. The struggle is with the *concept*, not the sounds. "Therefore my purpose is to remove purpose," spoke John Cage in a 1962 interview with Roger Reynolds.[1] The idea is to let sounds "happen," to free them from the composer's control. The religious implications are also noteworthy: can man learn to accept *all* sounds equally? Those which God or nature has created, and those which man has created unintentionally? Can he reject his ego and listen freely? This concept truly rejects the past twelve to fourteen centuries of Western thought; not the music itself, but the concept *of* that music.

Is man able to separate himself so completely from his acts, artistic or otherwise, through chance or "forced stupidity," to fully free sound rather than control it? It must be complete: any error in computation is as good as a thousand errors. That is, if *total* chance, *total* indeterminacy, is not possible, is it pointless to attempt merely to approach it? This

1. *Contemporary Composers on Contemporary Music*, Elliott Schwartz and Barney Childs, eds. (New York: Holt, Rinehart and Winston, 1967), p. 341.

question poses possibly the most serious and philosophical antithesis to indeterminacy. Cage has referred to his disappointment and compromise arising from the knowledge that he hasn't really "done it," but merely has been ". . . going along in that general direction."[2]

Indeterminacy is not a game or a passing fancy. It is *the* philosophical challenge to the aesthetics, art, and ego of history. Its antagonists are numerous (Hindemith refers to chance as "one of the ugliest modern musical diseases."[3]) However, what most antagonists (and some protagonists) fail to realize is that what must be dealt with is the *concept* of indeterminacy, *not* the sounds, *not* the forms, *not* the individuals involved. If it cannot be reckoned with in philosophical terms, then it will destroy (or possibly already has destroyed) the structure, terms, and aesthetics of music and art as contemporary Western civilization has come to know them.

Indeterminacy implies art as process. No beginning, no middle, no end; that is, no longer will "objects" of music exist in that sense, but each new performance, each new circumstance will create a continually variable process of ideas. As Cage has said, "If one is making an object and then proceeds in an indeterminate fashion, to let happen what will, outside of one's control, then one is simply being careless about the making of that object."[4] If art be process, however, then indeterminacy is the only viable way to proceed.

In "Indeterminacy," Cage notes that Bach's *Art of the Fugue* is an example of composition which is indeterminate with respect to its performance, based on lack of directions in regard to timbre, dynamics, sequence of the "determinate" notes, and duration, making available a wide range of possible realizations.[5] Indeterminacy philosophy must lie in a concept of disassociating man's significance as a creator, emphasizing the possibilities of man as creative performer/listener; understanding being something pedagogical and within the realm of language, not aesthetics.

The terminology surrounding chance operations involves certain basic American/European divisions. The term *aleatoric* (derived by Boulez from *aléa,* French for "chance") seems to be primarily a European concept which employs chance techniques within a controlled framework, therefore more related to improvisation than true indeterminacy. Of this, Morton Feldman has remarked: "This is true of Boulez. This is true of Stockhausen. You can see this in the way they have approached American

2. Ibid.
3. Ibid., p. 89.
4. Ibid., p. 345.
5. John Cage, *Silence* (Cambridge, Mass.: The M.I.T. Press, paperback edition, 1961), p. 35.

'chance' music. They began by finding rationalizations for how they could incorporate chance and still keep their precious integrity."[6] After reacting to the personality behind this statement, Boulez expanded on these basic differences between aleatoric and chance techniques:

G.W.: Feldman refers to "chance" here. Do you feel that you conceive of "chance" in the same way that, say, John Cage conceives of it?
P.B.: No, not at all. I find that so highly unproductive, because "chance" is not an aesthetic category. "Chance" can bring something interesting only one time in a million. . . . Most of the time you do not get that one time . . . and, if you do get it, you get it in the midst of a hundred thousand possibilities which are not interesting.
G.W.: Going to a "chance" concert, then, you feel would be like going to a baseball game, gambling for excitement?
P.B.: Yes, but even a baseball game has rules. Card games, which have much more chance, I suppose, still have rules. Can you imagine a card game with absolutely no rules?
D.C.: Like Mallarme saying, "A throw of the dice will not abolish chance," . . . you are saying that, while nothing can be totally chance, nothing can be totally without chance.
P.B.: Exactly. With the combination of the two, you must integrate, and it is much more difficult to compose in this way, integrating on a high level than in more traditional ways. Composing by chance is no composing at all. Composing . . . means to put things together. I am interested as to what chance sounds occur on the street, but I will never take them as a musical composition. There is a big difference between unorganized sounds and those placed within complete organization.[7]

The division between the American and European concepts of chance have grown deeper in the last several years. Pierre Boulez remarks: "Do you see what we are getting back to? Constantly to a refusal of choice. The first conception was purely mechanistic, automatic, fetishistic; the second is still fetishistic but one is freed from choice not by numbers but by the interpreter."[8] England's David Bedford and Brian Tilbury, however, have recently championed the American cause of experimental work in indeterminacy, mirroring in the late sixties much the same discoveries and excitement engendered by Cage and Feldman in the early fifties. Surviving, even thriving upon, the attacks from both here and abroad, the cause for freeing sounds continues.

Indeterminacy, as a step-by-step (even pedagogical) approach to erase or distribute that control over compositional elements which so many have fought to retain, must first transcend man's loss of individual and "racial" ego. As such, it is merely the first step to a far-reaching even-

6. Schwartz and Childs, *Contemporary Composers*, p. 365.
7. Galen Wilson and David Cope, "An Interview with Pierre Boulez," *The Composer* 1, no. 2 (September 1969):82-83.
8. Pierre Boulez, "Aléa," *Perspectives of New Music* 3, no. 1 (Winter 1964):42.

Figure 7.3. Morton Feldman.
BMI Archives. Used by permission.

tuality: rejection of *all* homocentered creativity, and acceptance of *all* of the life around us, with man no longer in control, no longer the creator or destroyer of images or ideals, real or imagined.

Composer Indeterminacy

Indeterminacy involves total lack of knowledge about the outcome of an action in respect to composition, performance, or both. A number of works are *indeterminate in respect to composition but determinate in respect to performance.* This is primarily music which is predictable before a performance but was composed with the use of some type of chance operations. Often these works come to the performer in very traditional notation. They always come to the performer in such notation implying *determinate* performance.

In his *Music of Changes* (1951), John Cage used twenty-six large charts indicating aspects of composition (duration, tempo, dynamics), following the *I Ching* procedure to "create" every aspect of the composition. Forty-three minutes (in music) and nine months later, *Music of*

Changes (every aspect except conception of which was based on coin tosses; a huge number) was completed. The restrictiveness of such rigid controls of composition technique (not unlike that of the twelve-tone school), and the dedication and care necessary for the creation of *Music of Changes,* cannot escape philosophical implications, regardless of intention. Possibly no other work in the history of music has received such exactness in its creation, its composer having purposely attempted to destroy his own control over it. Yet it shows little trace of either the composer or the *I Ching*: it is "merely" *sounds.*

Figure 7.4.   Iannis Xenakis. Photo courtesy of Indiana University.

The *stochastic* and mathematical approach to music as represented in the music of Iannis Xenakis is often deeply rooted in a chance framework: arbitrary materials are fed into an extremely determinate composition system, the resultant structure being composer indeterminacy written out in traditional notation for predictable results. Xenakis describes his concepts and procedures in his book *Formalized Music:*

As a result of the impasse in serial music, as well as other causes, I originated in 1954 a music constructed from the principle of indeterminism; two years later I named it "Stochastic Music." The laws of the calculus of probabilities entered composition through musical necessity.

But other paths also led to the same stochastic crossroads—first of all, natural events such as the collision of hail or rain with hard surfaces, or the song of cicadas in a summer field. These sonic events are made out of thousands of isolated sounds; this multitude of sounds, seen as a totality, is a new sonic event. This mass event is articulated and forms a plastic mold of time, which itself follows aleatory and stochastic laws. If one then wishes to form a large mass of point-notes, such as string pizzicati, one must know these mathematical laws, which, in any case, are no more than a tight and concise expression of chain of logical reasoning. Everyone has observed the sonic phenomena of a political crowd of dozens of hundreds of thousands of people. The human river shouts a slogan in a uniform rhythm. Then another slogan springs from the head of the demonstration; it spreads towards the tail, replacing the first. A wave of transition thus passes from the head to the tail. . . . The statistical laws of these events, separated from their political or moral context, are the same as those of the cicadas or the rain. They are the laws of the passage from complete order to total disorder in a continuous or explosive manner. They are stochastic laws.[9]

Some have argued that Xenakis's music is not indeterminate at all. Bernard Jacobson has written:

He uses chance, but his music leaves nothing to chance. This is not the paradox it might seem. To Xenakis—as indeed, to most philosophers—chance itself is a scientific concept. Central among the scientific laws he has applied to music is Bernoulli's Law of large numbers, which provides that as the number of repetitions of a given "chance" trial (such as flipping a coin) increases, so the probability that the results will tend to a determinate end approaches certainty.[10]

While many wonder why such determinate ends could not be achieved in more musical and less mathematical approaches, the enigmas around Xenakis and his ideas continue. His writings and the writings of those about him often contribute to these conflicts. The following is from a discussion between John Cage, Lukas Foss, and Iannis Xenakis:

Cage: I asked a Spanish lady scientist what she thought about the human mind in a world of computers. She said, "computers are always right but life isn't about being right." What do you say to that?
Xenakis: The opposite—life has reason and computers are often wrong.
Cage: You have been an architect and now you are a muscian. Are you going to go on to some other activity?
Xenakis: I'd like to but it is difficult.
Foss: Iannis, all the music of yours that I know is built on mathematical premise, mostly probability. Is there any aspect to chance that is not mathematical, that is, not probability theory?
Xenakis: All my music is not based on mathematics—there are parts of it which use mathematics. As to chance, it is not like dice or tossing a coin, this

9. Iannis Xenakis, *Formalized Music* (Bloomington: Indiana University Press, 1971), p. 9.
10. From the liner notes to Nonesuch Records H-71201 (*Akrata, Pithoprakta*).

is ignorance, as if there were impossibility of predicting. What does chance mean to you?

Foss: Anything I cannot control. You left architecture for music—why?

Xenakis: Mostly because architecture was a business and music is less business.

Foss: In order to compose you need time, solitude—what else?

Xenakis: To live in a big city.

Foss: If someone imitates you (I know of an instance) does it flatter you or make you angry or both?

Xenakis: I am angry . . . angry and depressed.

Foss: What did you want to be when you were a child?

Xenakis: An elephant.[11]

Dick Higgins's *Thousand Symphonies* involves the "machine-gunning" of one thousand pages of blank orchestra manuscript, the performance of which, though necessarily constituting some performer interpretation of the "holes," is basically determinate. Random number tables were used to construct *Indices* by Earle Brown, the result of which is a fixed relation of the materials and a determinate performance.

Performer Indeterminacy

Music which is *determinate in respect to composition but indeterminate in respect to performance* owes much of its development to the idea of "event." These works are "composed" in terms of individual sections or fragments yet mobile in the order of appearance, creating an unpredictability before and during performance.

The concept of sound-mass (see chap. 2), or the production of a vertical sound in which the individual components were inaudible or unimportant as entities in themselves, necessarily brought about a new consideration of sounds in horizontal relationships. With the occurrence of two sounds whose timbre, structure, and dynamics are so different as to avoid the traditional concept of melody, these entities become *events,* that is, equal in importance and not necessarily building to a climax or part of a cadence. The introduction of silence[12] as an integral part of a composition, to be treated as an equal with sound, becomes a help in identifying these events in time. The events become important in themselves, and contribute less to the phrase, period, or movement of the work. As these sounds separate, consideration of the significance of their order becomes immediately suspect; that is, if each "event," each unit, is predominantly important in itself, the order of these units becomes less and less important. This reflects much the same concept as a "mobile"

---

11. John Cage, Lukas Foss, and Iannis Xenakis, "Short Answers to Difficult Questions," *Composer* 2, no. 2 (September 1970):40.

12. Cage has often pointed out that "real" silence does not exist (see his book *Silence*). The author refers here to lack of intentional sound.

in art: that is, the shape, color, and design of each part is fixed, with the order and angle constantly changing.

Karlheinz Stockhausen's *Klavierstück XI, No. 7* (1957) is printed on a long roll (37 by 21 inches) and opened on a special wooden stand supplied with the score. It contains nineteen "events," which may be played in any order. Performer instructions require glancing at the score and performing whatever event may "catch the eye."

At the end of the first group, he reads the tempo, dynamic and attack indications that follow, and looks at random to any other group, which he then plays in accordance with the latter indications. "Looking at random to any other group" implies that the performer will never link up expressly-chosen groups or intentionally leave out others. Each group can be joined to any of the other 18: each can thus be played at any of the six tempi and dynamic levels and with any of the six types of attack.[13]

The composer allows that when a fragment is reached for the third time the piece is concluded. This would create anywhere from three fragments (the first one randomly observed three times in succession) to thirty-eight! (that is 38! —or 38 times 37 times 36 times 35 . . . etc. — a truly staggering number indeed: 10! is over 3.5 million).[14] This, along with the tempo, dynamic and attack variances, creates a work whose notes in terms of fragments are controlled by the composer, yet the resultant performance is totally unpredictable.

Figure 7.5 shows the score from measures 27 to 32 of Stockhausen's *Stop* (1965). This "Pariser Version" (the one shown in fig. 7.5—there is another version for full orchestra) is for eighteen performers in six groups (cued with the ◊ sign) of like timbres. This *recipe* work has determinate form (note the duration lengths at the top of each "measure") yet lacks "determinate" directions for performance ("noises" is hardly a predictable notation). The composer is obviously very much aware of the outcome in general terms of form, contrast, balance, and direction (note the occasional exact notation overlapping events) but extremely willing to allow performance unpredictability in terms of rhythm, entrance order, and pitch. This type of work, though very different from the *mobile* structures of his *Klavierstück XI, No. 7*, is still primarily composer-determined performer unpredictability.

Henri Pousseur's piano solo *Caractères* (1961) includes cutout windows and randomly placed score pages so that the order of the "events" is not composer-prescribed. Henry Cowell was among the first of composers to provide blocks of sound with which the performer constructed

---

13. From the composer's directions on the score. Universal Edition No. 12654 LW.
14. "!" here is not an exclamation point but rather a factorial sign in mathematics (the number preceding the sign multiplied by all those numbers in turn down to 1).

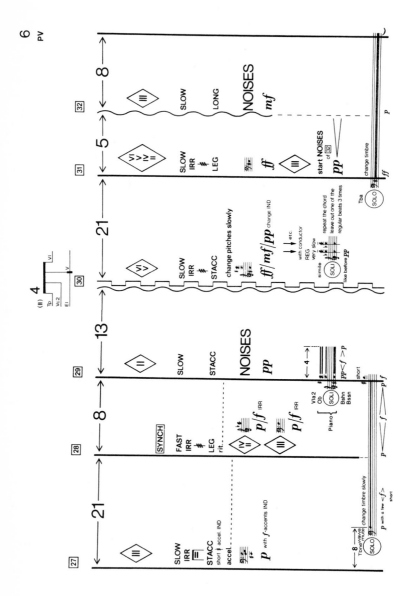

Figure 7.5. Karlheinz Stockhausen: *Stop.* © Copyright Universal Edition. All rights reserved. Used by permission.

the performance "form," in his *Mosaic Quartet* (1934). Affected by the mobiles of Alex Calder, Earle Brown has developed concepts of form and order in his music derived primarily from this "event" rationale. Referring to his *Available Forms I* and *II* (1961-62), Brown writes: "The title of the work refers to the availability of many possible forms which these composed elements may assume, spontaneously directed by the conductors in the process of performing the work. The individual musical events are rehearsed, but the performances are not."[15]

The antilyrical aspects of event concept represent one of the ideas most profoundly antagonistic to romantic thought. Barney Child's *Nonet* (*Source: Music of the Avant Garde* 3, no. 1 [January 1969]) includes an "event machine" (a numbered acetate overlay and two rotating color-coded discs) which provides the order, timing, and selection of events, each of which is provided by the composer. In Feldman's *Intersection 3*, the duration, number, and timbre of sounds are determined by the composer while the dynamics and range (*high, middle,* and *low* are the only terms given) are indeterminate during the performance situation.

John Cage's *Atlas Eclipticalis* (see fig. 7.6), first performed by the New York Philharmonic in 1962, includes the use of contact microphones placed in various locations on the instruments. Though somewhat graphic, this work is explicit in its pitch indications and directions of movement (a fact overlooked in the hissing of the arbitrary first performance). As is seen in figure 7.7, *34'46.776" for a Pianist* (1954) is also a graphic but explicit work.

Musical "games" (or "strategy") take a variety of forms (e.g., Subotnick's *Ritual* in chap. 5). Xenakis has characterized music detailed without in-performance "conflict" as *autonomous* (inclusive of most musics to the present day) and that music of games (introducing a concept of external conflict between groups or individuals in the performance situation) as *heteronomous* music. Xenakis's *Duel* (1958-59) comprises materials like that of the mobile structure: a set of six events, each written in the score in precise manner. Unlike mobiles, however, these strategic games employ definitive *tactics* with the events of length sufficient to permit interruption, and the choice of event a direct result of an "on the spot" performer decision. "At the end of a certain number of exchanges or minutes, as agreed upon by the conductors, one of the two is declared a winner and is awarded a prize."[16]

Roman Haubenstock-Ramati's *Mobile for Shakespeare* (for voice, piano, celeste, vibraphone, and three percussionists) is a prime example

15. From the program notes of the New York Philharmonic Society, February 1964.
16. Xenakis, *Formalized Music*, p. 122.

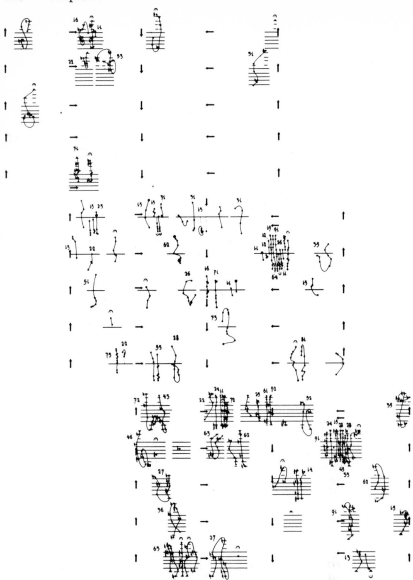

Atlas Eclipticalis, French Horn 5, Percussion 4, Cello 7, pages 245, 309, and 157

Figure 7.6. John Cage: *Atlas Eclipticalis, French Horn 5, Percussion 4,
Cello 7,* pages 245, 309, and 157.
Copyright by Henmar Press, Inc., 373
Park Avenue South, New York, N. Y.
10016. International Copyright Secured. All rights reserved. Permission
granted by the publisher.

Figure 7.7. John Cage: *34'46.776" for a Pianist*, page 50. Copyright by Henmar Press Inc., 373 Park Avenue South, New York, N. Y. 10016. International Copyright Secured. All rights reserved. Permission granted by the publisher.

of "mobile" type structure indeterminacy (see fig. 7.8). Each box gives a fairly straightforward, mostly traditionally notated (there are a few relatively explicit graphic symbols) fragment. The order of each box is not predetermined and therefore while the composer has indeed "composed" each note, the performances are quite different and unpredictable.[17]

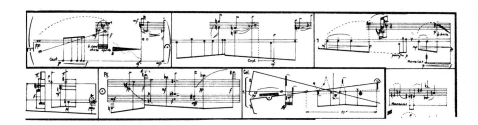

Figure 7.8. Roman Haubenstock-Ramati's *Mobile for Shakespeare*. © Copyright Universal Edition, 1968. All rights reserved. Used by permission.

Composer and Performer Indeterminacy

Music which is *indeterminate in respect to both composition and performance* is created by "chance" means which produce a "chance" score: at no time is there a predictable outcome. Christian Wolff's *Duo II for Pianists* (1958), for example, involves no score and all materials are indeterminate, the only indication for such being areas of limitation pro-

17. See the score for fuller explanation of complete performance.

vided by the composer (the use of pianos with no silences between performer responses). The work has no beginning or ending, these being
determined only by the situation under which performance takes place.

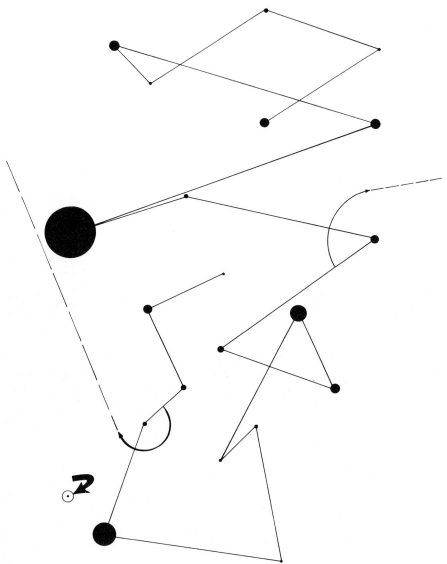

Figure 7.9.   John Mizelle: *Radial
Energy I*. Permission granted by
Source: Music of the Avant-Garde,
Composer/Performer Edition, Davis,
California.

Nam June Paik's *In Homage to John Cage* (1959) is equally indeterminate. In happening form, its first performance included Paik's leaping offstage to Cage's seat, removing Cage's jacket and, as Tomkins has it: "slashed his (Cage's) shirt with a wickedly long pair of scissors, cut off his necktie at the knot, poured a bottle of shampoo over his head, and then rushed out of the room."[18] Paik later telephoned the audience to let them know that the work was finished.

John Mizelle's *Radial Energy I* (see fig. 7.9) allows the greatest possible freedom in choice of sound sources, number of participants, location of performance, and interpretation (if any) of the score. In the sine chart and explanation accompanying the score, the composer describes in detail the silence periods between performances (six, seven, nine, twelve, fifteen, seventeen, eighteen, seventeen, fifteen, twelve, nine, seven, and six YEARS for the first phase of the chart, and the first point at which the piece may be concluded: i.e., one hundred fifty years). Other "complete" performances may last over 382 years, depending on initial performance time, with duration of the performances (between the periods of silence) computed by addition, squaring, cubing, etc., the

Figure 7.10.   Barney Childs. Photo credit: Mary Ellen Andrews.

18. Calvin Tomkins, *The Bride and the Bachelors* (New York: The Viking Press, 1965), p. 134.

initial performance duration (actual sound-producing performances could last over fifteen years). Likewise the area of performance could be expanded, as the composer states, "to other planets, galaxies, etc. When all of time and space are transformed into sound, the piece (and the Universe) ends."

Barney Childs' *The Roachville Project* (a sound sculpture for four to ten performers) verbally describes a situation in which performers *and* audience may create an instrument out of available materials and, during and after construction, improvise upon the realization in sound over which the composer has no control. Emphasis is directed *away* from sound and *toward* situation, theater, and total participation (see fig. 7.11).

Sylvano Bussotti's *Five Piano Pieces for David Tudor* (1959), on the other hand, reflects a totally graphic concept in which interpretation or noninterpretation is fully within the performer's realm (Xenakis uses standard music notation for most of his work, with performance predictability as exact as possible). The artistic drawings of Bussotti are conceived more within a visual than aural structure. The composer here becomes more an inciter than restrainer. Graphic scores such as this represent more than a breach with traditional symbols. Inherent in a nonsymbolic abstract representation is a concept of renewal of live creation. Bussotti's *Five Pieces* were performed in Los Angeles three times in one concert, by three different performers. More conservative members of the audience, obviously appalled by the lack of recognizable similarities among the performances in structure, length, instrumentation, or motive, reacted with real antagonism toward both performer and work. The problem here seemed to be rooted not in the sounds themselves, but in the categorization of who, in fact, is the creator of the sounds.

In reference to these performances Halsey Stevens has pointed out that:

. . . if Mr. Bussotti had wandered into the hall and didn't know what was going on, he would not have had the remotest idea that those three performances, or any one of them, might have been his own piece. They were so totally different in every respect that the only thing he could lay claim to was having designed the score, not to having composed the piece. Aleatoric music, it seems to me, as it is frequently pursued, is an amusing parlor game. . . .[19]

Egoless music, or music the composer of which has allowed unintentional or performer-initiated materials to be on equal or higher ground than himself, is only part of the point at hand. Had the sounds created during any one of these performances been recorded and subsequently

19. David Cope, "An Interview with Halsey Stevens," *Composer* 5, no. 1 (1973): 30.

"The Roachville Project"

4 to 10 performers, minimum duration 30 minutes.

Provide a great deal of material, most of which should be capable of soundproduction, either immediately (wires, pipes, blocks, tubes, containers, bits and pieces of musical instruments, junk, &c.) or potentially (material which when assembled or altered or worked with can be made, maybe, to produce sound in some fashion).

The piece begins with the arrival of the performers at the material. They begin to assemble the material, as they please, any way they wish, into a "musical instrument" of sorts. The complete construction is to be a unit—that is, separate people may work for a while on separate sub-units, but these must eventually be built into the complete construction. All that is necessary for assembly, finally, is ingenuity: the *means* of assembly (nails, staples, glue, string, sticky tape, leather straps, baling wire, rivets, &c.) are up to the performers. Performers may converse together concerning problems of assembly and sound potential, but this must be done very quietly, and other conversation is to be avoided; performers may test parts they are working on for sound as they are assembling (i.e. test string tension by plucking, test resonances by tapping, &c.) but this must also be done very quietly. At a stipulated time, or when all agree that the instrument is completed, the performers improvise music on it, for any length of time. The composition is finished with the completion, at a pre-arranged time or by agreement among the performers, of this "piece-within-a-piece." All material provided need not, or perhaps will not, be used. If passing members of the audience with to become performers they may, as long as the total working number of participants never exceeds 10.

Deep Springs
April 1967

*Roachville and White Mountain City were "settlements just over the White Mountain summit from Owens Valley. . . . A writer visiting there in 1864 tells all that we know of those would-be mining centers. The 'city' from which he wrote was on Wyman Creek, on the Deep Spring slope; its rival, Roachville, was on Cottonwood Creek, and was named by its proprietor, William Roach. . . ."

W. A. Chalfant, *The Story of Inyo*

Figure 7.11. *The Roachville Project* by Barney Childs. © Copyright Universal Edition, 1968. All rights reserved. Used by permission.

translated into traditional notation for performer "interpretation," with either or both of the composers' names attached, the same sounds would have resulted, but the antagonism would not have. Had the piece then been performed three times, only boredom would have resulted, this

being the substantive ideas rejected by the indeterminate composers presented here.

Figures 7.12 to 7.17 show the wide variety of notations John Cage
has used, and a cross section of the types of works he has composed.
Concert for Piano and Orchestra (fig. 7.12, Solo for Piano) was written
and first performed for the 1958 Cage Retrospective Concert in New York's
Town Hall, with the composer conducting. The staging included a large
battery of electronic equipment, with the conductor slowly bringing his
hands together over his head, in clocklike fashion, more to control the
duration of the piece than the individual events (which are more or less
indeterminate in sequence and number).

26'1.1499" for a String Player, 1955 (see fig. 7.13) is more graphic
and has recently been "realized" by Harold Budd for Bertram Turetzky's
Nonesuch recording of the work. Both *Variations I*, 1958 (see fig. 7.14) and
Fontana Mix, 1958 (see fig. 7.15) graphically plot the areas or physical
locations on which sound is to be made. The former belongs to a set of
works of which *Variations IV* (1963) involves the laying of the score
transparencies over a map of the performance area, determining not
what sounds will be heard, but where they will come from. The recording includes the strategic locations of the microphones throughout a Los
Angeles art gallery and, besides the various sounds of Cage at work with
electronic equipment, included the candid conversations of the audience-
performers. One microphone was placed outside the building to catch
street sounds. The final realization was composed when Cage, by splicing
and selecting, evaluated and manipulated the resultant tapes.

Possibly the most performed of his works, *Cartridge Music*, 1960 (see
fig. 7.16) employs a map translucent overlay to be placed on various
graphic charts in order to obtain an outline of the locations and directions
of movement of contact microphones on various performer-chosen objects.
Theatre Piece, 1960 (fig. 7.17), in the Cage "happening-type" tradition,
employs number charts significant both in their location graphically, and
their action representation.

Paintings (1965) by Louis Andriessen (fig. 7.18) is for recorder and
piano, and exemplifies a totally graphic indeterminate procedure. Even
with the instructions, the predictability of the performance is at a minimum. Neither the composer nor the performer is (or should be) expecting any distinct results except not-particularly-relevant sounds and
silences varying from one performance to the next.

Other composers employ varied degrees of *graphic* notations to
achieve equally varied ends. Anestis Logothetis's scores seem at first
glance to be totally works of visual art. If one reads carefully the instructions to his works, clues are found to at least partial determinacy

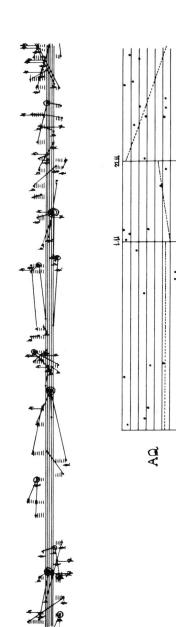

Figure 7.12. John Cage: *Solo for Piano* (*Concert for Piano and Orchestra*), p. 30. Copyright by Henmar Press Inc., 373 Park Avenue South, New York, N.Y. 10016. International Copyright Secured. All rights reserved. Permission granted by the publisher.

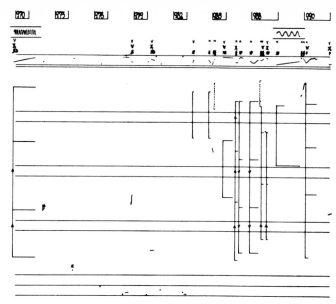

26'1.1499" for a String Player, pages 59 and 84

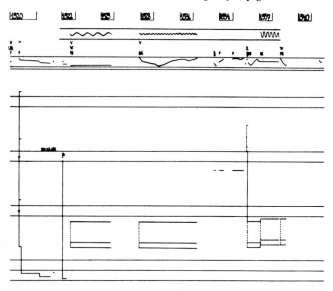

Figure 7.13.   John Cage: *26'1.1499"*
for a String Player, pages 59 and 84.
Copyright by Henmar Press Inc., 373
Park Avenue South, New York, N. Y.
10016. International Copyright
Secured. All rights reserved. Permission granted by the publisher.

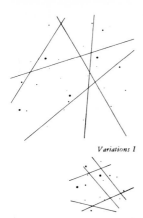

Variations I

Variations I. Extra Materials

Figure 7.14. John Cage:
Variations I. Copyright by
Henmar Press Inc.,
373 Park Avenue South,
New York, N.Y. 10016.
International Copyright
Secured. All rights re-
served. Permission granted
by the publisher.

Figure 7.16. John Cage:
Cartridge Music, superimpo-
sition using page 6. Copyright by Henmar Press Inc.,
373 Park Avenue South,
New York, N.Y. 10016. In-
ternational Copyright Secured
All rights reserved. Permission granted by the publisher.

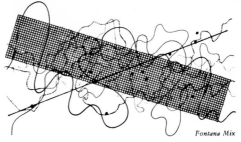

Fontana Mix

Figure 7.15. John Cage: *Fontana
Mix*. Copyright by Henmar Press
Inc., 373 Park Avenue South, New
York, N.Y. 10016. International
Copyright Secured. Permission granted
by the publisher.

Figure 7.17. John Cage:
Theatre Piece, Part VI (one of
eighteen unnumbered pages).
Copyright by Henmar Press
Inc., 373 Park Avenue South,
New York, N. Y. 10016. Inter-
national Copyright Secured.
All rights reserved. Permission
granted by the publisher.

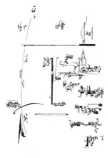

Figure 7.18. Louis Andriessen:
Paintings. Flötenpart, Blatt 1.
Copyright © 1965 by Herman
Moeck Verlag. Used with per-
mission. All rights reserved.

in terms of performer reaction and interpretation (e.g., *Clusters, Odyssee,* 1963, or *Ichnologia,* 1964). Robert Moran often utilizes *graphic* music, but like Logothetis, gives clear indication of instrumentation and "possible" interpretation of visual symbols (see *Four Visions,* 1963, in Karkoschka's *Notation in New Music,* or *Bombardments No. 2,* 1964, for one to five percussionists). Boguslaw Schäffer has pointed out a number of advantages of *graphic* music (at least for its usefulness to the mainstream of music) in his 1963 *Violin Concerto.* He has taken the cadenza (primarily thick black waves and twists of graphic art) and transcribed a possible traditionally-notated version. The result, based on a rather exact or literal translation, derives time in terms of left to right proportionality, pitch in terms of "up and down" relativity, and flow in terms of visual motion: an incredibly complex, nearly unplayable, concrete structure totally foreign to the direction of the work. The plasticity of the *graphic* notation allows for a free sound, every bit as complex as the traditionally notated one, yet without the studied end result (and, of course, without

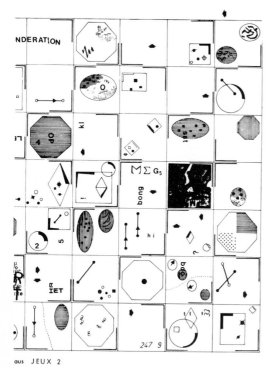

Figure 7.19.   Roman Haubenstock-Ramati:
Jeux 2 for two percussionists. © Copyright
Universal Edition, 1968. All rights reserved.
Used by permission.

the "performance-to-performance" variability). In Schäffer's *Concerto* one goes to hear the new elements, the surprises each performance offers and to judge a performer's mistakes or compare virtuosities in performance: it is indeed "composition in process."

Figure 7.19 is from Roman Haubenstock-Ramati's *Jeux 2*, 1968 (for two percussionists). Though a mobile in structure, the graphic nature of the fragments themselves makes determinacy on the part of the composer or performer an impossibility. Note the difference here between *Jeux 2* and *Mobile for Shakespeare*, 1959 (fig. 7.8), the latter having composer control over the fragments, thus falling distinctly under a different category (that of *performer-indeterminacy*). Possibly Europe's most experimental protagonist of the varieties of indeterminacy, Haubenstock-Ramati continues to explore the areas founded by John Cage, Earle Brown, and Barney Childs (unlike Stockhausen, for example, who now works with *conceptual music, antimusic,* etc., each new area as it comes into view).

The graphic score composer, however, cannot wholly escape a number of traditional performer approaches such as reading left to right, high pitch = up, low pitch = down, etc., and must either live with them or attempt to breach the gap by relenting to certain areas of determinacy while visibly rejecting others. William Bland's *Speed* (1968) for organ (see fig. 7.20) uses traditional left-to-right reading, up/down pitch level interpretation, and block-cluster chord representation, at the same time graphically encouraging nonpredictable performance possibilities (e.g., center triangle with ink blur). While manifestly constructing certain compositional elements, the composer has actively injected "live performance" situations with unpredictable results.

Other composers involved with indeterminate techniques include Folke Rabe, Bo Nilsson, Cornelius Cardew (though it should be noted that Cardew has recently disowned his former musics for that of "political-reformation" music), Roland Kayn, Allan Bryant, Joseph Byrd, Richard Maxfield, Philip Corner, Douglas Leedy, Robert Ashley, James Fulkerson, and many others.

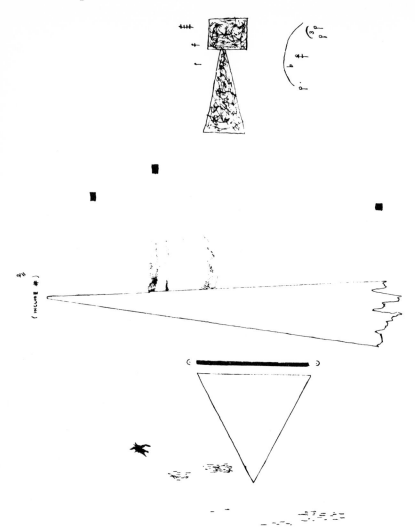

Figure 7.20.   William Bland: *Speed* for organ solo. (Published by Composers' Autograph Publications.)

Bibliography

*Further Readings**

*Addresses for record companies, periodicals, and music publishers mentioned in this Bibliography can be found in Appendix 4.

Behrman, David. "What Indeterminate Notation Determines." *Perspectives of New Music* 3, no. 2 (Spring 1964).

Boulez, Pierre. "Alèa." *Perspectives of New Music* 3, no. 1 (Winter 1964). A vivid attack on indeterminacy.

Brown, Earle. "Form in New Music." *Source* 1, no. 1 (January 1967). Excellent discussion of the "event" concept, mobile structure, and open form in music.

Cage, John. "History of Experimental Music in the United States." In *Silence: Lectures & Writings* (see details of publication in listing below). Examines the composers and ideas of "events" and musical continuity (especially Cowell, Wolff, Brown, and Cage on p. 71) and "getting rid of glue."

The John Cage Catalog. New York: C.F. Peters Co., 1962.

———. *M: Writings '67-'72.* Middletown, Conn.: Wesleyan University Press, 1973. Continuation of the "collected" forms of books that Cage has produced but begins to show a different side of Cage, especially in world and "semi-political" involvement.

———. *Notations.* New York: Something Else Press, 1969. A representation of 270 composers by single-page score reproductions.

———. *Silence: Lectures & Writings.* Cambridge, Mass.: The M.I.T. Press, 1966; first edition from Wesleyan University Press, 1961, paperback. See especially the article, "Indeterminacy."

———. *A Year from Monday.* Middletown, Conn.: Wesleyan University Press, 1967. (Note: The above writings of Cage are, in between the anecdotes, the most authoritative and explicit of materials available on the subject).

Cardew, Cornelius. "Notation-Interpretation, etc.," *Tempo* 58:24.

———, ed. *Scratch Music.* Cambridge, Massachusetts: The MIT Press; paperback edition, 1974. This is a book of scores and ideas by a great many composers involved with the *Scratch Orchestra* conducted by Cardew. Many of the works are indeterminate and quite a few belong to the antimusic category. Fascinating study for this area.

———. *Stockhausen Serves Imperialism.* London, England: Latimer New Dimensions Limited, 1974. Interesting account of this composer's about-face and repudiation of his own early works and those of other *avante-garde* composers.

Charles, Daniel. "Entr'acte: 'Formal' or 'Informal' Music." *Musical Quarterly* (1965). A good analysis of European/American differences over indeterminacy.

Childs, Barney. "Indeterminacy and Theory: Some Notes," *Composer* 1, no. 1 (June 1969):15. An excellent "objective" approach to the subject. See also his contribution "Indeterminacy" in Vinton's *Dictionary of Contemporary Music*. New York: E. P. Dutton & Co., 1974. A superb presentation of the definition, history, and aesthetics of the subject (although the dictionary itself does not discriminate between improvisation and indeterminacy).

Copland, Aaron. "The Music of Chance," In *Our New Music*. New York: W. W. Norton & Co., 1968. Quite fascinating though not as penetrating as the rest of the book is toward other areas of new music.

Dallin, Leon. *Techniques of Twentieth Century Composition*. 3rd ed. Dubuque, Iowa: Wm. C. Brown Company Publishers, 1974. This third edition has a chapter devoted to indeterminate procedures (pp. 237-49) which is a good introduction.

Feldman, Morton. "Predetermined/Indetermined." *Composer* (England, Fall 1966).

———. "Between Categories." *Composer* 1, no. 2 (1969):73. Fine article on *Time*, and indirectly relating to a philosophical construct of indeterminacy.

Fuller, R. Buckminster. *Operating Manual for Spaceship Earth*. Carbondale: Southern Illinois University Press, 1969. Though not directly relating to indeterminacy, this book indeed relates to Cage and more relevantly to the possible implosion of indeterminate procedures in relation to all events, musical and otherwise; truly fascinating reading (as are all his books).

Hansen, Al. *A Primer of Happenings and Time-Space Art*. New York: Something Else Press, 1968. Overlaps into media forms quite distinctly.

Higgins, Dick. *Postface*. New York: Something Else Press, 1964. Gives some very interesting ideas and insights into indeterminate concepts from a neo-Cage point of view though one must admit that his manner is much more violent in concept.

Kayn, Roland. "Random or not Random." *Horyzonty muzyki* (Cracow, 1966). Three lectures prepared for the Norddeutscher Rundfunk.

Kirby, Michael. *Happenings*. New York: E. P. Dutton & Co., 1965. Good historical survey of this indeterminate form.

Kostelanetz, Richard. *John Cage*. New York: Praeger, 1970. Superb in both text and pictures. A real must for any thorough study of Cage and indeterminacy.

———. *Master Minds*. New York: Macmillan, 1969. See especially "The American Avant-Garde," with part 2 relating particularly to John Cage and indeterminacy.

Layton, Billy Jim. "The New Liberalism." *Perspectives of New Music* 3, no. 2 (Spring 1964). Presents another attack on indeterminacy.

Logothetis, Anestis. "Gezeichnete Klänge." (*Neues Forum* 183, no. 1:177); "Kurze musikalische Spurenkunde." *Melos* 37:39.

MacKenzie, I. A. "The Critique." *Composer* 2, no. 4 (1971):92. Short but interesting letter to a critic with indeterminate procedures implied.

Reynolds, Roger. "It(')s Time." *Electronic Music Review* 7 (July 1968). "Indeterminacy: Some Considerations." *Perspectives of New Music* 4, no. 1 (Winter 1965). Both are exceedingly well written definitions of terms.

Tenney, James. *Meta ($^+$) Hodos: A Phenomenology of 20th-Century Music and an Approach to the Study of Form.* New Orleans, 1964. Related to a number of sections of this book in addition to indeterminacy.

Tomkins, Calvin. *The Bride and the Bachelors.* New York: Viking Press, 1965. Interesting biographical account of John Cage and related artists (Duchamp, Tinguely, and Rauschenberg).

Wolff, Christian. "On Form." *Die Reihe* 7:26. Relates to indeterminacy as does almost everything that Wolff writes, whether in words or music.

Xenakis, Iannis. *Formalized Music.* Bloomington: Indiana University Press, 1971. Quite interesting though mathematically complex even to those familiar with the subject.

Yates, Peter. *Twentieth Century Music.* New York: Pantheon Books, 1967. A bit outdated but does include some wonderful insights into Cage as well as into indeterminacy (see especially chaps. 30-32, pp. 303ff.).

Young, La Monte, and Mac Low, Jackson, eds. *An Anthology of Chance Operations.* New York: La Monte Young & Jackson Mac Low, 1963. Excellent source for readings in chance philosophy and procedures, and includes articles by Young, Mac Low, and Maxfield in particular.

Recordings and Publishers

Andriessen, Louis. *Ittrospezione II* (1963). Donemus. For orchestra.

———. *Paintings.* Belwin-Mills.

Ashley, Robert. *in memoriam Crazy Horse* (1963). Recorded on Advance 5.

———. *Wolfman* (1964). CPE-*Source* IV.

Austin, Larry. *Accidents* (1967). CPE-*Source.*

———. *Piano Set* and *Piano Variations* (1964). Recorded by Modern Jazz Quartet, Advance S-10.

Bedford, David. *Whitefield Music II.* For six to thirty-six players, concepts of music being for players not trained in music.

Boulez, Pierre. *Structures I for Two Pianos* (1952). Universal Edition. Incorporates the idea that works are no longer closed structures but are continually rewritten, i.e., always open.

Brown, Earle. *Available Forms I* and *II.* AMP. The former recorded on RCA Vics-1239.

———. *Four Systems.* Recorded on Columbia MS-7139. For amplified cymbals.

———. *Hodograph I.* Recorded on Mainstream 5007.

———. *Music for Violoncello, and Pianoforte* (1952). Recorded on Mainstream 5007.

———. *Quartet* (1965). Recorded on Mainstream 5009.

Bussotti, Sylvano. *Coeur pour Batteur—Positively Yes.* Universal Edition. Recorded on Columbia MS-7139.

———. *Frammento.* Ricordi. Recorded on Mainstream 5005.

———. *Five Pieces for David Tudor.* Universal Edition.

Cage, John. *Amores for Prepared Piano and Percussion.* Peters. Recorded on Mainstream 5011.

———. *Aria with Fontana Mix* (1958). Peters. Recorded on Mainstream 5005 (also includes works of Berio and Bussotti).

———. *Atlas Eclipticalis.* Peters. Recorded on DG-137009.

———. *Concert for Piano and Orchestra.* Peters.

———. *Cartridge Music* (1960). Peters. Recorded on Mainstream 5015.

———. *HPSCHD.* Peters. Recorded on Nonesuch 71224.

———. *Solo for Voice 2.* Peters. Recorded on Odyssey 32-160156.

———. *Fontana Mix.* Peters. Recorded on Columbia MS-7139.

———. *Indeterminacy.* (Cage, narrator; Tudor, piano). Recorded on Folkways 3704.

———. *Theatre Piece.* Peters.

———. *Variations I.* Peters. Recorded on Wergo 60033.

———. *Variations II.* Peters. Recorded on Columbia MS-7051.

———. *Variations III.* Peters. Recorded on DG-139442.

———. *Variations IV.* Peters. Recorded on Everest 3132.

———. *26'1.1499" for a String Player.* Peters. Recorded on Nonesuch 71237.

———. *34'46.776" for a Pianist.* Peters.

———. *4'33".* Peters.

Cardew, Cornelius. *Treatise* (1963-67). Buffalo: Gallery Upstairs Press. Graphic music for unspecified ensembles.

Feldman, Morton. *Chorus and Instruments.* Peters. Recorded on Odyssey 32-160156.

———. *Christian Wolff in Cambridge.* Peters. Recorded on Odyssey 32-160156.

———. *Durations.* Peters. Recorded on Mainstream 5007.

———. *False Relationships and the Extended Ending.* Peters. Recorded on CRI S-276.

———. *In Search of an Orchestration* (1967). Peters.

———. *Intersection 3.* Peters. Recorded on DG-139442.

———. *King of Denmark.* Peters. Recorded on Columbia MS-7139.

———. *Out of "Last Pieces."* Peters. Recorded on Columbia MS-6733.

———. *Viola in my Life.* Peters. Recorded on CRI S-276.

In addition, Odyssey 32-160302 includes the following Feldman works: *Structures, Three Pieces, Extensions I, Projections 4, Intersection 3, Two Pieces, Extensions 4,* and *Piece* (1957). All are published by Peters.

Foss, Lukas. *Geod.* Recorded on Candide 31042.

Haubenstock-Ramati, Roman. *Interpolation: a "Mobile" for Flute* (1,2,3), 1958. Universal Edition. Recorded on RCA Vics-1312.

———. *Jeux 2.* Universal Edition.

———. *Mobile for Shakespeare.* Universal Edition.
This composer's works are listed with examples in a brochure published by Universal Edition. Almost all deal in one way or another with indeterminate elements.

Higgins, Dick. *Thousand Symphonies.* CPE-*Source.*

Kayn, Roland. *Galaxis* (1962). Moeck. Uses variable instrumentation.

Logothetis, Anestis. *Ichnologia* (1964).

———. *Kulmination.* Edition Modern/Munich. Recorded on Wergo 60057.

———. *Labyrinthos* (1965). Universal Edition. For any soloists or any chamber orchestra.

———. *Odyssee* (1963). Universal Edition.

Mizelle, John. *Radial Energy.* CPE-*Source.*

Moran, Robert. *Bombardments No. 2.* Peters.

———. *Four Visions.* Universal Edition.

Mumma, Gordon. *Mesa for Cybersonic Bandoneon.* Recorded on Odyssey 32-160158.

Nilsson, Bo. *Reaktionen* (1960). Universal Edition. For four percussionists; uses open form structures.

Pousseur, Henri. *Caractères* (1961). Universal Edition.

———. *Votre Faust.* Universal Edition. Variable operatic fantasy.

Rabe, Folke. *Piéce* (1961). W. Hansen. For speaking chorus, done in collaboration with Lasse O'Mansson.

Schäffer, Boguslaw. *S'alto* (1963). PWM. For alto saxophone and orchestra.

———. *Violin Concerto* (1963). PWM.

Stockhausen, Karlheinz. *Klavierstück XI.* Universal Edition. Recorded on Phillips 6500101.

———. *STOP.* Universal Edition.

Wolff, Christian. *Duo, Duet* and *Summer.* Recorded on Mainstream 5015.

———. *Duo II for Pianists.* Peters.

———. *Edges* (1968). CPE-*Source.*

———. *For 1, 2 or 3 People.* Peters. Recorded on Odyssey 32-160158.

———. *Trio 2* (1961). Peters. Piano, four hands.

Xenakis, Iannis. *Akrata.* Boosey and Hawkes. Recorded on Nonesuch 71201.

———. *Duel.* Boosey and Hawkes.

8 Antimusic

Some Fundamentals

The end, toward which directions portend, is those sounds which destroy the mind (*danger music*), which don't exist (*minimal* and *concept music*), or which come about without the hand of man (*biomusic* and *soundscapes*). This is antimusic. It is (and must be) the final creation of the composer in search of the effective; the desperate search to invent that which truly has no alternative.

Antimusic is that concept beyond which no *avant-garde* can pass: the consummate effect. In search of the ultimate paradox goes the composer of antimusic, and nothing is exempt—suicide and death, danger—the rationality of it all escapes the essence of Western thought. It should be noted here that the term "antimusic" is in reality an "anti-Western-tradition-music." Many composers mentioned within this chapter indeed feel that their efforts are more "promusic" than that of mainstream composers.

The full focus of antimusic is intended to serve as a correlation with and the full integration of directions of new music with the world situation, which must exist if they are to have any plausible significance. To be specific, music has come full cycle: from the tower to the Colosseum. The ultimate freedom has, in antimusic, returned to the ultimate restriction: all is possible—consequently nothing is possible.

Art has been influential in many antimusics. Robert Rauschenberg, possibly more than any other artist (aside from Jackson Pollock and Marcel Duchamp), has sustained a creative "antiart" movement which has substantially affected a number of composers. His *Erased de Kooning Drawing* is exactly that: a de Kooning drawing (one he obtained directly from the artist himself) erased as completely as possible using a special selection of erasers collected by Rauschenberg. The act of "decomposing" the work of art becomes in this instance the "act" of creation (of a white sheet of paper only barely showing hints of lines, or even less—slight depressions in the paper where the original drawing once existed). If one can deal with art as *change*, beauty as totally *relative*, any *act* as plausibly artistic, then Rauschenberg's erasures can be (though are not necessarily) as significant as the original drawing. Whether one deals with it as such or not is of little consequence: it is antiart.

A similar act in music would not have quite the same effect. Indeed, however, one composer has come close but in an entirely different way. He has substituted an entire work of the past verbatim for his own. Paul Ignace indicates some of the rationale behind such actions in a recent letter:

When I was first asked to compose a piece for the orchestra I had no idea
what they wanted, except an experience of some kind. I wrote and asked for
a complete list of the other works included in concerts of the series, and
when I discovered that the concert preceding the night of my premiere included
Berlioz's *Symphonie Fantastique*, I made up my mind. I insisted that my
work be unrehearsed (there wouldn't have been much anyway, as those things
go) and that I would bring score and parts the night of the concert.
Imagine the shock when the conductor and players opened their music to find
the work that they had performed the night before . . . but they performed
it, much to the anger and horror of the audience and reviewers. They were
angry, of course, not at the sounds but at my plagiarism (legal, according
to copyright laws) but few realized they listened to the sounds in an entirely
new way—something very good, very creative, in my way of thinking.
No, I did not receive $$$ for my endeavor!
(The work, by the way, was titled *Symphonie Fantastique No. 2*.)[1]

Yehuda Yannay's *Houdini's Ninth* (1970) is antimusic theatre quite apropos of this genre. It is best summed up in this excerpt from *Stereo Review* by Bernard Jacobson:

A man cycled onto the stage, put a record of the (Beethoven) *Choral*
Symphony finale on a phonograph, and proceeded to mix some kind of culinary
concoction onto the surface of the actual disc, with bizarre effects on the
sound. This was interwoven with an episode involving a double-bass player in
a sort of straitjacket, and dominating the proceedings was a projection
of an incredibly stupid poem published in *Dwight's Journal of Music*,
Boston, on December 17, 1870. It was in honor of Beethoven's centenary, and
took a very encouraging view of his affliction of deafness: "A price how
small," it cheerily informed him, "for privilege how great, /When thy locked
sense groped upward and there/ The shining ladder reaching through
the air."[2]

Encouraged by the words of social philosopher Marshall McLuhan, R. Buckminster Fuller, and his own studies with Eastern philosopher Suzuki, John Cage has developed a personal philosophy expressed clearly in his sweeping statement: "Everything we do is music." His works encompass every aspect of the new concepts of the last twenty years: electronic, improvisatory, indeterminate, multimedia, exploration into new sounds, and antimusic. From his work in the thirties, when he originated

1. From a letter to the author.
2. Available on film from the composer: 4044 N. Downer Ave., Milwaukee, Wis. 53211 (as of December 1974).

the "prepared piano," to his present-day extension of multimedia "happenings," he has remained the remarkable enigma, his ideas and works amusing, startling, antagonizing, and somehow, also encouraging the worlds of music, dance, and art. If *change*, not idolatry, be the mark of greatness, then truly John Cage has reached this pinnacle. Nothing can or will be the same after him.

Aside from Cage, no other composer has achieved the shock value of, and relevance to, antiart, except perhaps La Monte Young. In particular, his *Composition 1960 #3*, in which the duration of the piece is announced and the audience told to do whatever they wished for the remainder of the composition; and *Composition 1960 #6*, in which the performers stare and react exactly as the audience would (as if the audience were the performers), are excellent examples of the "anti" aspect at work.[3]

Antiart is a returning to the soil. In the final analysis, even the term *theater* must exit the way the artificiality of art and music have. Again, works do not cease to exist, but a new awareness of *all* things, their disorder and order, their direction and nondirection in time, takes place. Man is no longer the center of the universe. He no longer attempts gymnastic representations of life, but becomes a part of it. Antimusic, like antijoke, relies on an audience expectancy of traditional forms; funny because it isn't funny, music because it isn't music: inherently temporary as awareness increases, constantly inevitable as all meaning requires opposites for significant identity.

Critics of these and other antimusics address themselves to the "dead end" and "pointless" philosophical ends implied. To these, I. A. MacKenzie has replied:

Art is imitation, repetition, memory, or rejection of life. Nothing is created by man, just recreated: a storeroom to collect the bits and pieces of the whole he feels worthy of saving, to be brought to life again whenever the need occurs, but never as good as the original. Art exists only as a refuge against new experience, un-recreated experience with reality: second-hand living.
The terms "musician," "painter," "writer," merely break these imitations down further for easier construction, assimilation and comfort. I am none of these.
I am not an artist. I do not imitate, or need of developing [sic] a memory with art for a thousand million possibilities of the present confront me, and I don't want that number diminished by one.
I am a mapmaker, a suggester of possible routes for those interested in experiences with what has already been created—everything. I am similar to the "artist" in that I do not create, dissimilar with him in that I do not pretend to.

3. Barney Childs discusses these works and others in an excellent article, "Indeterminacy and Theory: Some Notes," *The Composer* 1, no. 1 (June 1969):15-34.

Untouched by style, convenience, or tradition, the elements I observe
(not manipulate) I discovered, but only for myself and my discovery has style,
convenience just as yours.
I do nothing that anyone else could not do easily and do not pretend to.
I only give directions when someone wishes them and would be happy to stop
anytime. . . .
Everything exists: why should I mechanically alter one thing into another,
one thought into another? All exist—it is much more—to find the original.[4]

With these basic concepts and experiments, a transcendental form of
expression has emerged outside the realm of the arts: a communication
based more directly on the audience than on the creator, often philosophically—more often theatrically—directly antagonizing all possible reason and experience of man. Antimusic, antiart is *necessary, important,* and
contributive to art and man. It may be the flat tire which could possibly
spell an accident, or annihilation, but more often indicates care and understanding in progressing without artificial values or misdirected definitions
of terms: an annoyance which must be dealt with.

Cage speaks of this in *A Year from Monday*: "Art's in process of coming into its own: life."[5] and "We used to have the artist up on a pedestal.
Now he's no more extraordinary than we are."[6] Tzara states: "Art is not
the most precious manifestation of life. Art has not the celestial and
universal value that people like to attribute to it. Life is far more interesting."[7]

Danger Music

The history of *danger musics* is long indeed, and if one follows Paul
Nougé's thinking in *Music is Dangerous*,[8] all music has such potential.
While, as he points out, we may use it for "relaxation," "forgetting" or
"pleasure" it . . . "probably entails serious consequences."[9] This fascinating book describes a number of accounts of man's unfortunate encounters with the dangers of music:

4. I.A. MacKenzie, as paraphrased by David Cope in *Notes in Discontinuum* (Los
Angeles: Discant Music, 1970), p. 2.
5. John Cage, *A Year from Monday* (Middletown, Conn.: Wesleyan University
Press, 1967), p. 6.
6. Ibid., p. 50.
7. Robert Motherwell, *The Dada Painters and Poets: An Anthology* (New York:
Wittenborn, Schultz, Inc., 1951), p. 248.
8. Reprinted in *Soundings* as Book I in 1973. It first appeared in *View Magazine*,
December 1946 and Spring 1947 issues, but was originally written in 1929. Translation here is by Felix Giovanelli.
9. Ibid., p. 11.

Sometimes we find peculiar stories in a newspaper. A few weeks ago, a young American went home after coming out of a performance of *Tannhäuser*, and killed himself; not without having first written a note in which he explained that where Tannhäuser had weakened, he, yes he, would set a better example of courage and grandeur.[10]

Most current *danger musics* involve a more direct composer attack on the performer or spectator (e.g., Nam June Paik's *Danger Music for Dick Higgins* with the score reading: "Creep into the Vagina of a living Whale.").[11]

Art has certainly had a direct influence on *danger music* as it has in all areas of antimusic. Ay-o, for example, has created a number of finger boxes each containing a substance unknown to the "spectator." The art experience can only be obtained by placing one's fingers into these small creations some of which contain felt, fur, and similar "pleasantries." On the other hand, some contain razor blades, broken glass, and pocket knives. "Chance" has a new dimension here as one must certainly weigh his odds against the possible "curricular" losing of a small member of his body.

Though blood (and even death) are not unknown to *danger musics*, seldom do these occur as a direct result of composer notation. They rather occur as an indirect result of freed parameters so that "accidents" can occur or are welcomed. Such was the case of two happenings in 1962: the first involved a somewhat "bloodied" Robert Whitman at Bennington College; the second a more serious occasion of a woman spectator/performer falling from a window down a number of stories and eventually through a glass roof at an Al Hansen happening.

The environment around us provides another source of danger: sound pollution. While discussed in more depth later in this chapter under *soundscapes*, the aural dangers of even the average household cannot escape the artist's cognizance: turn the dial of a radio an inch too far to the right and a good percentage of one's hearing can easily be destroyed.

Robert Ashley's *Wolfman* (1964) needs *danger music* classification. Through use of a prerecorded tape and a voice "screaming" through a microphone involving electronic feedback, all turned to the highest possible level, the work easily reaches decibel counts above human ear danger level. The recording of this work, with instructions "to be played at the highest possible volume level" indeed constitutes ear annihilation to the uninitiated in a small "live" room.[12]

10. Ibid., p. 11.
11. See John Cage's *Notations* (New York: Something Else Press, 1969), unpaged, for a copy of the score in full.
12. *Wolfman* is published in *Source: Music of the Avant-Garde* 2, no. 2 (July 1968). Both the score and the recording are available there.

With 120 decibels the pain threshold for the average person, it is no wonder the artist has investigated the area of aural damage: even aside from 140-decibel "rock concerts," one can easily achieve his own *danger music* by stepping onto a busy downtown street.

Other musics directly attack the situation with little other than aggressive annihilation in mind. Dick Higgin's "*One antipersonnel type-CBU bomb will be thrown into the audience*" is simple but exact in notation, and the sound and audience reaction predictable.[13]

Antimusic is not sound; it is philosophy. The sounds, the lights, the actions are no longer important except in their conception. The arts have truly merged with reality. Antimusic is as the term denotes: war with music. War with the sanctity of sensual isolation; sound cannot be separated from the essence of all arts, all life functions. Daniel Lentz's comments in the Coda of his *Skeletons Don't Say Peek* (part of Harold Budd's *California 99* [1969], the instrument parts of which were composed by Turetzky, Oliveros, Austin, Childs, Lunetta, Mizelle, and Sherr) explicitly attack the hierarchy of traditional concert and instrument performance routine:

I too am sad. In fact, I am very sad. Men are still fighting wars and playing music. Some are guerilla wars, and some are guerilla compositions. But they are, nevertheless, war and music. They are fought with weapons and instruments. There is so little difference. One type is used for the defense of an army or nation; the other, for the defense of a vestigial culture. Do we need the protection of general and composers? Do we need their incredibly scary anti-ballistic-missile systems and synthesizers? Shouldn't we attempt their destruction, before they destroy us? From whom are they protecting us? From the Russians? The Princetonians? What, in the late-middle 20th century, does weaponry have to do with music? Can we eliminate one without first eliminating the other? Won't the metaphor be too powerful until it is taken away? Has there ever been an instrument built which wasn't used? Couldn't the players you saw in action tonight just as well have been aggressive soldiers of war? Did you watch closely their gestures? Is there a real difference between them and the Special Forces? Are they not identical mentalities? They are out to kill us and you sit there waiting. Are you all crazy? Can't you see, nor hear? But wait . . . don't blame the players. We are only cogs in the great hierarchy. We follow directions. The artistic generals tell us what to do and when to do it and the manner in which it is to be done. They are not even specific. Aren't they kind, as they destroy us? We are like you: just poor citizens caught up in the immense musical-industrial complex. Sure, if you threaten us or our friends, we will play for you. We have no recourse but to protect our "raison d'être."

Prior to this final "performer" announcement, all the instruments have been taken from the performers, placed in front of the piano, and *saluted.*

---

13. Published in *Source* 3, no. 2 (July 1969):5.

The act of not playing, the drama of attacking the performance istuation, are foremost in concept: acts which, without question, are directed at eliminating all vestige of traditional (and, for that matter, nontraditional) equipment, housing, instruments, and concepts.

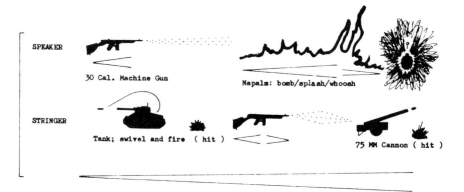

Figure 8.1.   Daniel Lentz: *Anti Bass Music,* p. 11.

Daniel Lentz's works are often antiwar as well as antimusic. *Anti Bass Music,* for example (see fig. 8.1), employs a number of notations used to best relate to the resultant sound, which brings to the level of equals the concert situation and a battlefield. The work is supplied with four optional endings (which may be performed in multiples, that is, more than one ending may be employed) which include a reading of a list of American composers not killed in Viet Nam, and the use of twenty-five to one hundred laughing machines. Thoroughly antagonistic to the traditions of both art and war, this work graphically and theatrically expresses the composer's intention without restriction.

Minimal and Concept Music

Minimal and *concept musics* are so closely related and so often resemble one another that separation becomes impossible (though both deserve distinct comments). Minimal art is the closest "art" relative to *minimal music.* Works such as Robert Rauschenberg's *White Paintings* (canvases covered as evenly as possible with white paint) are, for example, clearly related to such minimal works as John Cage's classic: *4'33".*

4'33" received its first performance in August, 1952, at Woodstock, New York by pianist David Tudor. Unfortunately, the brilliance of Tudor (using a stopwatch, he covered the piano keyboard at the beginning of each movement, playing nothing, but timing the silences of each period marked by Cage in the otherwise blank score) had the adverse effect of limiting this work to one for piano, which in fact (if one checks the score itself) it is not. Regardless of the composer's intention, then, the work has yet to reach its full potential. The title ("for any instrument or combination of instruments") makes realization practical on almost any conceivable plane of sound or nonsound. Virtually anything with a total duration of four minutes and thirty-three seconds (and movements of one minute, forty seconds; two minutes, twenty-three seconds; and thirty seconds respectively) could successfully serve as a realization of the score, from thinking-in-a-bathtub to silence by a symphony orchestra.[14] Cage has clarified the concept behind such works:

. . . where it is realized that sounds occur whether intended or not, one turns in the direction of those he does not intend. This turning is psychological and seems at first to be a giving up of everything that belongs to humanity— for a musician, the giving up of music. This psychological turning leads to the world of nature, where, gradually or suddenly, one sees that humanity and nature, not separate, are in this world together; that nothing was lost when everything was given away. In fact, everything is gained.[15]

The linkage between Rauschenberg's *White Paintings* and *4'33"* becomes apparent when one realizes that in the former the shadows of spectators, variance of lights, colored reflections, etc., turn the seemingly blank canvas into a veritable mass of visual activity. In the latter, the coughs, laughter, and other audible movements of the audience as well as the extraneous sounds from without the performance area become, in fact, the work. In both cases the act of the creator is minimal *and* conceptual: herein we see the great similarities between the two ideas.

In their extremes, the differences become more apparent. Minimal music (most often minimal in materials and not duration, as will be seen) is clearly defined in the works of La Monte Young with his *Compositions of 1960* (e.g., *Composition 1960 #7* which contains only the notes B and F♯ with the instructions: to be held for a "long time"; and *Composition 1960 #10*: "draw a straight line and follow it.")[16] and many others of that same year:

In 1960, at Berkeley, he presented a composition which consisted of turning loose a jar full of butterflies (they made a sound however inaudible). . . .[17]

14. This work is published in *Source: Music of the Avant-Garde* 1, no. 2 (July 1967): 46 ff.

15. John Cage, *Silence* (Cambridge, Mass.: The M.I.T. Press, paperback edition, 1961), p. 8.

16. A great deal of insight and material on and by La Monte Young can be had by reading *Selected Writings* by La Monte Young and Marian Zazeela (Munich: Heiner Friedrich, 1969).

17. Richard Kostelanetz, *The Theatre of Mixed Means* (New York: Dial Press, 1968), from the article (first page) on La Monte Young.

Figure 8.2.   Copyright © La Monte
Young & Marian Zazeela 1971.
Courtesy: Heiner Friedrich. (Photo
credit: Robert Adler.)

Others of that same year include his famous (infamous) "line piece":

My "Composition 1960 No. 9" consists of a straight line drawn on a piece
of paper. It is to be performed and comes with no instructions. The night I
met Jackson MacLow we went down to my apartment and he read
some of his poems for us. Later when he was going home, he said he'd write
out directions to get to his place so we could come and visit him sometime.
He happened to pick up "Composition No. 9" and said, "Can I write it here?"
I said, "No, wait, that's a piece. Don't write on that." He said, "Whadaya
mean a piece? That's just a line."[18]

Minimal music is as well very apparent in the music of Harold Budd
(especially: *Lovely Thing* (*Piano*), in which one chord is attempted many
times over a period of fifteen to twenty minutes, the performer trying
to play it as softly as possible; *One Sound* for string quartet; and *The
Candy Apple Revision* (1970), which states simply, "D-flat Major"). In
a letter to the author, Budd remarks:

18. Young and Zazeela, *Selected Writings,* unpaged (from the Lecture 1960, copyright 1965 by the Tulane Drama Review).

Ever since (a long time ago) I've pushed and pushed towards zero:
Running it all down, a kind of on-going process of removal. There's an enormous
difference, by the way, between Monotony and Boredom. Boredom, it
seems to me, is trying to make something interesting. Monotony is making
nothing interesting. And insofar as I feel all art to be utterly worthless (no
redeeming social values), I'm interested in that what I do is pretty—
("Terrifying," "Gripping," "Sensitive," "Relaxing," "Hypnotic," "Spiritual"
—all to the side for a moment) an existential *prettiness;* a kind of High-Art
Uselessness. . . .

A great number of minimal musics actually seem *maximal* in nature
(particularly in duration). La Monte Young's more recent New York City-
based *Dream Houses* (1968-   ) are media works of great duration (Alex
Dea singing, Jon Hassell on horn, David Rosenboom, viola, and De Fracia
Evans working slide projections). Like most minimal works these contain drones and slowly overlapping (focusing in and out) projections:
a minimum of material. Many of these works find precedent in Erik
Satie's *Vexations.* This 32-bar piece is to be played softly 840 times. Satie's
musique d'ameublement (1920) likewise gave impetus to minimal musics.
This "furnishing music" co-composed by Satie and Darius Milhaud
was played during intermission and the program announced: "We urge
you to take no notice of it and to behave during the intervals *as if it did
not exist.*"[19] Building on drones and/or slowly overlapping motives creating an ever-changing but slowly evolving *somnambulistic state* are
composers such as Charlemagne Palestine, Yoshima Wada (whose large
horns created from "plumbing pipes" are equally interesting), Max Neuhaus (whose underwater work, *Water Whistle,* utilizing 8-10 water driven
whistles which can be heard only if you are submerged in the same water
as the whistles: as well an overlap with *danger music*), Karlheinz Stockhausen (e.g., *aus den Sieben Tagen* [1968]: a verbal score containing
only very brief performance directions such as "play single sounds with
such dedication until you feel the warmth that radiates from you—play
on and sustain it as long as you can."), Frederic Rzewski (most notably
Coming Together, 1972), and Philip Glass (*Music in Fifths* and *Music in
Similar Motion,* both 1969). Philip Corner is especially noted for his work
with minimal concepts often lasting evenings, at other times lasting brief
seconds (of note here is his *One Note Once* which is indeed just exactly
that; the instrumentation being flexible). His *Metal Meditations* (often
collaborations with others involved in the *Sounds out of Silent Spaces*
series in New York City: Carole Weber, Julie Winter, Elaine Summers,

19. Pierre-Daniel Templier, *Erik Satie,* trans. Elena French and David French 1932.
(originally published by Presses Universitaires de France, Cambridge, Mass.: The
MIT Press, 1969), p. 45.

Anna Lockwood, Alison Knowles, Daniel Goode, and Charles Morrow, among others) are evening-long events involved with composer-constructed and traditional instruments struck softly with intense aural experience invited. These meditations also involve "total experience" with "ritual food events," slide projections, and lights. Corner's *One Note Once,* Cage's *4'33"* and Young's *Compositions of 1960* all approach the ultimate minimal structure: 0 duration, 0 instruments, 0 performers, 0 audience, etc.

As the anticomposer/artist progresses towards this zero state, "no-art," the circle will become complete. No further direction is possible except to begin anew the awareness of sound, the freshness of simplicity ungarnished by the vanities of highly ordered, monumentally structured "masterpieces." Many composers feel that the *avant-garde* as such is dead, and that the works in the 1960s point to a direction of return, of simplicity, in short, a return to the foundations of sound itself: pitch, duration, and silence. These composers and their works no longer achieve the "shock" immediacy and notoriety that *avant-garde* works of the 1950s characteristically received, nor the pretentious complexities of systems and scientific paraphernalia so in evidence with more mainstream academic-based composers. The "return" is an intellectual one: that is, not made without the careful consideration, and as a result, of a culmination of the many varied influences of a century of quick changes. In a sense it represents, not the "newest of the new," but the "oldest of the old."

Many of these works deal with tonal and/or modal formations and older instruments (gongs, etc.). Tonal and modal sounds abound in Terry Riley's *In C* (1964) which, utilizing a set of overlapping motives repeated at each performer's will, sets up a clear C-major tonality moving over a period of 45 to 90 minutes from C to E to C to G. Many of his other works evolve similarly: *Keyboard Studies* (1965), *Poppy Nogood and the Phantom Band* (1968), and *A Rainbow in Curved Air* (1969) are excellent examples.

Other composers using tonal materials include James Fulkerson (notably *Triad* which is a C-major triad performed over a 12-20 hour period), and Robert Moran (notably *Illuminatio Nocturna:* the building of a C-rooted major thirteenth chord softly sustained over a very long period of time). Similar in length and procedures but different in materials (not tonal or modal but more oriented in gradual changes in *time*), are the works of Steve Reich: *It's Gonna Rain* (1965), *Violin Phase*, and *Piano Phase* (both 1967), and *Pulse Music* for phase-shifting gate, an instrument invented by the composer (1968-69), are the most notable. Karlheinz Stockhausen's *Mikrophonie I* (1964) uses only one sound source, a large (about six feet) tam-tam upon which the performers manipulate the various verbal instructions of the score, "scraping, trumpeting," and so on *Concept music*, though often evident as an overlapping of many of the aforementioned works, is also occasioned by clearcut extremism (more powerful and often more interesting in concept than in the performance situation—if there is one—itself). Eric Andersen's *Opus 48* ("*Which turns anonymous when the instruction is carried out*") is sent through the mail on a piece of cardboard which states in total: "Place the chosen tautology." This is *concept art* (implication of music not being present). Tom Johnson, in his book *Imaginary Music*, includes a number of nonplayable concept pieces.[20] His *Celestial Music for Imaginary Trumpets* (see fig. 8.3) is clearly *concept music*, as performance is impossible; one is able to only "conceptualize" or imagine the work. Robert Moran's *Composition for Piano with Pianist* states: "A pianist comes onto the stage and goes directly to the concert grand piano. He climbs into the piano, and sits on the strings. The piano plays him."[21] This is likewise conceptual in character and, as is often the case, *message* becomes more important than any "real" act of sound production.

Concept philosophy is often implied only in the score and is not "real" to the audience. *Accidents* (1967) by Larry Austin, for example, contains instructions in which the pianist is given gestures to perform in the course of which he is to avoid creating sounds. The speed of performance make accidents in performance unavoidable. As if repenting his sins, the performer is requested to return to each gesture in which an accident occurred (i.e., a sound was made) and repeat that gesture until it is completely error-free (i.e., no sound has occurred).

The New York-based movement *Fluxus* (which included Paik, Young, Dick Higgins, Eric Andersen, Thomas Schmit, Jackson MacLow, and George Brecht) has represented the basic directions in this area for a number of years, finally becoming a publisher of art objects. Blank structures become the primary objectives and concepts in the experiments of these composers, poets, and artists. Often these works contain not the slightest hint as to what action is intended or what materials are to be used.[22]

Biomusic

Biomusic (music created by natural life functions rather than by necessarily conscious attempts at composition) has taken a number of

20. Tom Johnson, *Imaginary Music* (New York: Two-Eighteen Press [P.O. Box 218, Village Station, New York, N.Y. 10014], 1974).
21. Published in *Soundings* 1:44.
22. Other *Fluxus* movements have arisen in other countries, including Japan (Takehisa Kosugi, Chieko Shiomi) and Germany.

Figure 8.3.   Tom Johnson: *Celestial Music for Imaginary Trumpets.* © Copyright 1974 by Tom Johnson. All rights reserved. Used by permission. From *Imaginary Music* by Tom Johnson, Two Eighteen Press, N.Y.C.

very interesting turns in recent years. A number of composers have become interested in "brain-wave" music. Since human (and, for that matter, other advanced animals') brains function with bits of electric currents, it becomes a "natural" to attempt to amplify such functioning with the final product to be *active* control of sound by thinking in certain ways. By using these amplified currents as control voltages on synthesizer functions (utilizing normal electronic music gear such as oscillators, filters, etc.) the brain can indeed directly control sonic output.

The results of "brain-wave" music have brought conflicting ideas to the front. Stockhausen has reported:

. . . I attended a concert in which David Tudor, together with a composer at Davis, California, where I taught for six months, were performing a piece with "brain waves." The performance, in the beginning, seemed to be very magic-like, a table lifting society, and it seemed to promise quite a lot because of the way they were watching and looking at each other. The speakers' cardboard membranes were pushing the air, and these pulsations— a kind of colored low noise—were produced by the performers' brain waves. It's the same effect as if air were being pumped into a tire. So what? There's a certain periodicity which becomes more or less irregular, maybe interesting for doctors.[23]

Composer David Rosenboom has developed procedures far more sophisticated than those described by Stockhausen.[24] All success, of course, remains in the "heads" of the *performers* and their necessarily prac-

23. Jonathan Cott, *Stockhausen* (New York: Simon and Schuster, 1973), p. 43.

24. Prevalent in performances on such as the David Frost television show and others on NET (early 1970s).

ticed art of controlling such waves for more than gymnastic presentations.

Possibly one of the most fascinating areas to be uncovered under the heading of *biomusic* is that of the sounds of the humpback whale. At first glance seeming to be a preposterous joke, initial hearing proves quite the contrary; indeed these advanced mammals are highly creative:

Quite apart from any esthetic judgement one might make about them, the sounds produced by Humpback whales can properly be called songs because they occur in complete sequences that are repeated. . . . Humpback whale songs are far longer than bird songs. The shortest Humpback song recorded lasts six minutes and the longest is more than thirty minutes.[25]

Not only have recordings and tapes of the "songs" of the humpback whale become popular in and of themselves, but equally impressive is their ability to inspire human composers with their spirit. George Crumb's *Voice of the Whale* (*Vox Balaenae*, 1971), in the composer's words, ". . . was inspired by the singing of the humpback whale, a tape recording of which I had heard two or three years previously."[26] Likewise composers like Allen Strange and Gregory Allan have completed works influenced by this most highly developed of water mammals.

Works involving a "rediscovery" of bioenvironmental sounds include Pauline Oliveros's *Sonic Meditation XIII:*

Energy Changes
(for Elaine Summers's movement meditation, Energy Changes)
© Copyright 1974 by Smith Publications. Used by permission.
Listen to the environment as a drone. Establish contact mentally with all of the continuous external sounds and include all of your own continuous internal sounds, such as blood pressure, heart beat and nervous system. When you feel prepared, or when you are triggered by a random or intermittent sound from the external or internal environment, make any sound you like in one breath, or a cycle of sounds. When a sound or a cycle of sounds, is completed re-establish mental connection with the drone, which you first established before making another sound or cycle of like sounds.

In a slightly different manner, but definitely *biomusic*, Yehuda Yannay's *Bugpiece* involves yet another life form in the aural framework of, in this case, the concert hall. The work uses "live notation" in the form of:

. . . one beetle, one centipede, and five or six ants. These insects were in a real sense the "composers" and conductors, even if Yannay did set up the parameters as to how the chance operations would work. All the lights in the auditorium were turned off, the overhead projector was turned on so the audience and performers (with their backs to the audience) could see the bugs running around in a plastic box set on the projector. Different

25. Liner notes on Columbia ST-620, "Songs of the Humpback Whale."
26. Liner notes on Columbia M-32739.

Figure 8.4. "Training of musical consciousness is a large order." Composer Pauline Oliveros, assoc. professor, Music Dept. UCSD. Photo credit: Becky Cohen, Del Mar, Calif.

areas of the "playing field" represented varieties of loud and soft. Green, yellow, and blue gels represented high and low pitches. The ants did most of the running, even one was maimed. The beetle stayed around the sides, but did make one mad dash across the field. To spark things up, the centipede was a late entry, and he chased the beetle.[27]

An even later entry into the "bio" scene, *plant-created music,* is described vividly in an article from the *Rolling Stone:*

It could be said they were singing, but that is too anthropomorphic a way to describe the sounds the plants were emitting: strange electronic garglings, ethereal chirpings and shriekings to a mysterious nonlinear rhythm that reveals the secret life-pulse of the vegetable kingdom. Then something very strange happened. A spectator gently held a knife to one of the stalks and addressed the plant. "Hey you! Perk up or you get it." The words plunged the room into sudden silence. The plants stopped singing. Coleuses may be pretty but they certainly aren't dumb. Somehow the threatened plant conveyed a warning of danger to its pot-mates, and they responded by entering a sort of suspended animation . . . discovery of an early-warning system among plants is just one of the revelations that have come to three electronic music specialists at Sounds Reasonable, Inc., a recording studio in Washington, D.C. There Ed Barnett, Norman Lederman and Gary Burke have been experimenting with ways to create music from the silent vibes of plants. So far their efforts have yielded a single, called "*Stereofernic Orchidstra*" . . . the record is a studio mix of four plants, an Indian azalea, a philodendron, a Boston fern and an amaryllis, recorded at the National Botanical Gardens. The first side features the raw plant "voices" tuned to different pitches on an oscillator. It sounds like a demonic, atonal violin

27. Clifford Barnes, "Music: Melody sent into exile," *Cincinnati Post,* November 15, 1972.

section in electro-frenzy. On the second side the plants control the changes on an ARP music synthesizer. The result is more musical, but no less bizarre.[28]

Biomusic, while in and of itself representing some of the oldest forms of organized sound on earth, is still, remarkably, engendering a wide variety of emotions from its spectators. Obviously this, as with most of the musics described within this chapter, is primarily because what was once considered benign natural *artifact* is now considered by some as *art-in-fact.*

Soundscapes

Many composers have articulated their aural expression in terms of natural sound quite apart from *biomusic.* Among these articulations are many of Pauline Oliveros's *Sonic Meditations:*[29]

> V:
> Take a walk at night. Walk so silently that the bottoms of your feet become ears.

and

> XVII:
> Ear Ly
> (For Kenneth Gaburo's NMCE)
> 1. Enhance or paraphrase the auditory environment so perfectly that a listener cannot distinguish between the real sounds of the environment and the performed sounds.
> 2. Become performers by not performing.

the latter of which combines all possible available sounds of the organic and inorganic environments.

Other composers, such as I.A. MacKenzie, have verbally expressed actions, or concepts which often contain written directions toward action, but without any reference to sound other than that inherent in the environment of the situation (figs. 8.5, 8.6). His earlier "wind sound sculptures" (1930s) involved the principle of instruments which were played by wind (also water and fire sculptures) and needed neither performer nor audience. The wish, before he died, of having these placed at some point where man would not be able to hear them has been carried out, bearing close resemblance to the self-destructing sculptures of Jean Tinguely.

The following excerpts from an interview between the author and MacKenzie in 1968, just three months before his death, represent his direction towards anti-ego in art, the concert stage considered the arch-villain of true equality of sounds regardless of their origin.

---

28. Jim Wiggins, "Lily Sings the Blues," *Rolling Stone,* September 12, 1975, p. 12. © 1975 by Straight Arrow Publishers Inc. All Rights Reserved. Reprinted by Permission.
29. Copyright 1974 by Smith Publications. ALL RIGHTS RESERVED.

ATR E EWH   IC H AL O NEF AL   LS...

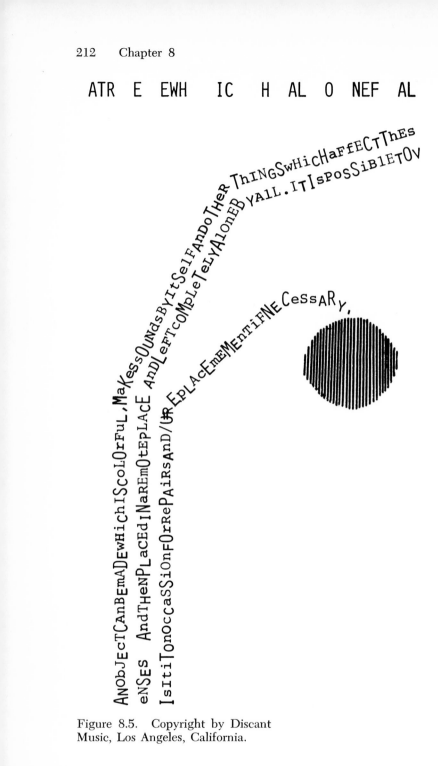

Figure 8.5.   Copyright by Discant
Music, Los Angeles, California.

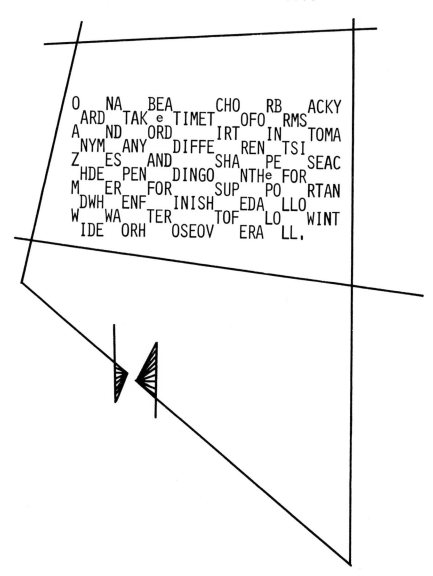

Figure 8.6. Copyright by Discant
Music, Los Angeles, California.

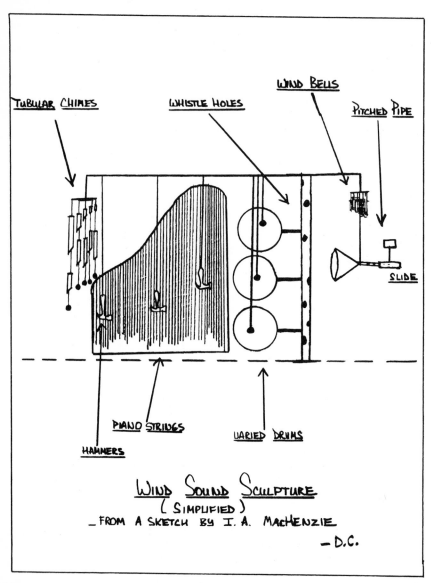

Figure 8.7.   From *The Composer*, 1,
no. 1 (June 1969). Copyright by
Composers' Autograph Publications,
1969.

I.A.: Basically, I was curious about the fundamental concept of whether
I, or mankind for that matter, was really important in the functioning of music.
. . . I still followed traditional notation . . . but demanded less and
less skill for the performer since it was not to be had anyway . . . my preoccupation seemed to be with creating instruments which played themselves.
. . . Musicians and composers . . . seem to delight in creating codes and
systems that will separate them more from the common man and, I'm afraid,
their audiences. . . .
D.C.: Was publication possible?
I.A.: Out of the question. By 1927 my music had become so involved
in new instruments of my own invention, the publisher would have had to
publish the instrument with the music. By 1930, I abandoned the written
music completely anyway, believing that I should be more interested in sound
than codes. . . .
D.C.: . . . What was your . . . reaction (to universities)?
I.A.: My reaction was harsh. . . . The teachers were very dull; more interested
in talking *about* sound than *in* sound; mostly more interested in themselves. Many times I would hear visiting composers lecture on their works . . .
only to find that the lecturer was just flesh and blood, not a god. . . .
I found quickly that for me, at least, the university and its intellect and
pomposity was creatively bankrupt: it offered nothing but security . . . and the
same old traditional claptrap. . . . As long as people continue to raise
gods, not people, the situation won't change. As long as so-called "great"
performers are regarded as towering musical figures, instead of rather grotesque
finger gymnasts, the situation won't change. The university has contributed
to this as well, creating a caste system. . . .
D.C.: . . . you say that around 1930 you began just creating instruments.
I.A.: Yes. But, more important, instruments without human performers.
By 1934, early spring, I had created my first wind-sound sculpture . . . an
elaboration of the old Chinese wind chimes . . . in fact, that's where I
got the idea. . . . I used to listen to storms approach through their sound
and somehow felt I was "tuning in" on nature (nature being something
I have always felt to be more impressive and profound than man or myself,
to be exact). . . .
D.C.: What do you consider yourself?
I.A.: I don't. Categorizing, defining and such limit creativity. . . . Whether
one thing is a work of art, and another not, is unimportant. This is cataloguing,
not problem-solving. Problems are: God, beauty, nature; creating with
or without them, or to them or from them. Creating is solving; cataloguing is
avoiding. . . . I don't dislike systems or codes any more than money;
but, as before, if these are used by someone to catalogue their own or someone
else's work, they have become destructive rather than helpful. . . .
I create what I like, in hopes that God, nature, and people (in that order) may
like some or all of them. . . .
. . . My sketches are, I suppose, my musical notation. However . . . when I
create the work, I let it go its own way, and I sort of follow along. Problems of
balance and so forth are worked out as I go along; intonation is achieved
through experimentation until I have what I want. . . . I am in complete control
of pitch, timbre, and . . . length. . . . I hope the sculpture will last forever,
though forever is a long time (I think).

D.C.: How do you regard the partially controlled aspects?
I.A.: With joy. Certainly rhythm is partially controlled . . . and the same
with harmony and melody, which are the least controlled.
D.C.: Does it disturb you when, leaving the instrument alone, it is performing
without human audience?
I.A.: Human audience? That's up to humans. It's never without an audience. . . .
. . . I have been moving toward something, not away from something.
I have never maintained that I am right or even important; I am just doing
what I think I can do best. . . . I have learned two very important things
about sound: (1) it exists, period. No more, no less. There is no good or bad
except in individual terms . . . and (2) music (sound) communicates
nothing. If I were to define (not categorize) Art, I would have to say it is
that which communicates nothing. Rather, it incites or creates something
new in each of us (I can say "Hello" and you can reply "Hello." This is
communication, bad as it is, but it is not Art. Art's beauty and importance is
that it does not communicate!) . . . *Sounds* hold an interest for me; I
don't give a damn how one produces them. . . .
. . . One last thing: if one should consider the nightingale and its music and
inspect closely the battery of technique in use, he might reconsider his
own bloated self-view: certainly music is sound (the existence of the former
term owes to social implications only) and man, or even his life, has
contributed little enough to expand its vocabulary.[30]

Other sculptors and artists have begun work in similar areas. The
German sculptor Hans Haacke, a member of *Atelier 17* in Paris and a
founder (along with Pene, Mack, and Vecker) of *Group Zero* (a group
dedicated to breaking ties with the past of nonobjective art), has created
wind and water sculptures. Japanese environmental artist Shinoda has
created elaborate metal sculptures with sound created as a by-product.
Composer Jon Hassell has recently explored acoustical environments and
objects, and large-scale outdoor sound-sculpture events (especially *Na-
dam,* a "sound-space"work).

Jon Hassell's *Landmusic Series* (1969-72) is a combination of minimal musics and *soundscapes*. Some are like the Oliveros *Sonic Meditations,*
being but brief suggestions: "Underground thunder spreading across an
open field." Another in the series calls for compact battery-powered
speaker, microphone, amplifier combinations to be planted in trees to
produce subtle sound amplifications of "wind, leaves, birds, and squirrels
who come near. . . ."[31]

The struggle, gaining intensity in the late sixties, for the safety and
revitalization of the environment, holds close ties with the antiart movement. Besides the creation of works which incorporate the environment

30. David Cope, "Chronicles of a Cause: I.A. MacKenzie," *The Composer* 1, no. 1
(June 1969):35-42.
31. Tom Johnson, "New Music," *Musical America* 24, no. 11 (November 1974):
MA-14.

as it is (without artistic distortion), the direction implies an immaculate concept of nature, with distrust of man's creations (and re-creations) in what appears to be their inherent destructiveness. Sound pollution, the technique of discounting the aural by-product of twentieth-century convenience living (e.g., the noise of freeways, airways, refrigeration), has arithmetically compounded the situation. The need for *intensity* of sound to compensate for the increased level of accepted background noise of living, subsequently leads to a battle over dominance between organized and unorganized sound; verification of determinate logic becomes so confused as to render reasonable decisions towards relative significance impossible.

The *World Soundscape Project* has been designed to explore and note trends in man's relation to his sonic environment. Based in Canada near Vancouver, and directed by R. Murray Schafer, the project attempts to bring together research on the scientific, sociological and aesthetic aspects of the environment and has five significant documents to date:

1. *The Book of Noise;*
2. *Okeanos* (a ninety-minute quadraphonic tape composition by Bruce Davis, Brian Fawcett, and R. Murray Schafer, dealing with the symbolism of the ocean);
3. *The Music of the Environment* (an article on the concept of the World Soundscape; the first treatment of the acoustic environment as a macrocultural composition);
4. *A Survey of Community Noise By-Laws in Canada;*
5. *The Vancouver Soundscape* (a combination two-record set and booklet detailing a sonic study of the city of Vancouver and its environs, and concluding with two most significant chapters dealing in turn with "Noise Pollution Problems" and "Toward Acoustic Design").[32]

The records of this latter document include a variety of sounds, from surf to suburban baseball games. Most remarkably notable are the extremes of everyday sounds pinpointed in this collection; sounds which ". . . too often people ignore (or think they ignore). . . ."[33] The thrust of these concepts is focused in these comments taken from an open letter called "a brief introduction . . .":

Acoustics as a design study has been limited to closed environments: concert halls, sound-proof rooms and the like. It is time that acoustic design

32. Available from Sonic Research Studio, Communication Studies, Simon Fraser University, Burnaby 2, British Columbia, Canada.
33. From "A Brief Introduction to the World Soundscape Project": open letter by R. Murray Schafer, Peter Huse, Bruce Davis, Howard Broomfield, Hildegarde Westerkamp, Barry Truax, and Adam Woog, Vancouver, 1973.

be applied to the environment as a great macro-cultural composition, of which man and nature are the composer/performers. To disguise an acoustic ambience with background music or masking noise, to block it out with ear muffs, cocoon-like sound-proof rooms or automobiles is not, in our view, a satisfactory solution to the problem of noise nor is it a creative approach to acoustic design.[34]

On the records, within the framework of "Moozak at the Oakridge Shopping Mall," and "A Ventilator at Eaton's Department Store," one can hardly escape the immediate intimacy and beauty of "Full Surf . . . on a Gusty March Afternoon," or "Children's Voices, Recorded on the Playground of Seymour School. . . ."

Though quite a few years must pass before the trials of many of the concepts and works of experimentalism included here expose their real contribution to man, their vitality and originality cannot be overlooked, regardless of their inherent threat to the systems of tradition and integrity.

34. Ibid.

Bibliography

*Further Readings**

Ahlstrom, David. "Footnotes for Mr. T." *Composer* 2, no. 1 (1970):24. Annotated bibliography of writings about the *avant-garde*.

Austin, Larry. "Music is Dead, Long Live Music." *New York Times* (July 6, 1969). Quite to the point.

Brown, Anthony. "An Introduction to the Music of Morton Feldman." * *asterisk* 1 (December 1974).

"An Interview with John Cage." * *asterisk* 1 (December 1974).

Cage, John. *Notations*. New York: Something Else Press, 1969. Many of the selections contained herein fall into the categories covered in this chapter.

———. "To Describe the Process of Composition 'Music for Piano 21-52.'" *Die Reihe* 3:41. A most important example of antimusic in process. Though "indeterminate" in initial look, a study deeper into the ramifications of this article lead one immediately to antimusic concepts and analogies.

———. "Lecture on Nothing." In *Silence: Lectures & Writings*. Cambridge, Mass.: The M.I.T. Press, 1966, p. 109.

Cope, David. *Notes in Discontinuum*. Los Angeles: Discant Music, 1970. Contains works and philosophy (especially that of MacKenzie on antimusic).

Cardew, Cornelius. ed. *Scratch Music*. Cambridge, Mass.: The MIT Press; paperback edition, 1974. This is a book of scores and ideas by a great many composers involved with the *Scratch Orchestra* conducted by Cardew. Many of the works are indeterminate and quite a few belong to the antimusic category. Fascinating study for this area.

Cardew, Cornelius. *Stockhausen Serves Imperialism*. London, England: Latimer New Dimensions Limited, 1974. Interesting account of this composer's about-face and repudiation of his own early works and those of other *avant-garde* composers.

Everett, Tom. "Five Questions: 35 Answers." *Composer* 2, no. 4 (1971):79. Quite contrasting views on a number of different subjects related to antimusic, by Earle Brown, Harold Budd, Philip Corner, Jim Fulkerson, William Hellermann, Karel Husa, and Elliott Schwartz.

Higgins, Dick. "Boredom and Danger." *Source* 3, no. 1 (January 1966). An excellent explanation of experiments in antimusic.

———. *Postface*. New York: Something Else Press, 1964. A very detailed history of *Fluxus* and its concerns and experiments.

*Addresses for record companies, periodicals, and music publishers mentioned in this Bibliography can be found in Appendix 4.

Huff, Jay. "On Interview with David Behrman." *Composer* 4, no. 1 (1972):29. Fascinating view of this man well-versed both as composer and "man of letters" in the *avant-garde*.

Henahan, Donal. "Music Draws Strains Direct from Brains." *New York Times* (November 25, 1970). Interesting account of David Rosenboom's work with brain music.

Johnson, Tom. *Imaginary Music*. New York: Two-Eighteen Press, 1974. An exceptional contribution to the various aspects discussed in this chapter. See also his extremely informative columns on expressions of antimusic, in both *Musical America* and *The Village Voice*.

Kostelanetz, Richard. *John Cage*. New York: Praeger, 1970.

———. *The Theatre of Mixed Means*. New York: Dial Press, 1968.

———. *Music of Today*. New York: Time-Life Books, 1967.

Lentz, Daniel. "Music Lib." *Composer* 4, no. 1 (1972):6. Interesting article on anti-music as well as the activities of the California Time Machine's European Tour of 1970.

Maconie, Robin. "Stockhausen's *Mikrophonie I*." *Perspectives of New Music* 10, no. 2:92. Interesting and sympathetic view of this piece.

Moore, Carmen. "The Sound of Mind." *Village Voice* (December 24, 1970). Another article about David Rosenboom's works with brain-wave music.

Motherwell, Robert. *The Dada Painters and Poets: An Anthology*. New York: Wittenborn, Schultz, 1951. Interesting as *art* background and insight into antimusic concepts.

Nougé, Paul. Music is Dangerous." *Soundings* 1 (1973). See this same issue for Andre Breton's *Silence is Golden*. Both are truly unique and well worth reading.

Oliveros, Pauline. "Many Strands." *Numus West* 3 (1973):6. By an active contributor and innovator in new music.

Paik, Nam June. See this author's articles in each of the first five numbers of *Decollage* (Cologne).

Partch, Harry. "Show Horses in the Concert Ring." *Soundings* 1:66. Good source for philosophical contributions to the subject area covered in this chapter.

Reich, Steve. "Music as a Gradual Process." In *Anti-Illusion Catalog of the Whitney Museum* (New York, 1969).

Rockwell, John. Refer to his column "What's New?" in *Musical America* (May 1974). In it he discusses minimalism in the music of Charlemagne Palestine. Tom Johnson now writes this column.

Rzewski, Frederick. "Prose Music." In *Dictionary of Contemporary Music*. edited by John Vinton. (New York: E. P. Dutton & Co., 1974), p. 593.

Schafer, R. Murray. "Ezra Pound and Music." *Canadian Music Journal* 4:15. Interesting view of this poet's relation to music and the integral effects those relationships that are inferred might have on such concepts as antimusic.

Stockhausen, Karlheinz. "Mikrophonie I and II." *Melos* 33:144.

Soundings 7/8. Contains several works valuable to this chapter, including Harold Budd's, *Madrigals of the Rose Angel* and Daniel Lentz's *You Can't See the Forest . . . Music (for three drinkers and eight echoes)*, as well as a large number of other highly interesting works.

Young, La Monte, and Mac Low, Jackson, eds. *An Anthology of Chance Operations.* New York: La Monte Young and Jackson Mac Low, 1963.

Young, La Monte, and Zazeela, Marian. *Selected Writings.* Munich: Heiner Friedrich, 1969. Excellent source for materials by this composer inclusive of interviews and the like. It also contains the concepts and drawings of *Dream House,* discussed in this chapter.

————. "Sound is God: The Singing of Pran Nath." *Village Voice* (April 30, 1970). Somehow more a study of the author than of the singer.

Recordings and Publishers

Ashley, Robert. *Wolfman.* CPE-*Source* 2, no. 2 (July 1968); special record issue. Recorded on Source Records 4.

Austin, Larry. *Accidents.* CPE-*Source* 2, no. 2 (July 1968). See Ashley, above.

Budd, Harold. *Coeur D'Orr* (1969). For tape, soprano saxophone, and/or voices. Recorded on Advance 16.

————. *Oak of Golden Dreams* (1970). Recorded on Advance 16.

Cage, John. *Variations IV.* Recorded on Everest 3132.

Corner, Philip. *Rounds. Soundings* 3, no. 4:92.

Crumb, George. *Voice of the Whale.* Peters. Recorded on Columbia M-32739.

Fulkerson, James. *Folio of Scores for the Composers Forum. Soundings* 3, no. 4:2.

Gibson, John. *Visitations.* Recorded on Chatham Square CS-LP-12. A 16-track multi-textured environmental soundscape.

Glass, Philip. *Music in Fifths.* Recorded on Chatham Square CS-LP-1003.

————. *Music in Similar Motion.* Recorded on Chatham Square CS-LP-1003.

————. *Music with Changing Parts.* Recorded on Chatham Square CS-LP-1001/2.

Leedy, Douglas. *Entropical Paradise.* Recorded on Seraphim S-6060.

Moran, Robert. *Four Visions.* Universal Edition. Graphic score for flute, harp, string quartet.

Mother Mallard's Portable Masterpiece Company. Steve Drews, Linda Fisher, and David Borden. Recorded on Earthquack EQ-0001. Drones and steady pulses.

Oliveros, Pauline. *Sonic Meditations* (1974). Smith Publications.

Reich, Steve. *Four Organs* (1970). Recorded on Angel S-36059.

————. *It's gonna Rain; Violin Phase.* Recorded on Columbia MS-7265.

Riley, Terry. *In C.* Recorded on Columbia MS-7178, and published with the recording.

————. *Poppy Nogood and the Phantom Band.* Recorded on Columbia MS-7315.

————. *A Rainbow in Curved Air.* Recorded on Columbia MS-7315.

Rosenboom, David. *Ecology of the Skin* (1970). Available from the composer, c/o York University, Downsview, Toronto, Canada. Bio-feedback for performer and audience brain-wave encounters.

Rzewski, Frederick. *Coming Together. Soundings* 3, no. 4, with composer commentary. Recorded on Opus One No. 20.

Satie, Erik. *Vexations* (1893). Salabert.

Songs of the Humpback Whale. Recorded on Columbia ST-620.

Stockhausen, Karlheinz. *Aus den Sieben Tagen*. Universal Edition.

———. *Mikrophonie I*. Universal Edition. Recorded on Columbia MS-7355.

The Vancouver Soundscape (Sonic Research Studio, Simon Fraser University, Burnaby 2, B.C., Canada). Recorded on EPN 186.

Winsor, Phil. *Melted Ears* (1967). Carl Fischer. Recorded on Advance S-14.

Related films include Andy Warhol's *Sleep* (eight hours of film showing a man sleeping) and *Empire* (an extended view of the Empire State Building in New York). Another film, *The Train,* presents humanist aspects of antiart: a German general, obsessed with the salvation of art works during World War II, attempts this at the cost of many lives. The classic struggle between art and life is brilliantly portrayed in the final scenes when a French underground agent wrecks the train carrying the art, and in disgust for a philosophy which can accept the works of man over man himself, leaves the paintings strewn along the tracks for what the audience presumes is destruction by elements.

9 The Post
Avant-Garde

Evaluation

The term *avant-garde,* as applied to music over the past several decades, has become a designation for those composers or works displaying the newest technique (often anti-technique, i.e., chance music) or sound (often lack of sound, i.e., silence). The apparent dead-end features of this experimental school, as projected by its critics and enthusiasts alike, become obvious when, as one composer stated, "anything goes." It is difficult to create something *new* within the framework of that philosophy.

The decay of any movement or social direction seems to begin when the thrust of its reason for existence is silenced. This "raison d'être" in the *avant-garde* movement seemed centered around supposed shock value and "newness" of purpose and effect. Certainly the movement would begin its death throes when an event in any of its art forms became so new, so shocking, as to virtually negate anything surpassing it.

Saying "anything goes" is still quite a far cry from *doing* "anything goes." Rudolf Schwarzkogler, a Viennese artist born in 1940, began his masterpiece in the late 1960s. It seems, as we pick up the story by Robert Hughes of *Time,* that Schwarzkogler, a prime mover of the *avant-garde* of his time, had decided that *his* art, at least, depended not on the application of paint, but on the removal of surplus flesh:

So he proceeded, inch by inch to amputate his own penis, while a photographer recorded the act as an art event. In 1972, the resulting prints were reverently exhibited in that biennial motor show of Western art, Documents 5 at Kassel. Successive acts of self-amputation finally did Schwarzkogler in. . . . No doubt it could be argued by the proponents of body art . . . that Schwarzkogler's self-editing was not indulgent but brave, taking the audience's castration fears and reducing them to their most threatening quiddity. That the man was clearly as mad as a hatter, sick beyond rebuke, is not thought important: wasn't Van Gogh crazy too? But Schwarzkogler's gesture has a certain emblematic value. Having nothing to say, and nowhere to go but further out, he lopped himself and called it art.[1]

As the article states, Schwarzkogler is indeed dead, a victim of his own art form. This is more than one small step beyond Ay-o's little finger

1. Robert Hughes, "The Decline and Fall of the Avant-Garde," *Time,* December 18, 1972, pp. 111-12.

boxes. One is often reminded of the aforementioned work of Dick Higgins entitled *One anti-personnel type CBU bomb will be thrown into the audience* (what kind of strange masochist would it take to attend a program which had announced that this work would be on it?). While one finds the composer's suggestions asking the performers not to fulfill the probably small audience's desires, at the same time one wonders why Mr. Higgins doesn't just consider the Korean war for his next piece. The shock factor here is death, the "newness" that either of these be considered as art in the first place. Whether the act be real (as with Schwarzkogler) or imagined (as with Higgins), it seems topped only by multi-deaths, war, and finally complete annihilation. Since none of these seems real (at least in the form of artistic development), one is led to believe that at least for those of us who are aware of what has been happening in the arts, "newness" and "shock" are over, and with them, the prime movers, the superstructure of the *avant-garde* movement.

Philosophically the *avant-garde* has remained one of the most conservative areas of musical thought: a concept in which, indeed, anything does *not* go. The very nature of the *avant-garde* concept binds the composer to reject the past and work within a multitude of limitations often surpassing those of the strictest of traditional contrapuntalists.

Sensing the oblivion inherent in such rejection of the past, a number of composers have begun to accept the philosophy projected, but not carried out, by the *avant-garde;* that is, truly "anything goes." Not a statement of rejection, this, but of affirmation: the post *avant-garde.* While the phrase "anything goes" may immediately alienate those of us intent on saving the arts for (and in some cases from) people and significance, the words *with purpose* may be added. It is no longer the new sound, the new device, the new trick, that becomes important, but the new *work;* no longer the shock value or esoteric meaning, but old-fashioned beauty, on every possible level.

Antagonists of this philosophy generally neglect the true depth of such a direction: once the composer has become unprejudiced toward sound, Bach is no longer an enemy; the major triad, tonality, need no longer be avoided; dissonance need not be a requirement to be contemporary. Redefined, the post *avant-garde* composer is *just* the composer: using anything that is necessary to fulfill his need to create music; accepting *all* sound and silence without being limited by the current style of his time.

It is the materials of music and sound, not their stylistic maneuvering, that the post *avant-garde* embraces. Likewise consistency, previously designated as the type of materials used (triads, noise, etc.) is implied and governed by the composer, not by his period, audience, or fellow composers. The post *avant-garde* composer has also challenged the listener's prejudices: can he truly accept all sound, all styles, all meaning in music? In effect, can he listen to Bach, to Webern, to Cage, to rock; not rejecting any?

Direction

There is no progress in music (or art). That is, while certainly an individual composer may get better and better with time, "newer" music (with its complex new instruments for creating much more diverse sounds) is no better than older music (or any worse for that matter). No invention, or creation, can "outdate" Machaut's *Mass* (c. 1360) as a newer car can, for instance, outdate the horse and buggy. A composer, an artist, should try to be *different* (different here not necessarily implying better, just different). Who indeed would really want him the same as another?

Notation, while a deeply rooted battle during the prolific years of the *avant-garde,* seems best when it communicates the most of its designer's intention. The new techniques of notation engendered by many of the more profitable experiments of the *avant-garde,* are just now becoming standardized (see Appendix 3). These developments, however, cannot be construed to supersede or replace previous notational techniques as "better" than they, but as different means of expression. The battles of improvisation and indeterminacy seem won, to the extent that we now agree—if a composer has no real intention, then unintentional notation would certainly be his best vehicle. The return to faith in honest technique and musicality, whatever form it may take (as long as the ultimate purpose is communication of composer intention), is now underway. Fortunately even the very patient have tired of the endless scribbles of masturbative visual art (as music notation) possessed of its own purposelessness.

Leakage

There seems to be a *leakage* between divergent schools, a new overlap of directions, which has been growing for some time. There has existed, alongside of the *avant-garde,* for the past twenty to forty years, a vast and somewhat sheltered mainstream of composers, often maddened, more often disgusted by what they saw and heard from the *avant-garde.* Nonetheless affected by it, they steadfastly held onto their historically justified techniques, and their ears. If it had been considered a battle, certainly the traditional composer must feel himself the victor, since he is still around. Yet it was not a battle and the split which developed between the camps was an unfortunate one, one which hurt both sides by its ever-widening walls of discrimination. True, the *avant-garde* is dead, but dead by its own hand and because its very life constantly shivered above a pit of self-destruction. But that difference, that canyon between the two divergent schools, is what is now the target of *leakage*: it is breaking down. The intelligent and talented composers on each side are beginning to realize that the radical claims of the initial proponents of both sides were not necessarily true.

One is reminded of two very radical claims set forth by two of the world's most renowned men of music: Igor Stravinsky, of *Le Sacre du Printemps* ("Very little tradition lies behind *Le Sacre*, and no theory. I had only my ear to help me. . . I am the vessel through which *Le Sacre* passed."[2]); and Pierre Boulez, the current conductor of the New York Philharmonic Orchestra ("Since the discovery by the Viennese, all composition other than twelve-tone is useless.").[3] Both men are, of course, incorrect; yet each viewpoint retains that grain of truth for which armies of artists and composers will clash for years. In the last few years there has occurred the collapse of these armed camps surrounding the ever new and the ever old.

We seem on the verge of one of the most creative and significant eras in the history of music. The prejudiced and insecure may still need shelter behind a mainstream door, yet those who now venture forth freely to take quiet advantage of the evident skills of both recent schools of thought (tradition and innovation, technique and intuition) are, will, and have been *braving an exciting new credible sensitivity into the world of music.*

Composers and Works

György Ligeti's *Requiem* is a four-movement work (around 26-minutes) for soprano and mezzo-soprano soloists, two choruses, and large orchestra. Composed during the years 1963-65, the *Requiem* fuses two basic concepts: *klangflächenkomposition* (sound-mass which ebbs and flows through constant overlapping of timbre and spatial modulations evident in the extreme in his later *Lontano*) and *mikropolyphonie* (highly complex densities of polyphonic motion in which no single voice dominates—only the overall fabric of resultant sound; notable in the extreme in his *Aventures*). There is as well a strong synthesis of traditional techniques (evidenced in the standard musical notation, text, extremely "determinate" articulations, and rhythmic complexities), and *avant-garde* notable in the use of the above *klängflachenkomposition* and *micropoly-*

---

2. Igor Stravinsky, "Apropos Le Sacre du Printemps," as printed on the cover of Columbia Records ML-5719.

3. David H. Cope and Galen Wilson, "An Interview with Pierre Boulez," *Composer* 1, no. 2 (September 1969):83.

Figure 9.1. György Ligeti.
With permission of
Universal Edition.

phonie and also special effects, from muting bassoons with handkerchiefs, to the "Langlois Effect" of squeezing the string with thumb and fore-finger rather than pressing it normally against the fingerboard). The score is accompanied by a 23-page booklet of incredibly exacting per-formance directions. Like his earlier *Aventures,* the *Requiem* occasionally moves from metered notation to "senza tempo" sections (especially in the third movement). Note that in figure 3.10 (in *Instrument Exploration*) his use of this effect is for *contrast;* in the *Requiem* the effect is quite the opposite with even the bar lines being in the composer's words ". . . purely a means of synchronizing the individual parts."[4] Aside from its obvious *leakage* of new and old, *Requiem* creates a composer-con-trolled "spatial movement." The composer has remarked about the work: "You have a drawing in two dimensions and you give it perspective. . . . I was constantly thinking of achieving this illusion of a musical space, which has only an acoustical existence in time."[5]

George Crumb's *Ancient Voices of Children* (1970) is a 27-minute work for soprano, boy soprano, oboe, mandolin, harp, electric piano, and three percussionists. The work consists of five basic vocal movements

4. From the "Introductory Remarks" of the score: C.F. Peters: 30285.
5. "Conversations with Ligeti at Stanford," *Numus West* 2 (1972):19.

Figure 9.2. George Crumb.
With permission.

separated twice by purely instrumental dances. The texts are by Federico
Garciá Lorca and sung in Spanish. The *leakage* present in this work is
evidenced by the composer's own words about the piece:

In composing *Ancient Voices of Children* I was conscious of an urge to
fuse various unrelated stylistic elements. I was intrigued by the idea of juxta-
posing the seemingly incongruous: a suggestion of Flamenco with a Baroque
quotation ("Bist du bei mir," from the Notebook of Anna Magdelena
Bach), or a reminiscence of Mahler with a breath of the Orient. It later occurred
to me that both Bach and Mahler drew upon many disparate sources in
their own music without sacrificing "stylistic purity."[6]

Crumb's "stylistic purity" does indeed remain intact in this as well
as his earlier (beginning with his *Five Pieces for Piano,* 1962) and later
works. It is characterized by three particularly distinct features: (1) extremely defined and thinly exposed textures often expressed as solo lines
(almost one-third of this work is solo lines), dramatic silences (often
expressed by Crumb's square fermatas with duration in seconds: see
fig. 9.3), and subtle motivic repetition and development; (2) the use
of instruments and voice equally for their pitch and "special" timbral
qualities:

Certain special instrumental effects are used to heighten the "expressive
intensity" e.g. "bending" the pitch of the piano by application of a chisel to
the strings; . . . the mandolin has one set of strings tuned a quarter-tone
low in order to give a special pungency to its tone.[7]

6. From the score: No. 66303. C.F. Peters.
7. Ibid.

Figure 9.3.   Luciano Berio. BMI
Archives. Used by permission.

(3) the musical imagery: a reflection of the texts without programmatic
connotations:

I feel that the essential meaning of this poetry is concerned with the most
primary things: life, death, love, the smell of the earth, the sounds of the wind
and sea. These "*ur*-concepts" are embodied in language which is primitive
and stark but which is capable of infinitely subtle nuance.[8]

Figure 9.4 shows the entirety of the fourth movement of *Ancient
Voices* and exemplifies the fusion and *leakage* referred to earlier. The
simple use of the whole-tone scale, the triadic harmonies and the simple
formal structure are all extremely traditional; while the marimba drones,
the percussionists singing, and a Bach work quoted on the toy piano, are
all very *avant-garde* in nature. The movement, and indeed the work,
holds together with a high degree of continuity despite the contrasting
material and styles.

Figure 9.5 is from Luciano Berio's *Sinfonia* (1968) for eight voices and
orchestra. The text here reads: "But now it's done, it's over, we've had
our chance. There was even, for a second, hope of resurrection, or almost." It seems to sum up almost the narrative "stream-of-conscious" flow
of this striking work. Eclecticism abounds in both text and music: (1) text
examples are drawn from sources such as Claude Levi-Strauss's book *Du
Cru et du Cuit* on Brazilian origin myths of water, Samuel Beckett and

8. Ibid.

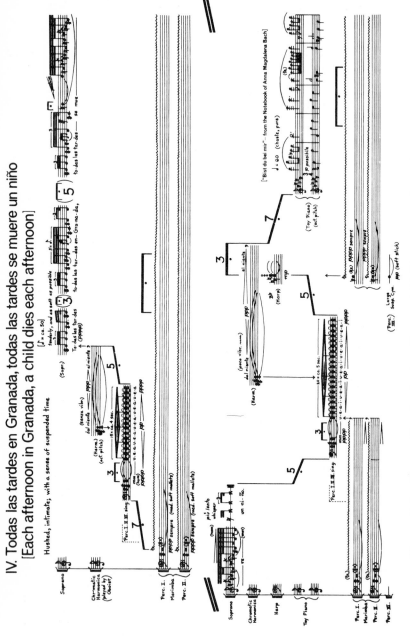

Figure 9.4.   George Crumb: *Ancient Voices of Children.* Copyright © by C. F. Peters Corp., 373 Park Avenue South, New York, N. Y. 10016. Reprint permission granted by the publisher.

Fig. 9.4 (continued)

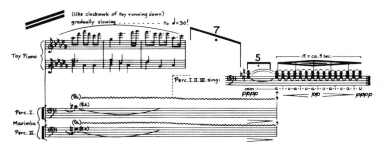

Berio's own words (all set with English performance directions such as "impatient," "indignant," and "bewildered"—these taken, for example, from just four bars on page 42); (2) music quotes are prevalent throughout the third movement and include fragments from Debussy's *La Mer* and the Scherzo from Mahler's *Second Symphony,* as well as references to Berio's own music (primarily *Epiphanie,* 1961 and *Sequenza 4,* 1966). For these, and other reasons only recognizable on hearing, *Sinfonia* has engaged both wrath and devotion comparable possibly to only one other work of this century: *Le Sacre du Printemps.* It would seem from any given chronicle of the work that such divisive elements as the work "talking about itself" ("Keep going, going on, call that going, call that on. But wait. He is barely moving, now, almost still. Should I make my introductions?"—at which point the singers are introduced by name while the music continues), the extensive quotation, exploring nearly every conceivable sonority (from major thirds, triads and lush ninth chords to panchromatic clusters) and the use of massive dramatic bursts of sound within delicate frames of textures (the first movement primarily) could not possibly work or even make sense. However, reflecting a society gone mad with self-preoccupation, *Sinfonia* forcefully drives its musical/dramatic point home, leaving few listeners with less than a profound disturbance borne of having indeed heard the through-composed "workings" of a man obsessed by the expression of *self* without restraint. The work does indeed have continuity and a kind of frightening "madness," a macrocosm of dramatic fusion and *leakage* quite unlike the aforementioned Crumb and Ligeti works. Traditional in notation, material for quotes, form, and rhythmic flow, it is as well a highly *avant-garde* work in text, "act" of quoting, and eclectic, harmonic, and melodic idioms, and is a well-defined member of the post *avant-garde.*

Apotheosis of This Earth (1970) by Karel Husa for concert band is, like the *Sinfonia,* a very "physical" work continually impelled by dynamic and textural momentum. Unlike the *Sinfonia,* its *leakage* is not easily heard (it is truly a work fused in every sense). Its three-movement struc-

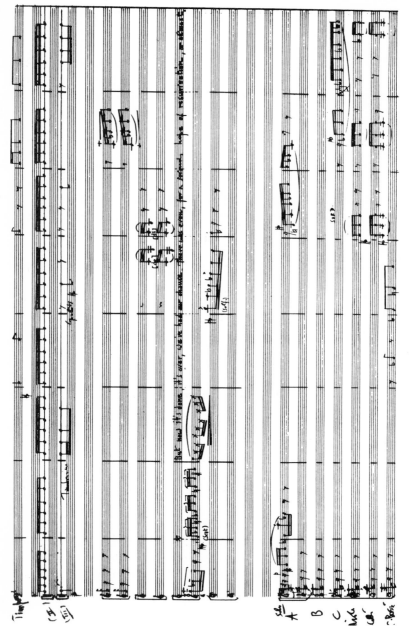

Figure 9.5.   Luciano Berio: *Sinfonia*. © Copyright 1969 Universal Edition. All rights reserved.

ture (Apotheosis, Tragedy of Destruction, Postscript) all employ sound-mass resultant of repetitive composite motives (see fig. 2.9 in *Sound Mass and Rhythm*) and cumulative sustained clusters (often panchromatic, e.g., measure 149, where the horns and trumpets attack and slowly "unvelope" a twelve-note cluster). The final movement employs whispering with both repetitive consonance attacks and text ("this beautiful earth"). In *Apotheosis* one finds the fusion of *avant-garde* and traditional techniques so complete that neither is visible: a work of unique and personal style.

Figure 9.6.   Karel Husa

Other works of varying degrees of *leakage* include Donald Erb's *Symphony of Overtures* (1964) and Richard Toensing's *Doxologies I*. Both these composers have evolved personal styles fused of elements equally *avant-garde* and traditional. The *leakage* is complete: these works no longer "espouse" a single thought or gimmick on the one hand, nor is the use of any sonic material for specific purpose feared, on the other.

The "toy of the idle rich," as some have labeled experimental music and art, has blossomed fully and is now capable of challenging the most simple or verbose of traditional rhetoric. There is no longer the time or the logic to avoid the implications of the directions discussed in this text. Whether they be, in the final analysis, friend or enemy (or both), we must know and acknowledge them. Nothing is gained by ignorance. Varèse's comments are most *apropos:*

My fight for the liberation of sound and for my right to make music with any sound and all sounds has sometimes been construed as a desire to disparage

and even to discard the great music of the past. But that is where my
roots are. No matter how original, how different a composer may seem, he
has only grafted a little bit of himself on the old plant. But this he should be
allowed to do without being accused of wanting to kill the plant. He
only wants to produce a new flower. . . .[9]

It is with this in mind that continued exploration must be carried out
in all *new directions in music.*

---

9. As quoted in *Contemporary Composers on Contemporary Music,* Elliott Schwartz
and Barney Childs, eds. (New York: Holt, Rinehart, and Winston, 1967), p. 201.

Bibliography

*Further Readings**

Burrows, David. "Music and the Biology of Time." *Perspectives of New Music.* (Fall-Winter 1972):241. A stimulating post *avant-garde* reference.

Cage, John. "The Future of Music." *Numus West* 5:6. An interesting article and, though garbed in the usual Cage linguistics, presents a different Cage than usual, and *his* future (". . . if there is one . . .") is one bred not so far from that described herein. Like Ives, there seems embodied in some engineers of change an equal if not stronger engineer of equalization.

Cope, David. "Footnotes." *Composer* 4, no. 2 (1973):52. Relates directly to the post *avant-garde.*

———. "A Post *Avant-Garde.*" *Composer* 3, no. 2 (1972):61.

Gilbert, Steven. "Carl Ruggles (1876-1971): An Appreciation." *Perspectives of New Music* (Fall-Winter 1972):224. A man of early "leakage."

Harbison, John. "Peter Maxwell Davies' *Taverner.*" *Perspectives of New Music.* (Fall-Winter 1972):233. About an active man in the area of the post *avant-garde.*

"Musician of the Month: Karel Husa." *Musical America.* (August 1969):5. A good but short biographical sketch.

Ives, Charles. "Music and Its Future." In *American Composers on American Music.* Edited by Henry Cowell. New York: Unger Publishing Co., 1962. Most prophetic.

Johnston, Ben. "On Context." *ASUC Proceedings* 3 (1968):32. Superbly optimistic article on this subject. See p. 35: "That's why I think it's spring." A most sincere and credible quote from this man of diverse musics.

Ligeti, György. "Metamorphosis of Musical Form." *Die Reihe* 7 (1960):5. An excellent article on this man's evolutionary and revolutionary process of thinking.

Petcock, Stuart. "Multiple Values in New Music." *ASUC Proceedings* 7, no. 8: 75. A most interesting and relevant article on the relativity in criticism of new music.

Poissenot, Jacques M. "Luciano Berio." In *Dictionary of Contemporary Music*, edited by John Vinton (New York: E. P. Dutton & Co., 1974), p. 78. Excellent in its breakup of the composer's styles into four major periods to date: "serial, electronic, aleatory, and eclectic."

*Addresses for record companies, periodicals, and music publishers mentioned in this Bibliography can be found in Appendix 4.

Rochberg, George. "The New Image of Music." *Perspectives of New Music 2,* no. 1:1. An interesting early approach to the concepts of unity in new music.

Salzman, Eric. *Twentieth-Century Music: An Introduction.* Englewood Cliffs: N.J.: Prentice-Hall, 1967. Has a fascinating post *avant-garde* ending (p. 186).

Santi, Piero. "Luciano Berio." *Die Reihe* 4:98. An interesting view of Luciano Berio at the time (1958).

Varèse, Edgard. "The Liberation of Sound." Edited by Chou Wen-chung. In *Contemporary Composers on Contemporary Music,* edited by Barney Childs and Elliott Schwartz (New York: Holt, Rinehart and Winston, 1967). An incredibly well-edited and "composed" article on the futures of music as diverse as they may be. It prophesies the post *avant-garde* with great clarity (the article is based on lectures given by Varese during the years 1936 to 1962).

Recordings and Publishers

Berio, Luciano. *Sinfonia.* Universal Edition. Recorded on Columbia MS-7268.

———. *Epiphanie.* Universal Edition. Recorded on RCA LSC-3189.

———. *Sequenza IV.* Universal Edition. Recorded on Candide 31015.

Cope, David. *Re-birth.* Seesaw Music Corp. Recorded on Cornell CUWE-16A. For Concert Band.

Crumb, George. *Ancient Voices of Children.* Peters. Recorded on Nonesuch 71255.

Davies, Peter Maxwell. *Eight Songs for a Mad King.* Boosey and Hawkes. Recorded on Nonesuch H-71285.

Erb, Donald. *Symphony of Overtures.* Galaxy Music. Recorded on Turnabout 34433.

Husa, Karel. *Apotheosis of This Earth.* Associated Music Publishers. Recorded on Golden Crest 4134.

Ives, Charles. *Central Park in the Dark* (1906). AMP. Recorded on Columbia MS-6843. Interesting "pre-logue" of the post *avant-garde.*

Ligeti, György. *Requiem.* Peters. Recorded on Wergo 60045.

———. *Lontano.* Schott. Recorded on Wergo 322.

———. *Aventures.* Peters. Recorded on Wergo 60022.

Stravinsky, Igor. *Variations* (*Aldous Huxley in Memoriam, 1954*). Boosey and Hawkes. Masterwork of a true man of "*leakage.*"

Takemitsu, Toru. *November Steps* (1967). Peters. Recorded on RCA LSC-7051. Interesting work of culminative opposites.

Toensing, Richard. *Doxologies I.* Recorded on Cornell University #9.

Appendix 1   Glossary of Terms

Here is an alphabetical listing of those terms used in the text which may need further clarification, with a brief definition of each. An asterisk (*) after a term within a definition signifies that the word so starred is itself defined within this glossary.

amplifier: an instrument used to expand or increase the power of a sound or signal.

amplitude: equivalent to the "loudness" of a pitch; the dynamics of sound.

amplitude modulation (AM):   a periodic variation of amplitude* creating tremolo.

analog computer: a computer whose information is stored and processed using electromagnetic energy on wires or tapes, as opposed to a digital computer,* which employs numbers.

antimusic: a term denoting those works the concept or implication of which is "opposed to" the traditional meaning of music. In current terms, it refers to those compositions which either (1) include no reference to sound in their scores; or (2) destroy one or more of the traditional composer/performer/audience relationships; or (3) are impossible to perform and exist only in concept.

atonality: literally, away from tonality, or no tonality. Atonality is truly impossible to obtain, as a group of sounds will by acoustical principles have one or more strongest tones (tone center = tonality), just as they will have form (intended or not). *Pantonality** (inclusive of all tonalities) has for the most part replaced the term *atonality* in reference to twelve-tone music (dodecaphony*).

augmentation: expanding the duration of a rhythmic set without disturbing the relationship of elements (e.g., doubling or tripling the value of each note).

autonomous music: Xenakis's term for music which does not employ "strategy" or "games" in its performance. This would include all of traditional music and all *indeterminate** music that does not result from group conflict (*heteronomous** music is the opposite term).

avant-garde: a French term literally meaning *advance guard* or *vanguard;* in the arts, applies to those who work in the newest areas of creativity. It may come to mean in music a certain period (such as "modern") roughly covering the years 1935-1972?; thus the term post *avant-garde,* meaning after the earlier period, implies that no longer can anything be really "new."

band-reject filter: an electronic filtering device that eliminates a particular band (group) of frequencies while allowing the remainder to pass through.

band-pass filter: an electronic filtering device which allows a certain band to pass while rejecting all the remaining frequencies; often applied to white sound° in order to obtain a wide variety of timbres.

Bauhaus: an art school in Germany (founded in 1919 by Walter Gropius, and closed in 1933) in which the various art forms and crafts were taught as a combined unit. Faculty included Paul Klee, Vasily Kandinsky, and Mies van der Rohe (among others of like prominence), and was instrumental in encouraging the development of many of the media-forms extant today.

black sound: used to denote silences as opposed to white sound° (inclusive of all frequencies).

brake drum: the housing of the braking mechanism of an automobile; also used as a percussion instrument.

chance music: often used synonymously with *indeterminate*° *music*, it means any music in which there is a "chance" result whether it be by composer, performer, or both.

circular bowing: on string instruments a procedure whereby the bow is kept in motion (regardless of bow direction change) by a circular action of the bow across the string.

circular breathing: on wind instruments the ability of the performer to breathe in through his nose while expelling air through his mouth thereby needing no rests or "breaks" to regain breath. Performers well-versed in this procedure can play continuously for great lengths of time with no stop in tone.

classic electronic music: that type of electronic music which is created primarily by "splicing" one sound to the next rather than by using keyboards, sequencers, sample-holds, and the like to create large sections of works in one "sitting."

cluster: a chord or sound which contains two or more intervals of a major second or less.

computer-generated sound: music with a high degree of composer determinacy produced by "programming" a computer with digital information and, through high-speed operation and information retrieval, the computer "performs" under the composer's directions. Through a digital-to-analog interface° an electromagnetic tape is produced that has from one sound up to an entire composition on it, depending on the stage of development in the work the composer has reached.

contact microphone: a certain type of microphone which requires physical contact before creating electric signals for reproduction as sound; either the object to which it is applied must be vibrating or the microphone itself must be moved across the surface before sound is created.

cross-coupling: a tape-recorder technique of attaching the playback of one channel to the record of the other and vice versa to create a reiteration of attack with built-in decay,° usually employed in live-electronic music.°

dada: international movement (beginning around 1916) which some feel originated with the poet Tristan Tzara. It included artists such as Man Ray and Marcel Duchamp among others, and attacked all conventional standards and aesthetics of "art." In art it was exemplified by such as the signing of machine-produced objects and thusly redefining them as works of art, by collages of newspaper, etc., on canvas with paints; indeed it was (and some still feel it still is) the generating force behind the *avant-garde*.

decay: that aspect of a tone's envelope° in which the amplitude is decreasing.

digital computer: a computer whose information is stored and processed in numbers (usually binary-input; that is, two states of a switch [on or off], a hole or no hole in a punch card, etc.).

dodecaphonic: a term commonly used to refer to twelve-tone music.

drift: in electronic music, any unintentional shift of frequency due to equipment failure or inaccuracy. All oscillators° and generators° necessarily include a small amount of drift.

envelope: the amplitude° characteristics of a signal: attack, initial decay,° sustain, and final decay.° Envelope generators can control both the amount and duration of each of these characteristics.

feedback: a result of cross-coupling.° Literally, any electronic device in which sound is fed back through the system one or more times to produce echoes or, depending on gain° adjustment, an increase of sound to limits of system tolerance.

filter: an electronic instrument designed to allow selection of frequencies from a signal: band-pass,° band-elimination.°

Fluxus: a group of *avante-garde*° composers of the 1960s with intentional direction toward danger and boredom as viable concepts within art.

frequency modulation (FM):   a periodic variation of frequency creating vibrato.

Futurists: Italian group of composers (1912-20) employing a wide variety of noise°-making instruments.

gain: amount of amplification. Variable gain would be the "loudness" knob on any sound-producing device (e.g., radio).

gate: an electronic instrument the purpose of which is to control the amplitude° of a signal.

generator: sound source of all types of electronic signals except sine waves.°

Gesamtkunstwerk: German term meaning literally "complete art work." Used to denote the nineteenth-century view of opera (particularly Wagner's), the composer controlling and creating all aspects of his work—staging, music, lyrics, dance, etc.—and all aspects contributing equally to the total effect.

graphic: in music, those scores which are more oriented toward visual incitement than communication of directions through symbols.

heteronomous music: music which utilizes "games" and "strategy" during performance, producing *conflict* and resultant indeterminate° results. Term primarily used by Xenakis.

hexachord: in its simplest form: a six-note chord. Commonly used in twelve-tone music to construct various further computations within the row. Also, trichord (three notes), etc.

improvisation: music which involves some performer freedom during performance within a certain set of parameters° drawn by the composer. As opposed to indeterminate° music, improvisation suggests (often demands) that the performer draw upon techniques and intuition (based on his previous experience) within a set stylistic framework. Nonscored cadenzas of the eighteenth-century concerto form are excellent examples of pre-twentieth-century improvisation.

indeterminacy: act of composer, performer, and/or both, in which the out-come is unpredictable. In general, unlike improvisation (where the per-former is "asked" to draw upon his previous experience and techniques), "indeterminacy" requires a *real* "letting of sounds be themselves" (as John Cage has put it) with performers and performing situations allowing any sound to exist within the framework set up by the composer. The term *aleatoric* music is often used for indeterminacy. It is, however, a term loosely applied to music allowing for varied degrees of indeterminacy and improvi-sation so that almost anything is "aleatoric." The term, therefore, is rarely used.

interface: in basic terms, any instrument which allows two instruments of different operating procedures to function together. In computer music (especially computer-generated sound*) it is the digital-to-analog (D/A) interface which allows the digital computer to produce analog sounds on tape. In the simplest of terms the digital computer "samples," for example, a sine-wave (the sampling rate being variable; for our example, say 10,000 per second) creating a set of points on a graph looking in general like the original sine-wave. These are, however, just points and it is through the D/A interface that analog unit "smooths" such points to create on tape an electromagnetic sound of continuous nature.

isorhythm: a compositional technique of Gothic music (c. twelfth- to fifteenth-century, primarily in Machaut) in which a set rhythm (usually very long) is repeated throughout the composition while an iso-melody of different duration and number of notes would be applied to the rhythm, causing an overlapping set of continuous variations.

Klangfarbenmelodien: German term denoting color pointillism*: individual notes receiving distinctly different timbre, and further separated by range.

Klangflachenkomposition: a sound-mass* which ebbs and flows through con-stant overlapping of timbre* and spatial* modulation.

laser: loosely, and as used in multimedia,* an intense beam of directed light usually connected by its beam to a receiving device which, in turn, usually leads to an oscillator.* When the beam is broken (by performer or object), the oscillator is triggered by the receiving device. It is also common to reverse the effect so that breaking the beam creates "no-sound." Other forms of laser use include voltage control of "colored" beams such that the elec-trical current activates movement of the laser apparatus, creating complex projections.

linear: literal meaning: line. In traditional music "linear" refers to melodic or contrapuntal flow. In electronic terminology "linear" refers to a "straight" line flow (increase or decrease) as opposed to exponential in which line flow increases or decreases in a sharply accelerated form.

live-electronic: music in which electronic sound is created by a performer working "live" using electronic instruments in a concert situation. "Live" also refers to an approach opposite to that of composing electronic music on tape directly to classical.* The composing in real-time, one-to-one pro-portion situation, using keyboards, sequencers, and the like.

microtone: any two tones which are less than an equal-tempered half-step. Quarter-tones* are one example.

mikropolyphonie: highly complex densities of polyphonic motion in which no single voice dominates—only the overall fabric of resultant sound.

mixer: an electronic instrument designed to combine signals by algebraically summing their amplitudes.

modulation: a process in which any aspect of a sound or signal is varied (e.g., amplitude modulation° and frequency modulation°).

montage: a visual overlapping of images.

multimedia: a work which employs two or more traditionally separate art forms. "Happenings" are multimedia events which are more or less aleatorically conceived. Often called mixed-media.

multiphonics: the technique (particularly on wind instruments) of obtaining two or more voices simultaneously. Obtained by control of the overtone° series in such a way that one or more of the partials becomes prominent enough to be heard as a separate tone. Another voice can be added by humming.

musique concréte: music which employs nonelectronic sounds on tape. The tape recorder is most commonly the compositional tool, and sounds are manipulated after recording to achieve the desired effect.

noise: traditionally defined as undesirable sound. Today, however, as composers continually employ sounds which were in the past "disliked," or considered "nonmusical," it has come roughly to mean those sounds whose complexity is such that individual frequencies are no longer determinable and/or audible. White sound° is often called "white noise."

oscillator: an electronic instrument designed to create sine waves.°

oscilloscope: a device used to show (via cathode-ray tube screen) the characteristics of incoming signals (amplitude,° frequency, etc.).

ostinato: a rhythmic grouping which is repeated many times.

overtone: all sounds except sinusoidal contain small secondary pitches called overtones, the alteration or filtering°of which alters timbre.

panchromatic: inclusive of all chromatic tones. Usually used to refer to cluster° chords in which all or most of the twelve (traditional) pitches occur.

pandiatonicism: inclusive of all diatonic (or key-scale) notes. Pandiatonic clusters° include all seven scale notes (e.g., a white key forearm cluster on piano = key of C pandiatonic cluster).

pantonality: inclusive of all tonalities. Like atonality° it is impossible to achieve, and thus very loosely applied to twelve-tone music.

parameter: any characteristic element (of sound) or a concept (of sound) which can be controlled.

pink sound: sound which contains all possible frequencies in the lower audible spectrum.

pointillism: a term derived from the graphic arts; as applied to music, each sound becomes more an entity in itself, separated distinctly from those before and after by space (frequency), distance (silence) and/or timbre.

potentiometer (pot): a variable resistor used to control the energy in a given system. Most usually found as a volume control.

prepared piano: a piano the timbre of which has been altered by the placing of various objects between, on, or around the strings inside the instrument.

program: a specialized computer "language." In composition, programs are set up in advance in order to create the parameters° of the computer's "musical" language as well as its interface° between the human "programmer" and the computer itself.

psycho-acoustics: the study of sound and its complexity, and its realistic communication both physically and psychologically to man.

pulse wave: any form of wave that instantaneously moves from a negative to positive function. This would include all square and rectangular wave-forms.

quarter-tone: the distance between two tones which are one-half of a semitone (half step) apart. Those instruments capable of variable intonation (e.g., string instruments) approach quarter-tones in correct performance of traditional tonal music (as D-flat should sound different from C-sharp in any other key than their own respective majors or minors).

real-time: a term used to denote composition time equivalent to performance time (as opposed to abstract or nonreal time, in which, due to notation requirements, conception and composition requires much more time than than performance). An important concept which is really for the first time attainable with the advent of electronic music: events, and even complex series of events, can be placed on tape in exactly the same amount of time as a performance would require. This opens many new avenues of composer experimentation and variation of his materials.

reverberation: quick repetitions of a sound which cannot be individually distinguished.

ring modulator: a signal multiplier circuit, combining signals to produce the sum and difference of their frequencies, with only the resultant sidebands exiting.

sampling: the ability of a computer to calculate as points the characteristics of a wave-form. The higher the sampling rate the better the resultant fidelity of sound in analog output through speakers.

sequencer: a device capable of storing programmed control voltages in order to "play" them at any given speed and rhythm. Sequencers vary from models with eight notes (three parameters per note) to huge quasi-computer models capable of storing and retrieving thousands of notes and their stored parameters (articulations, dynamics, duration, etc.). The sample-hold is a sort of "random" sequencer capable of many "sequencer-like" sounds but without the determinate composer control.

serialization: the ordered and intellectual logic applied to any or all aspects of compositional technique. This term no longer applies only to twelve-tone mechanics.

sine-wave: a tone which contains no overtones.°

sound-mass: a block of sound in which individual pitches no longer become important and/or perceptible. Used instead of *noise*° to avoid the negative connotations of the latter.

spatial modulation: sound which moves evenly and continuously from one physical location to another.

square wave: a pulse wave° with the positive and negative functions equal.

splicer: an instrument to cut and place together segments of tape for synchronization. It is used extensively in classic° electronic music.

stochastic music: mathematician Jacques Bernoulli's term from the Greek meaning, literally, "target." Stochastic laws state that the more numerous indeterminate* activities become, the more determinate their outcome. Stochastic music suggests that if enough "random" but similar-in-timbre activities occur the results will always be the same. While Xenakis was the first to apply the term to music, many composers utilize the basic concept of stochastic music, usually using huge "collages" of sounds often improvisatory or indeterminate in isolation, but in mass they create the same construct of sound-mass, mikropolyphonie and/or klangflachenkomposition.*

strategic music: heteronomous* music composed of "live-performance" games.

synthesizer: a loosely-applied term, literally meaning a device to build up or compose a larger idea or object from lesser ones, used in electronic music to refer to a more or less complete battery of smaller electronic units (such as oscillators*) placed together to form a larger or more complete unit.

timbre modulation: sound which moves continuously and evenly from one timbre to another.

triangle wave: wave form that, when viewed on an oscilliscope,* takes the shape of a triangle. It contains every other overtone.*

vibrato: in electronic music terms: frequency modulation.* This is different from the tremolo created by amplitude modulation.*

vocoder: an instrument designed to code sounds (speech) into digital information for communication over cables or by radio (subsequently decoded upon reception). It is now used by some composers to create new sounds by modifying traditional ones.

white sound: sometimes referred to as white noise; sound which contains all possible frequencies (called white, from white—inclusive of all colors—light). Often used in conjunction with various filters* to create a wide variety of timbres.

wind sound sculptures: sculptures designed to allow wind to create sound; similar to Oriental wind chimes in concept.

Appendix 2 Biographical Data

A listing of many of the composers discussed in this book, with brief biographies and/or current information about each, appear here in alphabetical sequence. Omissions are due either to lack of definite information concerning the composer, and/or necessarily limited space. Though by no means complete, the content will provide data concerning a cross section of composers and contributors to the *avant-garde*.

ANDRIESSEN, Louis (b. 1939, Utrecht) is a leading composer of Holland where he currently serves as musical advisor to the Globe theater group of Amsterdam.

ANTHEIL, George (1900-59) was noted as America's *Bad Boy of Music* (book by Antheil published in 1945), and during the twenties and thirties one of the most confusing figures in the world of music. His Ballet mecanique (inclusive of airplane motors, doorbells, and the like) is considered by many to be a milestone of the beginnings of the *avant-garde*. His music is as diverse as his character, and the predicting of the style of an unheard Antheil work is very difficult indeed. Charles Amirkhanian's *An Introduction to George Antheil* (*Soundings* 7-8:176) is an excellent beginning to the study of this man.

ASHLEY, Robert (b. 1930) is the cofounder of ONCE (at one time an annual festival of new music in Ann Arbor, Michigan) and coordinator of the ONCE Group. He is active as both composer and performer of new music and holds degrees from the University of Michigan and the Manhattan School of Music.

AUSTIN, Larry (b. 1930) is the editor of *Source: Music of the Avant-Garde* (a biannual publication devoted to the music of the *avant-garde* and Chairman of the Department of Music at the University of South Florida. His works have appeared as part of a number of important festivals, including the New York Philharmonic 1964 *Avant-Garde* Series and the 1965 Rome *Nuova Consonanza*. He cofounded the New Music Ensemble (NME) in which he also acted as a performer. His recent works include theatrical, multimedia, and live-electronic techniques.

BABBITT, Milton (b. 1916) is professor of music at Princeton University and a director of the Columbia-Princeton Electronic Music Center. Educated in mathematics as well as in music, he is particularly well suited for the complicated intricacies of programming and detailed acoustical knowledge necessary for composition using the Mark II Synthesizer. As one of the major representatives of American music, his work has received numerous performances throughout the world. He retains all possible control over compositional elements whether his materials be electronic or live in origin.

BEHRMAN, David (b. 1937) is cofounder of the Sonic Arts Group (performers of live-electronic music) and a producer of recordings of new music for CBS and Odyssey Records. As composer/performer, he has participated in many festivals of new music, including the Angry Arts Festival in New York, and the Lincoln Center Library New Music Concerts. He continues to organize and support concerts and recordings of *avant-garde* music both here and abroad.

BERIO, Luciano (b. 1925, Italy) founded the electronic studio at the Italian Radio in Milan with Bruno Maderna in 1955. A prolific composer and conductor, he lived in the U.S. and taught at Juilliard School of Music until 1973. He now conducts and composes in Europe and his music continues to rely on an intuitive "dramatic" approach, an emphasis not unlike the operatic heritage of his native Italy.

BOULEZ, Pierre (b. 1925, France) is founder (in 1953) of the now famous new music series *Domaine Musicale,* and continues to be active in his support of new music. In 1970, he took up duties as head conductor of the New York Philharmonic, replacing Leonard Bernstein. A prolific composer and author, his music and approach continues to be a major influence in the European *avant-garde.*

BRANT, Henry (b. 1913), whose first works appeared in the then *avant-garde* publication *New Music Quarterly* (early 1930s), continues to contribute as both theorist and composer to the spatial composing techniques now finding great popularity in the multimedia, electronic, and theatrical elements of *avant-garde* composers here and abroad.

BROWN, Earle (b. 1926) is on the staff of the Peabody Conservatory of Music. During the 1950s his association with John Cage led him to indeterminate techniques. This, together with influences derived from Alex Calder's mobiles, has led him further toward graphic and mobile-type structures, a composite of indeterminate and improvisatory techniques. His music is performed widely and he is acclaimed as one of the foremost exponents of the *avant-garde.* Notable among his writings about music is his "Form in New Music," *Source: Music of the Avant-Garde* 1, no. 1, (January 1967).

BUDD, Harold (b. 1936) holds a teaching position at the California Institute of the Arts in Los Angeles. His works have appeared at FFLEM (First Festival of Live Electronic Music), and he has enjoyed numerous performances by Bertram Turetzky among others. He has also composed for documentary and art films. His music and philosophies are influenced in part by recent art, especially "minimal art."

BUSSOTTI, Sylvano (b. 1931, Italy) is active as composer and promoter of *avant-garde* music, notably at the Cologne series *Music of our Time,* the Munich series *New Music,* and the Florence concerts *Vita Musicale Contemporanea.* His scores are primarily graphic in nature with emphasis on live performing/composing situations.

CAGE, John (b. 1912) is unquestionably the world's leading exponent of the *avant-garde.* His writings (*Silence, A Year from Monday* and *Notation,* among others) and music continue to explore and experiment with the basic concepts, techniques, and philosophy of all the *avant-garde* forms presented here. His percussion concerts in early 1936 (Seattle), experiments about the same time with prepared piano techniques, and his first compositions on tape (1951), simultaneous with the inclusion of chance operations involved in compositional process, culminated in a 25-year retrospective concert of his music in Town Hall (New York) in 1958. He continues to make extensive United States and European lecture tours with David Tudor and Merce Cunningham. Very few concerts of new music have failed to include the name and music of John Cage.

CARTER, Elliott   (b. 1908), under the encouragement of Charles Ives, studied at Harvard with Walter Piston and in Paris with Nadia Boulanger. He has taught at Juilliard, Columbia, Cornell, Yale, and other schools and is particularly noted for his rigid and iconoclastic views of rhythm (metric-modulation) and harmonic space. His works, like those of Carl Ruggles, come very slowly (usually at the rate of one every one or two years), and are regarded by their performers (he does not compose electronic music) as *extremely* difficult. His *Double Concerto,* and the *Concerto for Orchestra,* are considered by many to be the most difficult in orchestral literature.

CHIARI, Giuseppe   (b. 1926, Italy) is coorganizer (with Bussotti) of the *Musica e Segno* and a member of *Gruppo 70* in Florence. An active member of the European *avant-garde* movement, his works have been performed at the 1963 *Internazionale Nuova Musica* at Palermo, the Festival of the *Avant-Garde* in New York, and several *Fluxus* festivals. His concepts point towards a new theatrical form of music dependent on inclusion of all aural materials.

CHILDS, Barney   (b. 1926) is a graduate of Stanford University (Ph. D.) and studied at Oxford University as a Rhodes Scholar. His many awards include the Koussevitsky Memorial Award in 1954, and he was an associate editor of *Genesis West.* His book (coedited with Elliott Schwartz) *Contemporary Composers on Contemporary Music* is a most important contribution to contemporary music literature and, with his endeavors for Advance Records, he has achieved a foremost position among those furthering the cause and works of new music. His *avant-garde* works (his list of works also includes many mainstream compositions) involve improvisatory and some indeterminate methods, often including audience participation but avoiding the overly-theatrical. He currently teaches at the University of Redlands in California.

COWELL, Henry   (1897-1965) was editor of *New Music* from 1927 until 1936 (the periodical continued until 1950 with Cowell on the executive board), a publication devoted to the innovative scores of that period (not once did he include a work of his own). His 1930 book *New Musical Resources* is devoted to the new possibilities of harmony and rhythm which would later form a cornerstone for *avant-garde* experimentation. Until his death, he promoted new music with great vitality and composed prolifically in countless styles and with considerable diversity, freely open to new and creative ideas.

CRUMB, George   (b. 1929) studied at the University of Michigan with Ross Lee Finney and currently teaches at the University of Pennsylvania in Philadelphia. His *Echoes of Time and the River* for orchestra won the 1968 Pulitzer Prize. His scores are unique both musically and in notation (all of his published works are autograph scores, as his manuscript is both incredibly neat and his notations unique [see examples in the body of this book]).

CURRAN, Alvin   (b. 1938) has been a recipient of both the Bearns Prize and BMI Student Composers award. An active member of *Musica Elettronica Viva* in Italy (live electronic performance group), his recent music is theatrical and concerned with new sounds, both electronic and nonelectronic in origin.

DAVIDOVSKY, Mario   (b. 1934, Argentina) currently composes and teaches in New York City. His *Synchronisms No. 6* for piano and tape won the 1971 Pulitzer Prize. He, like Carter and Ruggles, composes very slowly and his electronic works are *classical* in construction. He has been active for many years in the Columbia-Princeton Electronic Music Center.

DAVIES, Peter Maxwell   (b. 1934, England) is a composer and conductor in England who has been active with *The Fires of London* and the *Pierrot Players*. His music, like that of Berio, is highly eclectic and dramatic.

DRUCKMAN, Jacob   (b. 1928) teaches at the Juilliard School of Music and has been active in the Columbia-Princeton Electronic Music Center. His *Windows* for orchestra won him a Pulitzer Prize. A great deal of his music, especially the *Animus* series, has been for traditional instruments and tape. He has also been involved in the creation of new sounds for traditional instruments, and their resultant notations.

DUCKWORTH, William   (b. 1943) founded and was president of the Association of Independent Composers and Performers, dedicated to the performance of new music. His music often employs experimental sounds from both percussion and electronic sources and is published by both Composers' Autograph Publications and Media Press.

ERB, Donald   (b. 1927) has received grants from the Ford and Guggenheim Foundations and from the National Council on the Arts. He is currently Composer-in-Residence at the Cleveland Institute of Music. His music often employs both live and taped electronic sounds in combination with performers on traditional instruments. His works are performed widely both here and abroad and are recorded on Nonesuch and Ars Nova discs.

FELCIANO, Richard   (b. 1930) currently teaches at the University of California at Berkeley, and has received grants from the Ford Foundation (two), Fulbright Foundation, and Guggenheim Foundation. Since 1967 he has been resident composer to the National Center for Experiments in Television in San Francisco. His works are primarily for traditional instruments and tape and are published by E. C. Schirmer in Boston.

FELDMAN, Morton   (b. 1926) is one of the major influences on young composers today, through both his music and his writings about music. His music (often graphic), generally requiring very soft dynamics, is published by C.F. Peters and recorded on Columbia, Odyssey, and Time Records. His work, though influenced by painting (especially the works of Pollock and Kline) and dance (Merce Cunningham), constantly underplays the theatrical and dynamics of traditional directions.

FOSS, Lukas   (b. 1922) is currently conductor of the Brooklyn Philharmonic and codirector of the Center of the Creative and Performing Arts in Buffalo. His music revolves around a controlled concept of improvisation based on historical concepts of live performance-creation combined with intentionally used "non-musical" sounds for drama and expression.

HAUBENSTOCK-RAMATI, Roman   (b. 1919, Poland) studied at the University of Cracow and is presently living as a free-lance composer in Vienna.

His music is predominantly indeterminate in nature and explores, both in technique and notation, its almost limitless varieties.

HILLER, Lejaren   (b. 1924) studied with Milton Babbitt and Roger Sessions at Princeton while achieving his Ph.D. in chemistry. After 1955 his work turned toward composition and with Leonard Isaacson he began experiments in computer music with which he is still very much active (first at the University of Illinois and later at the State University of New York at Buffalo). A great deal of his most recent composition is *inter-media* in nature.

HUSA, Karel   (b. 1921, Prague) studied at the Prague Conservatory as well as at the Ecole Normale de Musique in Paris (composition with Arthur Honegger). Since 1954 he has taught at Cornell University. His music is a strong fusion of the traditional and *avant-garde*, and his *Music for Prague* and *Apotheosis of this Earth* have made the concert band idiom a more viable ensemble for which contemporary music can and will be written.

ICHIYANAGI, Toshi   (b. 1933, Japan) formed a new music performing group called *New Direction* in 1963. His works have been performed both here and abroad, notably by David Tudor. His music often is graphic and live-electronic. In the last few years, his concepts have turned to mixed-media in the form of environmental works.

IVES, Charles   (1874-1954) was (and still is) a major influence on almost every facet of *avant-garde* tradition. His music has already become *standard* concert literature, and the fact that almost everything done in the *avant-garde* (whether directly traceable to him or not in terms of linkage) was done by Ives many years before their so-called discovery, have made him without question the most remarkable innovator in music history. Laurence Wallach's article on Ives in *The Dictionary of Contemporary Music* is excellent both in and of itself, and useful as well for the bibliographical references it gives of *Ivesian* biographies.

JOHNSTON, Ben   (b. 1926) teaches at the University of Illinois and has received a Guggenheim Fellowship and grants from the University of Illinois and the National Council on the Arts and Humanities. His writings have appeared in *Perspectives of New Music* and *The Composer*. His music is highly structured and often utilizes unique sound sources and microtones.

KAGEL, Mauricio   (b. 1931, Argentina) currently resides in Cologne, where he serves as composer/conductor for the *Ensemble for New Music*. Many of his recent works involve written directions rather than notes, employ some improvisatory and aleatoric elements, and are based primarily on theatrical concepts. His music can be heard on Odyssey Records.

KRAFT, William   (b. 1923) is currently percussionist with the Los Angeles Philharmonic Orchestra. He has studied with Otto Luening, Vladimir Ussachevsky and Henry Cowell, among others, and has written extensively not only for percussion, but for full orchestra as well. His *Contextures: Riots-Decade '60* is a classic inter-media orchestral composition.

KRENEK, Ernst   (b. 1900, Germany) began his composing career as a twelve-tone composer. He has never ceased to explore all available materials and concepts of his craft. This prolific composer is widely published and performed, and his music is intellectual and complex with an approach directed towards individualizing each work both in concept and sound.

LENTZ, Daniel   (b. 1942) has had numerous performances of his works both here and abroad. His music, generally graphic and dramatic (multimedia), often expresses political messages, and his unusual use of colors to represent instrument and/or effect gives both the visual and aural image of his works a marked individuality.

LIGETI, György   (b. 1923, Transylvania) worked from 1957 to 1958 in the Studio for Electronic Music of WDR in Cologne. Since 1961 he has been professor of Composition at the Hochschule fur Musik in Stockholm. Though largely nonelectronic, his music has explored the vast sonic possibilities of traditional orchestral and choral instruments. Despite the fact that his ideas are extremely complex, he continues to employ traditional notation and exact composer control. He has attained wide acclaim as a leader of the *avant-garde* both through his recordings on DGG and exposure in the sound track of the motion picture *2001: A Space Odyssey.*

LUENING, Otto   (b. 1900) is a foremost representative of electronic music in America. His models and ideas of the early 1950s continue to represent effective techniques and procedures for contemporary composers. His historical surveys of electronic music remain the sole source of information on the origins and development of this medium. He is currently codirector of the Columbia-Princeton Electronic Center. His music freely includes all sound sources available, especially *musique concrete.*

LUNETTA, Stanley   (b. 1937) was a member of the *New Music Ensemble* and, aside from his work as percussionist (Sacramento Symphony Orchestra), has composed a large variety of *avant-garde* works. His music is theatrical and employs many multimedia techniques. Through his association and performances with David Tudor and Larry Austin, he has been instrumental in advancing the cause of New Music in America.

LUTOSLAWSKI, Witold   (b. 1913, Poland) is both an active conductor and a composer in Poland. Most of his early works were destroyed in World War II but show a strong traditionalism. His works today are a strong fusion of *avant-garde* and traditional techniques. He works very slowly (a large work every two years or so) and has used indeterminate procedures to a degree. He attributes much of his current style to a hearing of Cage's *Concert for Piano and Orchestra* (divulged in a conversation with this author).

MacKENZIE, I.A.   (1894-1969) as a composer was an early exponent of experimental ideas involved with novel instrument exploration and philosophical concepts of ego and art. His music, though for the most part without notation or significant audience approval, continues to motivate polarization of *avant-garde* ideals: fancy vs. reality.

MADERNA, Bruno   (b. 1920, Italy-d. 1974) was an active conductor of new music (testament are the large number of recordings he has done and the premieres of new works he conducted in both Europe and America), as well as a composer of many different types of musics (inclusive of almost all listed in this book). In 1961 he founded the Darmstadt International Chamber Ensemble which he conducted until his death.

MORAN, Robert   (b. 1937) is currently Composer-in-Residence for the city of Berlin. His works often involve a great deal of humor as well as drama. Primarily a composer of *mixed-media* compositions, Moran has also been active in performing a good deal of new music (such as the puppet operas of Satie and many others when he was director of the West Coast Music Ensemble, 1968-73).

MUMMA, Gordon   (b. 1935) is a member of the Sonic Arts Group (live-electronic music) and a composer/performer actively concerned with the preservation of live performance and a controlled theatrical/gesture situation. His music is found on the *Music of Our Time* series (Odyssey Records).

OLIVEROS, Pauline   (b. 1932) is currently a member of the staff of the University of California at San Diego. She is an avid composer of electronic, live-electronic, and multimedia compositions and an articulate experimentalist. Her works appear on the *Music of Our Times* series (Odyssey Records) and Columbia Records, and her writings in *Source* and *The Composer.*

PARTCH, Harry   (1901-1974) received many grants, including those from Carnegie Corporation, Fromm Foundation, and the University of Illinois. A virtually unknown experimentalist in new tunings and instruments for many years, his works and ideas have recently gained wide notice, consideration, and success. His book *Genesis of a Music* and his works serve as a storehouse of new concepts and performing techniques. He lived in San Diego and taught part-time at the University of California there until his death.

PENDERECKI, Krzysztof   (b. 1933, Poland) has won awards from the Polish Union of Composers and UNESCO (1960) and is a graduate of the University of Cracow. His music explores the vast possibilities of sonic material available within traditional concert bodies (e.g., orchestra, choir). He currently teaches at Yale University.

POUSSEUR, Henri   (b. 1929, Belgium) works at the Brussels electronic music studio and conducts theory classes in Darmstadt. He is a graduate of the Liege and Brussels Conservatories. Most of his music is electronic, and much of it explores the numerous sonic and acoustical possibilities of tape with live performers (especially orchestra).

REYNOLDS, Roger   (b. 1934) is cofounder of ONCE and has received Fulbright, Guggenheim, and Rockefeller Foundation fellowships. He is now on the staff at the University of California in San Diego. His works are available from C. F. Peters and are recorded on Nonesuch Records. His music is primarily live-electronic multimedia, and his writings explicit and articulate.

ROCHBERG, George   (b. 1918) has, since 1960, been on the staff at the University of Pennsylvania in Philadelphia. His music is surprisingly *avant-garde* though he does not use electronic sound sources. He uses "quotes" liberally throughout his more recent music.

SATIE, Erik   (b. 1866, France-d. 1925) was one of the most influential composers of the *avant-garde.* Composers such as John Cage, Robert Moran, and many others have given Satie the highest plaudits in terms of his influence on new music. These influences take the form of ultra-simplicity, new time concepts (i.e., *Vexations*) and Inter-media. A number of biographical books are available and have been listed in the appropriate chapter bibliographies.

SCRIABIN, Alexander   (b. 1872, Russia-d. 1915) has been influential in the use of media forms. Biographical information is available in almost any book on twentieth-century music.

STOCKHAUSEN, Karlheinz   (b. 1928, Germany) resides in Cologne. His experiments with electronic music in the mid-fifties, co-editorship of *Die Reihe,* and prolific compositions utilizing electronic sound sources on tape performed over numerous speakers placed acoustically and compositionally in and around the audience, have placed him at the forefront of the European *avant-garde.* His life and works are discussed at length in *Kontrapunkte #6* (P.J. Tonger-Rodenkirchen/Rhein). His writings about his music are prolific and complex. His recorded works appear on DG. Fascinating books about Stockhausen include: Karl H. Worner, *Stockhausen,* trans. Bill Hopkins (Berkeley: University off California Press, 1973) and Jonathan Cott, *Stockhausen, Conservations with the Composer* (New York: Simon and Schuster, 1973).

SUBOTNICK, Morton   (b. 1933) teaches at the California Institute of the Arts in Valencia. He was one of the founders of the San Francisco Tape Center and has worked in the Columbia (New York) electronic studio. Aside from his electronic music (recorded on Columbia and Nonesuch Records), he is currently working in multimedia and theater with some improvisation/interaction involved.

USSACHEVSKY, Vladimir   (b. 1911, Russia), together with Luening, presented one of the first American tape music concerts in 1952, and continues to be one of the foremost exponents of *musique concrete* in this country. He teaches at Columbia University in New York, and was recently visiting composer at the University of Utah.

VARÈSE, Edgard   (b. 1885, France-d. 1965) spent the latter forty years of his life working in New York City. His early predictions and pioneering work with tape and electronic sounds, along with his original approach to concepts of music, mark him as one of the major experimentalists and creators of our time. His music is available from G. Schirmer and is recorded on Columbia.

WOLFF, Christian   (b. 1934, France) is teaching classics at Harvard University. His association in the early fifties with Cage and Feldman led to the development of his very personal borderline indeterminate procedures, often notated graphically but sometimes traditionally. His works are published by C. F. Peters and recorded on Time and Odyssey Records.

WUORINEN, Charles   (b. 1938) is an active composer and pianist. Most of his works (recorded on CRI, Nonesuch, and Advance Records) require immense performer virtuosity and are explicit in notation. He has, more recently, explored more nontheatrical and formally complex electronic music than most of his American contemporaries.

XENAKIS, Iannis   (b. 1922, Rumania) until recently taught at Indiana University. He received his early training in science at the Ausbildung am Polytechnikaus in Athens, Greece. From 1947 until 1959 he worked with the famed architect Le Corbusier. His approach to composition is founded primarily on mathematical principles and explores fields of new sounds using traditional instruments and notation. His music is recorded on Columbia, Angel, Vanguard, and Nonesuch Records.

YOUNG, La Monte   (b. 1935) is one of the most highly original composers of the *avant-garde*. He did most of his studying in Los Angeles, briefly with Karlheinz Stockhausen in Germany, and currently resides as a free-lance composer in New York City. His *Dream Houses* and other mixed-media works, as well as the innovative compositions of 1960, have made him along with John Cage one of the most energetic exponents of new music in both America and abroad.

A great deal of further biographical information on these as well as many other contemporary composers listed in this book is available in *Dictionary of Contemporary Music*, edited by John Vinton. New York: E. P. Dutton & Co., 1974 (834 pp.).

Appendix 3　　　　　Notations

The objective of this Appendix is to provide a skeleton outline of a few of the new music notations developed over the past fifteen to thirty years which have become somewhat standard in usage. It is just a minimal sketch, and is intended to illuminate some of the examples in the book, to give samples of viable solutions to problems posed by *avant-garde* music, and hopefully to stimulate the reader to research this area in greater depth.

Most scores over the past thirty years include a "performance instructions" page which describes the new symbols evolved by the composer for the work, usually separate, sometimes multipaged, and often full of symbols in direct conflict with similar symbols of other composers working in the same area. Until the late sixties there seemed an almost endless stream of "artistic" endeavors—as numerous as composers and works attempting New Directions. Since the publication of the *Darmstadter Beitrage zur Neuen Musik* in 1965 there has been a slow but steady pull toward codification of symbology. There has been more and more attention paid to this area and, as the short bibliography that follows this introduction indicates, a host of articles and books dedicated to at least focusing attention on the problem. It should be remembered, however, that all notation is an ever-changing animal and the word "codified" here must always be taken with caution and a necessary temporal prefix.

One of the most important new[1] *concepts* employed in new music is that of *proportional notation*. In most musics since 1600 there exist bar lines intended to serve a variety of purposes:

1. keep performers together:
2. provide (in some musics) primary and secondary implied accents for *dance suites* and the like;
3. make the *reading* of music more feasible (even a Clementi *Sonatina* becomes a "nightmare" upon the removal of bar lines).

Contemporary composers have felt that these bar lines conflict with their ideas of freeing musical line, form, drive, and especially rhythm from imposed "square-ness" and repetition. While some of these composers have solved their problems within a metered structure (i.e., Elliott Carter: *metric modulation;*

---

1. The word "new" is used here with caution: indeed proportionality existed *before* metered notations in many medieval works, etc. In fact, it is probably the oldest concept of music notation. However, it is the new "ways" in which the term is used that concerns us here, as does the fact that "metered" notation has been common and standard for so long that proportional notation seems "new."

György Ligeti: involved and intricate rhythmic entrances; etc.) others have felt that the only solution was to dispense with the bar line entirely. *Proportional notation* is basically a bar-less structure in which the rhythm of the work is derived from the performer "proportioning" his left-to-right visual reading speed with the time allotted for the given section. Some do it as Toru Takemitsu did it in *Voice* (fig. 3.5), wherein each small vertical slash through the upper portion of the staff is the end of approximately 4½ seconds of playing time. Others, like Penderecki (see fig. 2.7—*Threnody*), use large blocks of space which equal a certain duration of time. The performer then reads at a speed *proportional* to the time given for performance (i.e., if an entrance began about one-third through a 30-second section the performer would wait about 10 seconds before entering, etc.). This system eradicates the limits and implied accents of bar lines. At the same time, however, it introduces a certain degree of flexibility in the way in which each performer reads the score (therefore giving more "chance" possibilities to the performance).

Some composers, like George Crumb for example (see fig. 9.3), use tempo marks without bar lines and are successful; at the same time most of these composers write in a very *thin* soloistic style so that the need for bar lines is less (less than, say, trying to perform *Le Sacre du Printemps* without bar lines). In any event, different composers use notations for different reasons and a number mix proportional and metered notations within the same work (see fig. 3.10—Ligeti's *Aventures*), thereby taking advantage of the benefits of both systems. While to the untrained eye these types of scores may appear unnecessarily difficult and/or obscure they represent, in fact, an excellent solution to the problems at hand and will probably become standard practice before long. Certainly the extent to which composers are stylistically limited due to their notational systems is a fascinating subject area for future research, and will be a central subject for twenty-first-century musicologists.

Following a short bibliography of notation sources (and brief it is due both to space limitations and the fact that large, completely annotated bibliographies on the subject are available in many other sources) is a list of somewhat standard new music notations. To repeat, this is a bare outline only, and does not in any way pretend to be comprehensive, in fact comprehensiveness would require a huge 2,000-page book in itself, as you might gather from the Gardner Read entry in the bibliography), or to make any major codifying suggestions (this is the subject of another of this author's books: *New Music Notation*, referred to below).

Brief Bibliography

Bartolozzi, Bruno. *New Sounds for Woodwind*. London: Oxford University Press, 1967.

———. "Proposals for Changes in Musical Notation." *Journal of Music Theory* 5, no. 2 (1961).

Behrman, David. "What Indeterminate Notation Determines." *Perspectives of New Music*. (Spring-Summer 1965).

Brindle, Reginald Smith. *Contemporary Percussion*. London: Oxford University Press, 1970.

Bunger, Richard. *The Well-Prepared Piano*. Colorado Springs: Colorado College Music Press, 1973.

Cage, John. *Notations*. New York: Something Else Press, 1969.

Cope, David. *New Music Notation*. Dubuque, Iowa: Kendall/Hunt, 1976.

Cowell, Henry. *New Musical Resources*. New York: Alfred A. Knopf, 1930.

Eimert, Herbert; Enkel, Fritz; and Stockhausen, Karlheinz. *Problems of Electronic Music Notation*. Ottawa: National Research Council of Canada, 1956.

Darmstädter Beiträge zur Neuen Musik. Mainz: B. Schott's Söhne, 1965.

Howell, Thomas. *The Avant-Garde Flute: A Handbook for Composers and Flutists*. Berkeley: University of California Press, 1974.

Karkoschka, Erhard. *Notation in New Music*. New York: Praeger Publishers, 1972.

Kontarsky, Aloys. "Notation for Piano." *Perspectives of New Music* 10, no. 2 (1972).

Pooler, Frank and Pierce, Brent. *New Choral Notation*. New York: Walton Music Corp., 1973.

Read, Gardner. *Twentieth-Century Music Notation*. (Unpublished as of this writing, unfortunately).

Rehfeldt, Phillip. "Clarinet Resources and Performance." *Proceedings* 7/8, American Society of University Composers (1974).

Salzedo, Carlos. *Modern Study of the Harp*. New York: G. Schirmer, 1921.

Stone, Kurt. "New Music Notation: Why?" *Musical America* 24, no. 7 (July 1974.)

———. "Notation." In *Dictionary of Contemporary Music*. Edited by John Vinton. New York: E. P. Dutton & Co., 1974.

Turetzky, Bertram. *The Contemporary Contrabass*. Berkeley: University of California Press, 1974.

Yates, Peter. "The Proof of the Notation." *Twentieth-Century Music*. New York: Pantheon Books, 1967.

New Music Notations

A) Pitch

meaning	symbol	one composer among the many who use this type of notation.
quarter-tones:	↓ ↑ = (¼ up or down)	*Béla Bartók*
	♯ ♭ ♮ = (¼ up) (sharpen) (flatten)	*Mauricio Kagel*
	↑ ♯ ♭ ↓ (¼) (¾) (¼) (¾)	*Krzysztof Penderecki*

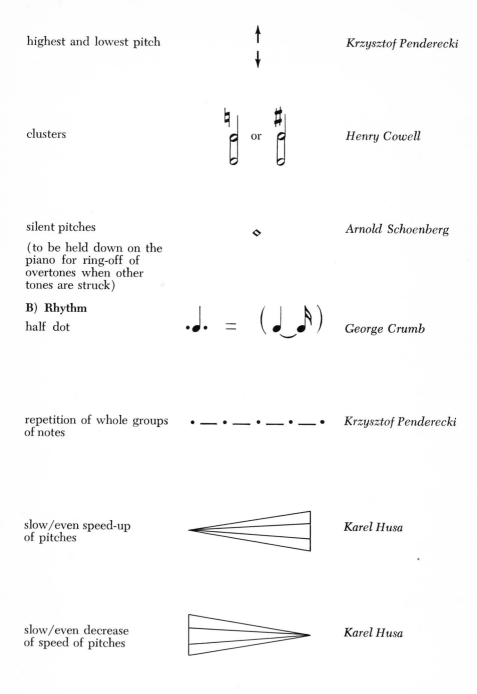

highest and lowest pitch — *Krzysztof Penderecki*

clusters — *Henry Cowell*

silent pitches — *Arnold Schoenberg*
(to be held down on the piano for ring-off of overtones when other tones are struck)

B) Rhythm

half dot — *George Crumb*

repetition of whole groups of notes — *Krzysztof Penderecki*

slow/even speed-up of pitches — *Karel Husa*

slow/even decrease of speed of pitches — *Karel Husa*

long fermata with
duration shown in seconds

5

George Crumb

irregular tremolo

Krzysztof Penderecki

C) Dynamics

refined dynamic changes

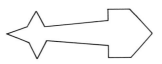

Henry Gorecki

ad lib dynamics and flux

John Cage

D) Articulation

articulation of ends
of notes

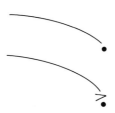

Richard Bunger

E) Timbre effects

1. *Winds*

sing while playing

♩ = play

♩ = sing

David Cope

multiphonics

Toru Takemitsu

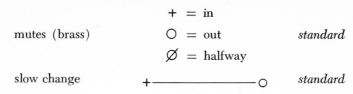

	+ = in	
mutes (brass)	O = out	*standard*
	Ø = halfway	
slow change	+ ——————— O	*standard*

2. *Percussion*

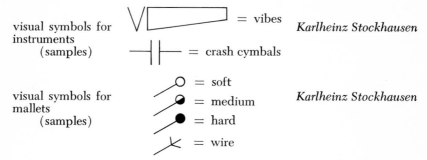

visual symbols for instruments (samples)	= vibes / = crash cymbals	*Karlheinz Stockhausen*
visual symbols for mallets (samples)	O = soft / ◑ = medium / ● = hard / ⤬ = wire	*Karlheinz Stockhausen*

(for these last two see Reginald Brindle's book for complete listing)

3. *Harp*

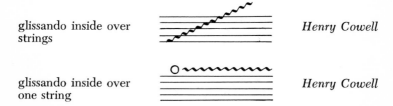

rolling surf effect   *Carlos Salzedo*

(for a complete listing of such effects and notations, see Carlos Salzedo's book in the preceding bibliography)

4. *Piano*

glissando inside over strings   *Henry Cowell*

glissando inside over one string   *Henry Cowell*

(for a complete listing of preparations, etc., see Richard Bunger's book in the preceding bibliography)

mute   *George Crumb*

5. *Strings*

    mute on

    mute off

    play between tailpiece
    and bridge

6. *Vocal*

    falsetto

    spoken

    breath inhale

    breath exhale

    laughter

Pierre Boulez

Krzysztof Penderecki

Krzysztof Penderecki

György Ligeti

György Ligeti

Krzysztof Penderecki

Note also that a number of contemporary scores leave out staves of instruments with empty bars. This contributes to the "new" look of many of the scores of Crumb, Penderecki, and many others shown in this book. Likewise, when non-pitch-related activity is being employed, one-line staves are often used— quite unfamiliar in appearance to those who are used to the standard five-line staff for all but percussion instruments.

Appendix 4   Source Addresses

The purpose of this appendix is to furnish addresses of record companies, new music periodicals, and music publishers, which emphasize new music and dedicate a large part of their services to the promotion of contemporary and *avant-garde* music. The lists are provided to aid the reader in these ways:

1. to obtain catalogs of materials and works for further study and research (since the author has by no means been comprehensive in coverage of *all* works in given areas) and to make purchases;
2. to become acquainted with the large number of sources not ordinarily found in record and book stores or even in many university libraries;
3. to help support the dissemination of new music by making the names and addresses of its supporters that much more available.

The lists are by no means complete for a variety of reasons:

1. lack of space (and for this our apologies to all those companies who do support new music yet whose names, for one reason or another, were not included in the lists);
2. the names of some companies are very readily available to the general public (i.e., Columbia Records does indeed support new music, but their name has not been included in our lists as their records are available at any retail record store);
3. many companies produce materials of new music but only a very small proportion to their complete output: the emphasis here must of necessity be on companies which devote a *major* portion of their output to new music;
4. a considerable degree of emphasis has been placed on listing those companies from which the examples in the book were taken, thus giving the reader the opportunity to obtain the score, record, or book with comparative ease.

Record Companies

Advance: Box 17072, Rincon Station, Tucson, Ariz. 85731
Advent: 23366 Commerce Pk. Rd., Cleveland, Ohio 44122
AMG: Box 2866, Sta. A, Champaign, Ill. 61820
Avant: Box 65661, Los Angeles, Calif. 90065
Avant-Garde: 250 W. 57th St., New York, N.Y. 10019
Bowdoin College Music: 6 W. 95th St., New York, N.Y. 10025
Brewster: 1822 Monroe St., Evanston, Ill. 60202

CAPRA: 6 W. 95th St., New York, N.Y. 10025

Chatham Square: 6 W. 95th St., New York, N.Y. 10025

Concept: 6 W. 95th St., New York, N.Y. 10025

Cornell University: Lincoln Hall, Ithaca, N.Y. 14850

CRI: 170 W. 74th St., New York, N.Y. 10023

Crystal: Box 65661, Los Angeles, Calif. 90065

Desto: 14 Warren St., New York, N.Y .10007

Deutsche Grammophone: 810 7th Ave., New York, N.Y. 10019

Discant: 6 W. 95th St., New York, N.Y. 10025

Earthquack: 6 W. 95th St., New York, N.Y. 10025

Finnadar: 75 Rockefeller Plaza, New York, N.Y. 10019

Folkways: 43 W. 61st St., New York, N.Y. 10023

Golden Crest: 220 Broadway, Huntington Station, N.Y. 11746

Kama-Sutra: 810 7th Ave., New York, N.Y. 10019

Louisville: 333 W. Broadway, Louisville, Ky. 40202

Mach: 539 W. 25th St., New York, N.Y. 10001

Mainstream: 1700 Broadway, New York, N.Y. 10019

Nonesuch: 15 Columbus Circle, New York, N.Y. 10023

Now: 224 S. Lebanon St., Lebanon, Ind. 46052

Odyssey: 51 W. 52nd St., New York, N.Y. 10019

Opus One: Box 604, Greenville, Maine 04441

Orion: 3802 Castlerock Road, Malibu, California 90265

Owl: Box 4536, Boulder, Colo. 80302

Point Park: Wood and Blvd. of the Allies, Pittsburgh, Pa. 15222

Redwood: 8 Redwood Lane, Ithaca, N. Y. 14850

Serenus: Box 267, Hastings-on-Hudson, N.Y. 10706

Trilogy: 723 7th Ave., New York, N.Y. 10017

Turnabout: 211 E. 42nd St., New York, N.Y. 10019

UBRES: P.O. Box 2374, Champaign, Ill. 61020

Varèse: Box 148, Glendale, Calif. 91209

Wergo: 65 Mainz, Postfach 3640, Weihergarten, Germany

WIM: Box 65661, Los Angeles, Calif. 90065

Note: Special thanks for the addresses on the list go to the Schwann Record Catalog who graciously supplied most of them.

Periodicals

° *asterisk:* 1215 Kuehnle Ave., Ann Arbor, Mich. 48103

American Society of University Composers: Journal of Music Scores: c/o Joseph Boonin, P.O. Box 2124, South Hackensack, N.J. 07606

Canadian Composer: 159 Bay St., Toronto 1, Canada

Composer Magazine: P.O. Box 671, Hamilton, Ohio 45012

Composium: P.O. Box 65661, Los Angeles, Calif. 90065

Contemporary Music Newsletter: Dept. of Music, New York University, Washington Square, New York, N.Y. 10003

Darmstädter Beiträge zur Neuen Musik: B. Schotts Söhne, Weihergarten 12, Postfach 1403, 6500 Mainz, Germany

Electronotes: 60 Sheraton Drive, Ithaca, N.Y. 14850

Interface: heerweg 347b Lisse, Netherlands

Journal of Music Theory: Yale University, New Haven, Conn. 06520

Konzerte Mit Neuer Musik: Rundfunkplatz 1, 8 Munich 2, Germany

Melos: B. Schotts Söhne, Weihergarten 12, Postfach 1403, 6500 Mainz, Germany

Music in Poland: ZAIKS 2, Hupoteczna Str., Warsaw, Poland

Musical America: 1 Astor Plaza, New York, N.Y. 10036

Numus-West: P.O. Box 135, Mercer Island, Wash. 98040

Nutida Musik: Sveriges Radio, S-105, 10 Stockholm, Sweden

Perspectives of New Music: Princeton University Press, Princeton University, Princeton, N.J. 08540

Proceedings: American Society of University Composers: c/o American Music Center, 2109 Broadway, Suite 15-79, New York, N.Y. 10023

die Reihe (back issues): c/o Theodore Presser Co., Bryn Mawr, Pa.

Sonda: Juventudes Musicales, Madrid, Spain

Sonorum Speculum: Donemus 51, Jacob Obrechtstraat, Amsterdam, Netherlands

Sonological Reports: Utrecht State University, Utrecht, Netherlands

Soundings: The Athenian School, Danville, Calif. 94526.

Source: Music of the Avant Garde: 2101 22nd St., Sacramento, Calif. 95818

Tempo: c/o Boosey and Hawkes Ltd., 295 Regent St., London, England W1A 1BR

There are a number of other magazines which carry regular columns dealing with new music and/or magazines dealing with more mainstream musical trends. Names and addresses of such magazines can be found in either: *Directory of the Music Industry,* 1418 Lake St., Evanston, Ill. 60204, or *Directory of the World of Music,* Music Information Service, 310 Madison Ave., New York, N.Y. 10017.

Music Publishers

It is very difficult to be complete in this area without filling several hundred pages with addresses. To avoid this, the author has listed the major U.S. music publishers, many of which handle in addition the music of numerous European companies dealing with new music (C.F. Peters, for example, aside from their own nine inner companies, represent forty publishers of new music from around the world); these "umbrella" publishers are noted as such with an asterisk. Catalogs and lists of music available from almost all of the new music publishers in the world can be had by writing these "major" companies.

Music distributors are also included in this list and each is likewise designated by an asterisk. Among these companies are many who hold and distribute catalogs of a great many publishers around the world, and information about almost any work is obtainable by writing them.

The Internationales Musikinstitut Darmstädt Informationszentrum für zeitgenossische Musik Katalog der Abteilung Noten (Druck und Herstellung: Druckerei und Verlag Jacob Helene KG., Pfungstadt, Ostendstrasse 10, Germany) is a fairly comprehensive listing of new music and publishers of such (issued annually) and serves considerable purpose in making information on publishers available.

Along with the listing of major publishers and distributors are a number of smaller companies which deal almost exclusively in new and *avant-garde* musics. These companies for the most part would not be represented through the distributors. Other such publisher addresses may be obtained from the *Directory of the World of Music*, Music Information Service, 310 Madison Ave., New York, N.Y. 10017, or *Directory of the Music Industry*, 1418 Lake St., Evanston, Illinois 60204.

ASCAP (1 Lincoln Plaza, New York, N.Y. 10023), BMI (40 W. 57th St., New York, N.Y. 10019), and Sesac (10 Columbus Circle, New York, N.Y. 10019) all have publishers' names and addresses (of their own affiliated "performance rights" publishers).

Associated Music Publishers: 866 3rd. Ave., New York, N.Y. 10022

Augsburg: 426 S. 5th St., Minneapolis, Minn. 55415

Baerenreiter-Verlag: Heindrich Schutz Allee 35, 35 Kossel, Germany

B. H. Blackwell Ltd.: 48-51 Broudstreet, Oxford, England OX1 3BQ

Belwin Mills: 16 W. 61st. St., New York, N.Y. 10023

Bowdoin College Music Press: Brunswick, Maine 04011

Brass Press: 159 Eighth Ave. North, Nashville, Tenn. 37203

Composers' Autograph Publications (CAP): P.O. Box 671, Hamilton, Ohio 45012

Composers' Facsimile Edition: 170 W. 74th St., New York, N.Y. 10023

Composers' Press, Inc.: 1211 Ditmas Ave., Brooklyn, N.Y. 10018

J. W. Chester, Ltd.: Eagle Court, London, E.C.1, England

Dorn Productions: P.O. Box 704, Islington, Mass. 02090

Carl Fischer, Inc.: 62 Cooper Square, New York, N.Y. 10003

Galaxy Music: 2121 Broadway, New York, N.Y. 10023

Otto Harrassowitz: Postfach 349, 6200 Wiesbaben 1, Germany

Edward Marks: 1790 Broadway, New York, N.Y. 10019

Media Press: Box 895, Champaign, Ill. 61820

Mills Music, Inc.: 1619 Broadway, New York, N.Y. 10019

Moeck Verlag: D31 Celle, Postfach 143, Germany

MCA Music: 225 Park Ave. South, New York, N.Y. 10003

C.F. Peters: 373 Park Ave. South, New York, N.Y. 10016

Theodore Presser: Bryn Mawr, Pennsylvania 19010

E. C. Schirmer Music Co.: 112 S. St., Boston, Mass. 02111

G. Schirmer: 866 3rd Ave., New York, N.Y. 10022

Seesaw Music Corp.: 177 E. 87th St., New York, N.Y. 10028

Smith Publications: 906 E. Water Street, Urbana, Ill. 61801

Source: 2101 22nd St., Sacramento, Calif. 95818

Universal Edition: Postfach 3 A-1015, Vienna, Austria

Walton Music: 17 W. 60th St., New York, N.Y. 10023

Wilhelm Hansen Group: Gothersgade 9-11, DK 1123 Copenhagen K, Denmark.

Index